PRAISE FOR THE AUTHOR

"SESTO plays with language in new and exciting ways. Fascinating twists and turns of an engaging plot…"
~Renaissance Magazine

∽

"ANTICIPATE struggles, achievements and failure…of entwined lives which emerge in this fast-paced story."
~Library Bookwatch

∽

"BE prepared for intrigue and an unexpected ending that shakes the foundations of the [characters'] lives."
~Dominic Cibrario, author *The Pomelo Tree trilogy*

"THIS talented novelist...takes us into a world most of us would otherwise not experience. One of those surprising pleasures that might otherwise be overlooked by most critics."
~Bookviews

"CLEVER dialogue and fast-paced suspense create a bold new story... The novel's prose is tight and crisp, the turns of plot effectively manipulated to create suspense."
~Emeritus Professor Andrew McLean
University of Wisconsin-Parkside

COSMIC ENTANGLEMENT

A novel by GENEVIEVE SESTO

scritta
PRESS

ALSO BY GENEVIEVE SESTO

FICTION
Flight: When Someone Disappears
A Door in the Road
Corpse Pose

scritta
PRESS

This is a work of fiction. Names, characters, places, and incidents either are the product of the author's imagination or are used fictitiously. Any resemblance to actual persons, living or dead, events, or locales is entirely coincidental.

Copyright ©2019 by Genevieve Sesto

All rights reserved, including the right of reproduction in whole or in part in any form.

Published in the United States by Scritta Press.
www.scrittapress.com.

Printed and manufactured in the United States of America

ISBN 978-0-578-53793-1

Printed in the Unites States of America

Cover and book design by Lucia Lozano, Process2Creative

First Edition

COSMIC ENTANGLEMENT

ONE

WHEN Simon Butler one night mistook gunshots for car backfire, Janey Leduc recognized Darwinian natural selection at work. It meant that the tribe of Simon was on the fast track to extinction. Wicked booms in the hot summer darkness, had sounded to Simon like ordinary car backfires. No matter that this was Chicago at the city's all-time worst in gun violence. Even after Janey had said it's gunfire, Simon wouldn't smarten up. She had shaken her head in annoyance. Though Simon's insistence on always being right rankled Janey more than anything else about him, she decided to drop it. Let Simon's blithering win for now. Truth will out. Anyway, Janey never liked to preach. However, this seemingly negligible event during an ordinary evening portended trouble ahead.

Janey reared off the sofa cushions scurried over to the

open window and said, "That gunfire sounds awfully close."

"Only a car backfiring. Don't be scared. You're safe with me."

Simon stroked her warm, soft shoulder and tried to reassure his jitter lady. Again sharp, short explosions nearby, sounded almost under the window.

Janey jumped on her high horse, asked how could he mix-up gun shots with car farts? In a patronizing way he assured her that he was an expert in these matters. Because of his job, for one thing, he knew about cars.

"Hey, come on," he said. "That's backfire. Hey, I understand you mixing them up. The two sounds are easy to confuse."

"Anyone who's heard gunfire up close wouldn't get them mixed-up. And I have. Guns send shock waves for miles right along with their killer coils. Guns emit death like viral pathogens."

"Don't get moody on me," Simon laughed at her. "I've been on a shooting range. It's easy to get the two mixed up." End of conversation.

"There's no way…if you've ever been near a…an automatic discharged, you'd feel fear first at such a bloodthirsty battery—"

"A cylinder hiccough." Diverted by his own humor,

"Is that what you think? Sorry. It sounds just like some old car needs tuning." No, Simon Butler, level-headed, unreligious, apolitical and a decent guy, was not cut out to survive in the blood-red jungle of tooth and claw.

"Like hell, listen." A sudden racket of deep prolonged roars, harrowing reflexive cracks, split the wall of dense night air.

Then eerie silence closed in the night.

Janey bit at her lower lip. "That's a freakin' gun going off."

Next morning as Simon poured his second cup of coffee WBBM Radio reported that Wong Fat Chinese Provisions, a few blocks from Janey's house, had been broken into. When police arrived, shots were exchanged and the gunmen had been killed.

On his way to work Simon took a detour and very excited, swerved into Lutheran Social Services' parking lot. Janey would be busy. But he could not wait until tonight to tell her. He hustled in and caught her shuffling a rotund man with a fuzzy scowl down the hall toward her office. A bedraggled woman in a dingy yellow housedress and black velveteen vest tugged on Janey's arm, trying to get her attention. Sorry-looking bunch this morning, Simon thought.

Janey had seen Simon enter the lobby, so she plied

the big frightened man into her office and flew back out. She beckoned Simon into the short hall next to the entrance.

"What are you doing here?" Janey's gaze, genuine, wide-eyed, appealed on an instinctive level. Her upturned nose, freckles, molded cheek bones, seemed seductive yet assured, calm. Dark blonde hair traced her oval face. An attractive package to many men. While Simon with his static, ordinary good looks, his lack of vitality, did only average with women. Until Janey came along he'd been an indifferent lover. In these four months they'd been dating he thought he'd turned into a tiger. A lucky man, he considered himself, among the luckiest of men.

"Hey, Janey, I had to come tell you. Want to see the look on your face. " He leaned against the wall, tried out his impish grin. "You were right. Those shots, last night, they were gun shots. On the radio—"

"I know that."

"Yeah, but listen, you got it right. On the news this morning it said that a Chinese food distribution warehouse was broken into and the cops had a shoot-out with the thugs. I know the owner's brother, Wing Fat. His law office is in the mall next to the dealership. Not usual for that kind of shit going down in your neighborhood."

"Becoming endemic." She waggled her head side to side the way she did at a client's tale of woe.

"You were so certain about the gunfire. Nobody sneaks a thing past my Janey."

He wanted to hug her.

"The shooting?" She's being obtuse, Simon thought. It grated that he'd raced here with big news and she seemed indifferent to it.

"I lived in Manhattan for a few years. Once I witnessed a drive-by shooting. The sound of the…Jesus. Some guy not more than a hundred feet from where I was waiting for the bus, got shot in the front tooth."

"Give me a break, Janey," Simon snickered thoroughly put off. He tries to credit her with a little street cred, and she turns her life into an action movie.

Not daunted by his disdain Janey said, "It was like everything hung in suspended animation. Then traffic whipped off when the light turned green, cars jammed around the corner from all directions. One bus rumbled up but like it was filmed in time-lapse. Behind it the van the shooter rode in, it jumped the curb, raked the underbody, probably flooded the engine, sat dead still a split second. Then a grinding screech and gone. A send-off of blue smoke all I could see. And the guy on the ground blood spurting out of his mouth.

Oh Lordy, come on, thought Simon. Now he wanted a fast exit. So he gave her a quick kiss and told her he knew she had to go counsel that fat guy.

After Janey, Simon drove to the car dealership where he was service manager. Not being mechanical, Simon had found a white-collar job in charge of those who were. All in all, Simon shined at his job. He knew automobile repair in the abstract, pistons, transmissions, brake calipers, struts. He could be diplomatic in order to handle customer complaints. These qualities had made him a valuable employee, and the work was just taxing and varied enough to satisfy him. Simon liked to work alongside people who got their hands dirty. But he would prefer to have clean hands himself. He enjoyed new cars, but he had been lousy at sales when he tried it. Selling, he considered on the whole superfluous work. Customers were either intent on buying a car when they walked in or were only there to browse. In his mind the salesperson was almost superfluous. The business world in general wouldn't have suited him. He had found the perfect job that made him happy.

When Simon strolled into the service bay, cars were already up on lifts. Around him the bangs of giant tools and rasp of metal on metal, shrieks of air compressors. Shouts of the mechanics in grease-smeared tee shirts echoed off high metal walls. Gas fumes permeated his computer stand, even with the oversized doors rolled up as cars curled around the back-showroom lot to be admitted for repair or maintenance. A husky brown man in bib coveralls threaded over to Simon, wiping his permanently stained hands on an oily cloth.

"Morning, Simon."

Simon pressed his thumbs into his temples and turned to face the chief mechanic. "Hey, Hank. Did you hear the news? Shoot-out right around the corner from Janey's house late last night. At the Chinese food warehouse. I heard it going down."

"Oh? Right." If it didn't have an engine, he wasn't interested. "We got a customer been here since seven, pitching a fit. The guy's in the waiting room. Wants to talk to the manager. He said there's a problem in his Porsche's fuel line. I tested it. Nothing wrong. Really cool car. Running like a million bucks."

"Who checked him in?"

"Margaret Ann."

"Okay. What's the guy's name? I'll see what he wants." Second glitch of the day. This sort of thing runs in threes. Simon had a streak of superstition.

"Don't know his name. Nobody else in there right now."

Simon went first to his computer station, punched in

his code, pulled up the day's work orders, and began on the lineup of cars in the concourse. After he cleared the congestion, he wandered into the waiting area adjacent to the showroom, cup of coffee in hand. From a chair against the bank of windows back-lit by glary sunlight, a blond man stood up when Simon approached as if he recognized here was the manager.

Slender, short-haired, chiseled featured, he wore charcoal pinstripes, glistening wingtips, and a silk red tie.

"Hank said you were asking for me. Our chief mechanic hasn't found a thing wrong with your Porsche." He smiled, "A beautiful car."

"I know it. So you're the service manager. Simon Butler?"

"That's right. If you're questioning his result—"

"No, I'm not." The way the guy grinned blurred his sharply limned face, setting off an alarm in Simon.

His normal diplomacy fled. "You don't need your car serviced then why you hanging around?"

The spiffy man blinked languid eyelids over wispy blue eyes. "I used to be married to Janey Leduc." A casual, flippant declaration which struck Simon a horse-kick in the gut.

"You're lying." Simon blurted. Before his words had warped the air, Simon sensed the other man's ultimate victory, and tried to turn it. He pushed his jaw out,

"Janey's never been married," for a fraction of a second completely convinced. The man was a liar. Simon had met Janey's mother when she visited last month. Heard them talking about Janey's old friends. Janey's nosey sister, Isabelle, wouldn't have passed up spilling the beans about a thing like a husband. And Janey. Of course, Janey would have told him.

The guy stood unmoved. "I'm Arthur Kane, and Janey was my wife. Why would I lie?"

"Why would you come here at all?"

Simon ignored a persistent itch, an insistent urge to explain to this arrogant schmuck how Janey had recognized the gun shots for what they were. Instead he settled for a good loud laugh.

"You're lying, Mr. Arthur Kane, because if you had been married to Janey, she would have told me.

"Yeah, sure, and you know a whole lot about her." Another smear fogged his unblemished face. Kane had come to see this boyfriend of hers, thinking he might smooth the way for him with Janey. Strange fidgety guy hadn't even known she was married. Didn't cross Artie's mind to think that odd or not.

Simon proceeded as if this son-of-a-bitch was running a con on him. Then he could handle it. "If you haven't got an issue with your automobile, I've gotta get back to work." Flipped down his eyelids and pretended to look at the service report still clutched in his hand.

Kane twisted around without apparent movement. He seemed to glide to the showroom entrance. Over one tilted shoulder he called back to Simon. "Listen, tell Janey I need to see her. I'll be in Chicago couple of days, and I'll look her up."

The showroom doors pulled closed with a long hiss. Through the sun's harsh glare on the window, Simon squinted as the cocky Mr. Kane disappeared among the glitter of new car models in the lot.

"Screw the bastard." He said and returned to work.

As the day wore on, Simon Butler immersed himself in the minutiae of auto repair, like doctors or financial planners or cops, the mundane diagnoses, the causes and symptoms, the hundreds of decisions, oil changes, broken rods — MRIs, stock forecasts, futures, hedge funds, crime scene investigations. When a job gets done, a laborer is worthy of his hire.

Wistfulness settled over Simon when the work day closed, a mixture of longing, envy, nostalgia for the time when he was too young to have to earn a living — putting away a school day and looking forward to dinner, freedom for a while, a gladness for the late afternoon, inspiration from the renewing night.

Simon bounded out of the service area, climbed in his own car, and then, single-minded, phoned Janey. He wanted to relieve his left-over anxiety from weird Mr. Arthur Kane's visit. He had convinced himself Kane was either a con man or a demented jokester. Anyway, an out-and-out liar. But denial came at a cost. By the end of this day, he was encased in a nagging, free-floating anxiety. To believe and not to believe at the same time, is hard on a person's psyche.

No answer on her cell. Maybe she'd turned it off. She did that sometimes at work. She had a landline. No answer there either. Simon shook his head against the creep of dread. What had come over him? He was normally a calm guy, mellow and unhurried. He really was — no matter his friends might not see him that way. Maybe she was held up at work. Some more-or-less emergency. That was probably it.

Switching on the engine he pulled off, drove down the highway, dashed in and out of lanes, took his exit, all in a resolute manner. Aimless ideas, floating bits of detail from the day dulled his anxiety. Loud music on the radio distracted him as usual. By the time he reached Janey's house, an arts-and-crafts bungalow, cream-stuccoed with bright red window shutters, he felt sweaty and nauseated. His mind had closed shut at the possibility that Janey had been married. That she had kept the fact of her marriage from him would be no small thing. Then his mind did a somersault. For what reason would she hide such a thing?

Then, as a saving grace, Simon began to intellectualize. What would it matter if she had been married? And not told him. She had simply not gotten around to telling him yet. Anyway, people, everyone comes with baggage. Even so, he was sure Janey's explanation would suffice with him. All would once again be well. At Janey's house he raced to the door and let himself in with the key she had given him. Normally, he knocked before entering, but Janey not answering her phone gave him a reason to use the key. He called her name, but no response. The house felt empty, so he stepped back onto the porch, relocked the door, and sat on a wicker chair to wait. At least he hadn't found that walnuto Arthur Kane in there with her.

He thought, slowed his heartbeat, thought some more. This was an ordinary relationship setback. Failure to communicate, didn't all couples suffer from that, time to time? But he couldn't let go of the senselessness of what he'd been told. Janey had been married. It shook him up. While he fought with this niggling bitterness, this gall, a shift occurred as if the ocean floor had buckled, and the coast within seconds was inundated with a wall of sea. Everything crushed and washed away, but not only that. Everything from that time forward was seen through shape-distorting water. Eventually, all would appear back to normal, but transformed, covered in brine and seaweed and sand. Simon squelched a noise at the bottom of his throat. A rise of despair slithered up his spine. He straightened with a mental jerk, rapped his right-hand knuckles against his left palm.

The arrival of an unknown husband hadn't done Simon in. It was his pathetic reaction to him. He called himself a toad, a sucker, a hypocrite. This wasn't he. But the fear of not having Janey, the Janey he had had this morning, made him rear in panic like a horse that spotted a rattler. When Simon couldn't wait a moment longer, he heard Janey's clippy gait, smelt her almond presence. She stood at the top of the steps, tousled curls, brown jersey and striped — yellow, green, blue, orange — scarf over a long slick azure skirt, the one she often wore when she had to appear in court. She hefted bags of groceries by the handles, jingling a bunch of keys against her hip to get the right one in a position to stick in the lock.

She lifted her brows and smiled, open, happy although smudged with fatigue. Obviously, she suspected nothing. For Janey the world had not done a swift disconnect.

"Hey, Simon." Something about him looked wrong. "Why didn't you go in? Did you just get here?" He followed her into the house. In a moment she came back from the kitchen and plopped on her soft Cyrene blue sofa. Instead of joining her there, he perched like a guest at the teak dining table.

"I thought we were all meeting at Braden's around eight? You know, to plan Carol's party... Did something happen?" He shook his head which she took as a "no" to there being anything wrong, although she thought he seemed a little testy.

"Well, I'm not ready obviously. If you wanna wait, turn on the TV, the *Trib*'s over there... I have to put all the groceries away and take a shower..." She meandered to the kitchen, kissing the top of his head as she went by.

His empty mind echoed the ruckus she was creating in the kitchen. Simon slunk to the front windows and gazed at the trees and the flickering street lights about to go on. He watched as the cars slid by. Slowly, the echo dissipated, and he began to think clearly again.

Out from the shower Janey tip-toed across the room in bare feet, her hair in wet ringlets, her curves snuggled inside a big, floppy bathrobe. Simon left his window lookout and settled back into the teak chair. At the sight of her normal, sexy self, he felt the stirrings not of desire, but anger. She was being obtuse, ignoring his obvious distress. He had never liked to bother her if a problem came up at his job. Janey worked all day with troubled people, so he hadn't thought it fair to dump his petty troubles on her. She should be good at listening, but seemed callous right now.

In fact, Janey was giving him time. Soon he would vent whatever had made him so moody and listless. After she dressed, when he still didn't speak she chatted uneasily at him. Lord, she hated silent standoffs. Some social workers were good at them, but not she. Passive-aggression frustrated the hell out of her.

"You wouldn't believe how crowded the Daily Grind is getting these mornings. All I wanted was a cup of coffee before court…ended up overhearing Sally talking while she took an old couple's order. She said she works from six in the morning to two in the afternoon seven days a week, which is good timing for her kids in school, but awful in the summer. Now get this, Simon, she told them what she hates about her shift is that she never gets to go out to breakfast anymore."

He glared while she hooted, then said, "What the hell do I care?"

"Good god, Simon." She pushed herself upright on the sofa where she'd flung back laughing. "Something is bothering you. There you were hanging outside my door. You looked like the ranting preacher man in my hometown—"

"Spare me his goddamn story—"

"What are you so upset about?"

"Listen to me once in a while. You get so tired handling those losers and dimwits, you don't have anything left for me." Hadn't meant to raise his voice.

"Well, tell me what's the matter." Her voice penetrated his pose. She was patting the cushion next to her, inviting him to sit where her nearness would melt him. In that moment he believed everything would work out. There must be a way to slough through this miasma.

"A guy came into the service bay this morning driving a Porsche." The dark hot mist in his chest congealed in his throat. He coughed. Janey waited. An unnatural, forced patience extruded from her. "He said he used to be your husband." He spit out then took a deep breath, expected a sign of indignation from her.

"Artie… I thought he might be dead."

Hope squeezed out of Simon, a collapsed crescendo. Hope that Simon had held to against all odds, clung to, hope — that slimy rock.

"So, so this Arthur Kane guy, he was your husband?" For that single moment he didn't think it would matter what she answered. But, of course, it would.

"Well, yes. Artie and I were married for a little while. About a thousand years ago." She eyed him for signs of distress and saw many. Still, this wasn't a client sitting there. "I had heard — must not have been true — that he had been in a bad crash and didn't survive."

Without understanding, except that things had changed, some other reality had arrived. Without feeling more than disenchantment, Simon lifted off the hard dining room chair and shifted to the indigo settee which put him closer to her. He lowered his haunches into its smooth curvature. Brief gust of relief went poof caused by Janey's indifference. She didn't seem to think his finding out about Kane indicated a breach between them.

Then the full force of it hit him as if he were a drowning body under stolid ice in a winter lake, that slipped beneath a glacial fissure, disoriented and about to freeze the moment before he would drown. He could not verbalize why he felt devastated.

He struggled to make sense of his turmoil. "But, you never told me about this guy. You never said you'd been married. All these months, Jesus… You went on about your mother, your sister, in Toronto. Hell, I even met them. They never said a word."

"They don't talk about my ill-fated marriage."

"How you worked for the mayor of Brampton. About, about, your dad's heart attack. Went on and on about that."

"It's natural we should tell each other those things. You talked about your family, too."

"That's my point. Being married, holy shit. You missed telling me that little detail? What a thing to skip." Maybe he was talking to himself, but it didn't matter. Didn't matter one bit.

Suddenly, Janey felt cold and vulnerable. She got up from the sofa and said, "You're upset and hey, obviously we've got to talk. We can go get something to eat and discuss this."

He stared in her direction without looking at her. "Not hungry."

"Yeah, well, I'm starving. You can eat or not, suit yourself. Let's go." She made ready to leave, reached into the little hall closet and grabbed her coat. As she opened the front door, she said, "Oh, and I better tell you… I've got an eight-year-old son."

That was the kicker. Furious, Simon pounced across the carpet, pushed past her, and stalked out. She thought she heard him mutter, "treacherous" and maybe "bitchy."

Used to people exhibiting hissy-fits, Janey mostly ignored Simon's. After getting herself a sandwich, she drove to Braden's house where they were to join a few of

Simon's friends to plan a party for Braden's girlfriend, Carol. Too much alone when she'd first come to Chicago, Janey had fit herself into Simon's crowd. She assumed Simon would cool off and show up there. She might have a chance to talk to him later.

They were drinking margaritas when she got there. Right off she let them know why Simon wasn't with her.

"What did you expect, Janey?" said Carol, looking for confirmation from Braden. "He's gonna be pissed about that."

Braden O'Neill with deep-set blue eyes bracketing a prominent nose, looked serene and thoughtful. His black hair sprinkled with premature gray, hung unfashionably, above his collar. When he sat, his legs looked about to trip him up if he rose too fast. Carol often, with affection, but pointedly, criticized his laid-back attitude. A cool, self-assured woman, Carol Quinn shone well-coiffed and twinkly. She was in her prime. She had had a bad marriage to an alcoholic who drank himself to death. Had no use for mental health workers, as she had told Janey when they first met. Braden said nothing. His opinions always arrived late.

"Oh, come on, Carol," said Janey, "He acted like it was a betrayal. I tell things at my own pace, in my own time. I would have gotten around to it."

"What? When did you think is the proper time? A former husband should be the first thing you mention in a new relationship. I'm not a therapist, of course," smile and ingratiating nod, "but wouldn't it be part of getting off on the right foot?"

"Hold on, Carol. You and Braden didn't know about Artie or Paulie either. I don't see you two carrying on like I've compromised our friendship."

"Paulie?"

"My eight-year-old. He'll be coming soon. He's with my mother in Toronto. I wanted him to finish his school year first. Less disruption—"

"My God," said Carol, her head spun like an eggbeater. "That's a lot for Simon to take in. It's different with friends versus lovers, anyway, of course. Don't you get it? Yes, you're Simo's girl, and we all get along. Great. But we're not going to get upset like Simo would. Our group of friends is close. Hell, Braden and Simo were in kindergarten together. There's not much we don't know about each other." Braden turned and raised his eyebrows at her. "Yeah, I suppose there are things about Braden I don't know. But I hope to God he'd tell me if he had an ex-wife."

"I don't have one."

When Janey laughed, said, "I see what you mean, "

Carol thought she'd hit home. She saw Janey wince.

"You could've told me. I thought we were getting along well. I like some new blood once in a while. And you'd come from Canada. I don't ask that much of people. I'm satisfied if they don't talk about me behind my back. Now Simon, he's always looking for a soul-mate. I don't even believe in soul-mates. Neither does Braden."

"I don't know what that means."

"Braden and I have a simple, uncomplicated kind of faith." She grinned at him, turned face-to-face with Janey. "Simon might equate this secret of yours with telling a lie. Don't you think holding things back might be like a lie?"

"No. It's in the law. If you lie you perjure yourself. You have a right to remain silent. Silence isn't consent, it's not a lie. It's silence." She'd gone far afield and was uncertain. "Anyway, he has to get over it. I didn't pretend anything. I'm not a criminal in a terrorist cell or something. This place, you all call — Chicagoland, it differs from my hometown…"

"People are people wherever. You act like Ottawa—"

"Toronto. I've been fair with Simon. We're dating, ah, going out. We aren't engaged."

Half-deflated, Carol said, "So why worry about it then?"

"I'm not, Simon is." It occurred to her that she didn't know why Artie had appeared out of nowhere. Been two years since he stopped calling Paulie. The boy had quit asking why. A few weeks ago she'd heard a rumor about Art's death. Not able to confirm it, she hadn't said anything to Paulie. She shivered at what it might mean.

"So, your son's coming?"

"Yes. He'll move here in June."

"How much better if you'd told Simon."

Late the next afternoon Simon Butler walked into the computer repair company where Braden worked. Braden wasn't surprised to see him. Trouble wasn't over when last night ended. Although Carol was forever trying to get him to lighten up, Braden at his core lived far happier than she fathomed. Where Carol had to seek out happiness, Braden had it sewn up inside him. He might sound cynical at times, and pessimistic about all life's adverse events, but daily living suited him.

Simon's eyes were wandering over all the computers and accessories, digital electronics galore.

"Simo, I'm on my way out."

"Where you going?"

"Darts with Biff and Carlo and Por'chop."

"Biff Saint James?"

"What other Biff?"

"Sounds good. I'll join you guys."

Simon flung up his arms and scampered out as Braden pushed the door closed behind them. They hurried down the busy, dusky city street.

"You don't like darts, Simo."

"I take 'em or leave 'em." His eyes flitted up and down the crowded avenue, people scattered every which way, cars backed up, pushing a few feet ahead or crimping along clogged streets, halo lights incrementally bluing for the dark. "Hey, Braden, you must've read about the shooting at the Chinese restaurant supply place… Know anything about that? Isn't the owner a customer of yours?"

"Wang Fat, sure. Multimillionaire. Don't know what they expected to get, burglars, if that's who it was. He's got a state-of-the-art security system."

"I heard the gunshots."

"Once, Wang told me 'fat' means riches in Chinese. That's why he's got so damn much money. It was fate."

"I thought they were backfires, but Janey…" At the crosswalk Braden stopped for the walk signal instead of plunging into the congested traffic. Simon shook his head.

"Stop being so skittish, Simo, and go talk to Janey. She told us about it last night. You didn't show, Dude. How could we plan Carol's party without you, huh? Go take her out for a drink. You don't wanna play darts."

Put off by Braden, Simon hustled back to where he'd parked his car. Funny guy, Braden. He'd known him forever, and still the guy got things he told him fouled up. He wasn't going to run after Janey. He needed some time to think.

It didn't take Simon many days to decide to call Janey. The week was creeping to its end, and he began to feel lonely. Janey must be devastated that she hadn't heard from him. Must be what Braden had meant. He hadn't given Janey a chance to make her point. He'd rushed out on her, and that wasn't like him. He who was fair-minded. He hadn't let her finish her explanation. Might be, there could be, an acceptable reason for her silence about Arthur Kane. If Kane threatened her maybe, and she had run away and hidden her son. So Simon called, asked Janey to dinner. He now felt sure there had been some horrid misunderstanding. She'd explain it to his satisfaction.

Simon chose Cyrano's, a romantic, toney restaurant. It seemed perfect, with a classy meal Janey would make his distress vanish. Cyrano's it turned out wasn't right. Quiet and mildly posh, the bistro's waiters hanging about ready to service every want, the ambiance hampered his deposing of Janey which was his real plan. Instead he put up with desultory talk about work and friends in intervals between courses.

This chatting, he mused, was uncharacteristic of her. Simon found he couldn't eat. Nothing left for it but to start the interrogation. After Janey enjoyed her grilled salmon, and the silence stretched out, he determined to make her talk.

"…Do you want to tell me about Arthur Kane now?" He implied 'about time' in his tone.

She sighed. "First off…I don't see it as very important… the way you do."

He let that pass. "I want the reason you didn't tell me, that's all. I know an ex-husband is no big deal to you. So why the hell didn't you tell me? You never explained that." His voice had raised; he lowered it and looked around him. "You didn't tell me about any goddamned husband."

"Artie and I are divorced. That's the long and short of it. I didn't want to go over that time in my life."

"But why not?"

"I didn't want to yet. I wasn't hiding anything, so Art would have come up in the normal course of events."

Simon swung his head side to side monkey-like in his biggest outward show of disbelief. Never had he imagined such calumny, so his mind was emptied of an authentic response. He kept swinging his head and cursing, "Jesus Christ."

"Stop it, Simon," she hissed. "I've only been in Chicago a few months. My son is coming in June. I would have told you about Artie then. You'll get to meet him, Paulie—"

His eyes crackled. "I will not. I'm not meeting any son unless you stop hiding things from me."

She drained the splash of white wine left in her goblet, and breathed out into the heated air.

"Want to know the gory details? Why I divorced Artie for a start? That I can tell you right now. One would think that in my line of work I would have anticipated this response of yours…this, this lacuna. So sue me, I didn't. I must be a lousy therapist." Unwisely, she started to laugh, loosed by two glasses of wine. "I had no idea…" Like the Margaritaville song, "hell it could be my fault." She shook back her hair, a frazzle of strands fell along her cheek. Simon didn't speak, let her dangle in the wind.

Janey took her time. "But to the point, yours. I see your annoyance and think I know what it means. You feel betrayed." She was being logical, professional. She knew that approach wouldn't work with him. But…what else was there?

"That's it, you got it," he said, and met her eyes with a

hardened stare. She resisted the urge to get up and walk out. Get this over with. But, leaving now wouldn't do it.

"I did not intentionally keep Artie's existence secret. I do not like to talk about those years." Spoken in separate words. Simon's discovery had pushed her toward a premature disclosure. He said nothing, let her dangle twisting like a bed sheet on her mother's summer clothesline.

At last he ended the impasse. "How can you say that — not meaning to keep it from me? You meant to or you wouldn't have done it."

"Not like…not like a secret I didn't want you to know. When I was fifteen, I broke my collarbone in a softball game. Year before last I spent twelve days in Lisbon with Stuart Blegen who got pneumonia, was laid up most of that so-called vacation. My mother had four children, the twins died in infancy before I was born. You didn't know any of this stuff either, not because I was holding it back. We've only gone out a couple of months. Lordy, we haven't gotten around to everything. Given time a couple learns a ton about each other, not all at once."

"Very good," he snarled, "sounds like a professional social worker calming a client. Well, I'm not your client, and it doesn't pass the smell test. I'm not a fool, Janey. There are things that couples say right away."

"Yes. I've been married. You would have known from the start if Paulie had been with me, or if I was the kind who jabbers about her kid all the time."

"Too bad you weren't a better mother."

That brought relief in a painful stab. She would have pled guilty to his charge of being thoughtless, or careless of his feelings. Not this last assault. She prepared to leave, digging money out of her bag because she didn't want him to pay a cent for her meal.

Simon was flush with victory. In truth, nothing she could have said to him, nothing would have satisfied except if the events of the last week had never happened. If only Janey had made Arthur Kane and her son magically disappear, no, not disappear — never have been — nullified. Nothing short of that would have done.

He watched her throw some cash down and leave without looking back.

TWO

ART Kane and Janey Leduc had been married for five years. Although Art made a high-risk living on the racing circuit, Janey had been misinformed about his demise. He continued to be successful and lucky. After competing in the Can-Am series, he had switched to IndyCars and won more than a dozen races there. Kane was a well-known and celebrated driver. In their five wedded years, she had come to terms with his compulsion to tempt death until he dragged her into his obsession. Why she had decided to leave him was the crucial part of her aversion to mentioning his existence.

During a vacation in Washington State they had taken a harrowing route up Mount Olympus, a winding, narrow, tortuous road which, of course, Art drove at as fast as is possible to go and still make the curves. Through her squinting eyes, a ribbon-thin of asphalt spiraled flush against the sheered rock face up one side. Skittering tires clinging to the gravel edge of a three-thousand-foot drop, screamed along the other side. A wired energy of adrenaline tricked her fear into a dangerous thrill as Arthur cradled the pulling wheel and up the speed even faster. His grim, game face on, his gut always aware how fragile a control his body had over the tons of steel, he steered the car with manic detachment, a fatalistic bravado.

A sickening terror gripped her throat and clawed her stomach as Artie pumped the rental's strained brakes without the car even slowing. They were spongy, Arthur later said, couldn't breach the curve's swing back. In a static moment of horror, the box of steel plunged down an escarpment, dug out huge roots, flung mounds of earth over stunted pine and scrub oak, screeching against outcrop boulders, until the car caught, trembled. It balanced perilously on a huge sequoia limb, a fat monstrous branch which creaked and bent but held the juggling automobile. Inside the car, almost insensate, Janey screamed and screamed.

"We went over the cliff and fell. And the car caught on a tree," she would tell her mother, "...suspended over the abyss by a tangle of fragile threads." For three hours until they were found and rescue workers could reach them and extract them, they hung there. Swaying, terrified, shivering in shock, swaying over the tops of trees above the ravine. They were plucked out the of the dangling wreck as the disturbance of removing them jarred lose the car's precarious balance. The death trap went rappelling in sickening smashes to the bottom of the mountain. Still, at moments Janey couldn't stop the dreaded memory coming back to her in real time, but with muted affect, the way fear becomes absorbed into the skin like a toxic waste which isn't deadly but settles into the body's tissues forever.

It changed her. To an ineffable degree, it changed her. It was the wait more than anything else.

She had lain safe, lingering in euphoric relief in the ambulance when out of nowhere hot shivers of terror began coursing through her. On and on they went. She came out of the panic attack at last by making a compact she would not compromise and that she adhered to the rest of her life. As soon as she was out of the hospital, she gathered up their little son and left Art Kane. He was quicker to heal from his injuries, but it took him awhile to figure out she had left. From that moment on she lived with intention. She felt the authenticity of not sleepwalking through life. She swore never, not ever, to spend even an hour unaware. Not ever again. She could see that it would be impossible to impress on anyone what had lit up in her. Lit up in colors of bright transcendence which soaked her being. It would be impossible to explain to anyone why she had bolted from her old life.

Simon's response, if she had told him her story, would be negligible. Would it work for him if she said that a bad accident on Mount Olympia was why she put Arthur Kane out of her mind? If filtered through to the essence of things a germ of truth could evolve into words. Later when she took a leap of faith and spoke of it to Braden, she knew there had been a fundamental shift. No longer did she exist in the silent drip drip drip of ordinary life. But all that was to come. Simon Butler, she confessed to herself tonight, might have been a mistake.

∽

It burst like shrapnel from nowhere. As if a piece of illusion scraped open a crevice in the boulders blocking the hidden cavern's entrance. A streak of white light — torn jagged-edged silver — an escape opening. There seemed a way out. A refrain, a jingle, danced after the blink of thought from elsewhere, flicker words: "Desperate hopes are sureties in the land of make-believe," strangely,

strangely. Gone now. Nudged aside by a waterfall of musical notes designed beyond the cavern, faraway but heard. If only she could hold out long enough to reach it.

Leah Campion had been laid low by profound loss. Her only child, Jonathan, had been killed in action in Afghanistan and her grief was inconsolable. It had been nine months since his death, as much time as she had carried him in her womb. She had become aware of that irony when she went to bed. Each morning's return to consciousness was hell. Never a moment of relief. She woke to the fact that her son was dead.

From beneath her ribs, Leah drew cautious, shallow breaths. Today a reprieve. Alive. All checked out. Yet no sharp claws at her heart. Her abdominal muscles took a deeper breath. She flicked open her eyes and sought the glow that had awakened her. Under a window shade the daylight seeped in. Turning over, Leah curled up fetal-style and hid her head under her flattened pillow to be numbed again in sleep. No need today. An analgesic shield seemed to be holding. That lacquer of remembrance, not stupor but coherent, self-aware, attainable through her senses, hardened her waking up. She pedaled further into her mind. Must locate where the breach was, the fissure through which the balm flowed. It had assuaged her wake-up misery.

Fully awake she struggled to move out of the bed. Cold. But only from the chill in the room, not localized in her psyche, not clammy to the touch. A thought was slipping around. If she moved her body perhaps — although it seemed improbable she could get decisively out of bed.

An image of sorrow — the underside of wrinkled bat wings, ugly stretches of skin — she dashed it away. If he had managed to live despite his horrible wounds he would have been shattered, body and mind mangled, eyeless, face scarred, his beautiful face. Worse than death, she thought, then her mind shut down. Sat on the edge of her bed, a blank. Betrayal, sorrow's so despicable consolation. Unbidden a calmness cloaked her. No. She would not let the grief lessen. That would be the end if she let time begin to erase her pain. That her son was dead — the cruel actuality of it — from that there was never a reprieve. She had stopped denying he was dead, even before they sent his body home. The Guard money was going to send him to school.

She hoisted herself up off the side of the bed, put on robe and slippers, moved like a turtle to open the door — get to the bathroom. A fierce pain hit her as a vanquished image returned, only a vapor of itself, the Improvised Explosive Device in the road. What she'd seen when the Lieutenant spoke to her. When his body came home. In the crushing, blindingly dark night in front of the curtained bay window. A hidden mine meant for anyone. An indiscriminate exploding device, what were the odds? Shut it out of her mind. Don't fall back onto the bed, into the abyss.

Slowly, Leah washed, lugged herself into the kitchen. The gist of it was whether she was going to get dressed today and go out. Head drooping over the coffee maker, Leah heard the phone ringing. Her sister, Merry Alice, checking up on her again. Once a day, sometimes twice. She lifted the phone to her ear.

"I've been calling for an hour."

"I was in bed."

"It's almost noon. Leah, what are you doing to yourself? You haven't stepped outside in days. Good lord, listen to me. You have to snap out of it."

Leah wiped perspiration off her forehead with a napkin. "Don't be daft. You talk without thinking, Merry, always did…bad habit. Makes people think you're an idiot."

"You can't shut yourself in forever." Merry Alice lived up to her name, sanguine, positive, her long blonde hair pulled up in a topknot, eyebrows penciled in, she'd be cheerful and optimistic at eighty.

"I can, if I want."

"Oh, I know, it's gotta be too much for you to bear." They both knew what Merry Alice had said was inane. Of course, Merry Alice couldn't fully comprehend Leah's loss. Out of a remnant of mercy, Leah prayed she never would.

"I'm all right at this minute. And that's enough…"

"The farmers' market, come with me to the farmers' market this morning. Will you? There'll be flowers, sweet corn, preserves, fresh veggies. Homemade bread. Huh? Will you?"

Although Merry Alice couldn't see her, Leah shook her head. She shivered. A look of agony swept her blue eyes. Only a few years past forty, slender and attractive before this burden had made her too thin, had sapped her energy, Leah had been strong, vivacious. The darkness deepened, crushing her.

"Come on, Leah, you've been cooped up for weeks and weeks. I'm going to this stupid market and…you are, too. You can't stay like this forever. I'll come get you."

"I'm not—"

"Yes, you've got to—"

"I'm not staying in. I'm going someplace. The office

called yesterday. They can't extend my leave any longer… so I quit."

"You quit your job? Oh, Leah. They've bent over twice backward to help you."

"I've made up my mind, Merry Sweetie, hear me."

"But you don't seem—"

"Myself? I never will be that again. But, I'm enduring it, Merry."

Relieved and panicked, Merry Alice said, "What you going to do?"

"I'm going to go out and find a new job. I've been off work for months. I need to support myself."

"Oh," panic dissipated. "I see." Somewhat mollified, the owl-eyed Merry Alice allowed Leah to end the conversation.

Leah Campion started a practical train of thought as if this morning her water of sorrow had broken as a quickening water had done when Jonathan was born. Today, her despair had given way to an idea of continuation, the need to keep Jonathan with her. She must figure out a way to do that. If she meant never to bow to losing her son, irrationally she felt a need to find out where he was. He had suffered a sea change, could never be created as Jonathan another way, nor destroyed.

He was somewhere. To find him she had to come alive.

She dug through the newspaper recycle bag and pulled out yesterday's classified section. Yesterday she had noticed a classified ad seeking someone for a curiously worded position. Even in her malaise it had intrigued her. A job with something hidden in it. A job proper to her search. This ad had appealed, unusual work, not bizarre or peculiar, but it went with a hint of the exotic in its job description. A jewelry store owner was looking to train an associate, it read. Followed by a list of what she might be expected to do: appraise gemstones, choose settings, clean and repair clocks and watches. Then the kicker: No prior experience necessary. She thought that last bit must have been written tongue-in-cheek. It said he was willing to train. Yeah, she thought, serious training at that.

Leah, as she drove away from her bungalow, unconsciously enjoyed the motion of her body, the kinetic muscles, smooth moving joints. She was taking comfort from the buffeting wind and warming sunlight. Early afternoon in June could be too sultry. But the heat against her back and arms soothed her today. She felt a lift at the sight of the whitecaps on Lake Michigan, far-out waves of roiling argent tipped with topaz. Allowed herself to inhale prickles of living, as she followed the Chicago skyline, dropping into the curve of the shore, elbowing the water into the sky. Alive, what it meant, in the beginning. It was enough to bring a smile. Her body tensed, breathing halted. Jonathan could not. The cheery moment flashed to a burned-out filament. Life force, though, still fluttered inside her. Her hands clutched the steering wheel with purpose. All the thought, all the movement, all the goings-and-comings had taken great energy. Leah stretched out her arms and leaned backward, rounded the corner and headed west on Dempster, revving the car into the flow of traffic.

In a small strip-mall over the North Shore Channel, she searched for the name from the want-ad. The jewelry store's front windows glittered in a natty red brick building amidst a string of commercial shops. Its sign read "Claymore Mandebrote, Fine Gems" and below that "In-House Bench and Jewelry Service." Before entering Leah gazed at the front display. She stood unsure, considered going home. Like the centipede, she thought, I know how to do this, I don't have to think about it. Then she pulled the heavy beveled glass door open and walked in.

Iridescent colors played inside the glass counters along two sides of the entrance and on island showcases in the middle of the carpeted floor. Her eyes danced around, brilliant earrings, a heart-shaped peridot, star diamonds, an emerald pendant, gold hoops, an oval amethyst ring,

South Sea pearls, an array of birthstones, both high-end watches, and throw-aways. In one corner of the shop sat grandfather clocks, elegantly numbered faces in shining hardwoods. As if she were a customer, she took a turn around the store, ignored by the elderly man behind the back counter, staring at his computer.

On artistically rumpled velvet sat a gold, lariat necklace, a Byzantine cross, and a ruby encrusted watch with the face of a bulldog. A bit like the Field Museum, she thought, what endless beauty… Then, it all became tiring, precious, semiprecious stones, she recognized or they were labeled, all soured to baubles and trinkets. Each glistening piece had given off its unique tint, hue, patina. A bell had tinkled when she walked in. The old man hadn't looked up when she came so most likely wouldn't when she left. She was only a customer who hadn't found what she was looking for.

As she turned to leave, the man lifted his head and asked if he could help her. She saw a shortish figure in a brown cardigan, grey hair that flopped sideways over his forehead, hazel eyes behind wire-rimmed spectacles, a large, handsome head, prominent, slender nose, quizzical expression. The bell tinkled as customers sauntered in, a blonde, pink-faced, matron-looking woman in a dark suit. A young man and woman in jeans stopped at the big clocks in the front alcove and began talking fast. The older woman went to the revolving swivel displays of costume earrings.

While Leah hesitated, the owner — it was he — had left his computer and approached her, a jeweler's loupe clutched in his fingers.

He was cut off by the matronly woman who insinuated herself between him and Leah and demanded attention.

"I'm rather in a hurry. I wonder if you can help me," she said to him. "I have to get a preliminary appraisal of a diamond. Could you take a look at this?" Dragged him to his station at the back of the shop. Leah hung around and listened. The young couple chirping happily had left the store.

"It's large, yah, sure." The diamond lay on a suede pad in front of him. He pulled at his sweater, unsure what to say. These were delicate cases, family heirlooms. "I wouldn't worry too much about size, Mrs. Van Hooten."

"A couple of carats, my great-aunt said. An antique, as you can see. She never married. She bought it as an investment, and it's come down to me."

"Size is only one indication of worth, Ma'am."

Mrs. Van Hooten looked warily at him. "Oh?"

"You see the table..." Tepid smile. "Has a girdle through it."

"What does that mean?" The woman appeared offended, plucked up the ring and caressed it.

"The stone's been cut too shallow," he said. "And it draws a little color. That detracts from its quality, maybe D grade. Wear it, Mrs. Van Hooten, it's very pretty. And a diamond it is. But as an investment… A thousand dollars."

To the woman the jeweler's voice sounded contentious, words askew. "I don't believe it. She must have paid too much. Was she cheated?"

"Difficult to say. Wise not to buy diamonds without knowing your seller."

"Really, she paid a great deal for it."

"It's a lovely ring. Wear it. Pave diamond, torque, eighteen-carat, yellow-rose and white-gold. Wear it, Ma'am in good health."

Leah turned and looked up after quick footsteps trod past her, then heavier walking seemed to sneak up on her.

"Can I help you, Miss?" He shrugged one shoulder, kept it elevated under his ear. She gave off sadness, a drawn, harrowed, suffering face.

At his first words, Leah thought better of asking for this job. What were stones and color to her? But she had appeared to be waiting for something and felt stuck.

"I'd like to look at necklaces…for my niece," dug herself deeper, "To match her party dress." Ill-chosen words, however the jeweler didn't seem to notice.

"Color?"

"Ah, what?"

"Of your niece's dress? We start with color."

"I'm not sure."

"Pearls? For instance… Many teenagers like the accent of pearls these days."

"No, not pearls."

"So, there's—"

"I'll look around a little."

That threw the old man. She'd been in here long enough to memorize his available stock of necklaces.

"Of course. Sure." He moved to the end of the counter and slid open the back of a case, rooted through his displayed wares.

Leah had begun to sidle toward the door when the jeweler jerked upright and slid quickly over to her, a necklace laced in his fingers.

He held up a string of shimmering violet stones, each graded size seductively grew larger in a serpentine motif. Beguiling. Leah couldn't take her eyes off the brilliant color.

"What is it?" she said.

"Tanzanite," he nodded. "It's called a journey necklace."

"I have to tell you… I didn't come here to buy anything."

She saw the old man's face harden, with maybe a trace of suspicion. She hurried on — don't sound as fraught and nutty as you feel. "Actually, I came to apply for the position you advertised about. In the *Trib*. But now...I'm not sure it's right..." Her eyes drifted back to the dazzling necklace. "I don't know anything about jewelry."

"Good. Yes." He took up the necklace as if she might snatch it. "I don't mind that. I'll go get you an application." Now not so agile the old man shuffled off and shuffled back a few minutes later with a sheet of paper and an apologetic smile.

"I'm not so sure either. I put the notice in the help wanted like I needed an assistant. It's really an apprentice I'm looking for. Someone to teach. Well, and wait on the customers naturally." He studied the movement of Leah's eyes. Did she look distraught or only cautious? He trusted his instinct in this matter more than what she would put on an application. He added, "You know?"

Leah snapped up the application from him not looking at him, like a rude adolescent forced to take make-up homework. It didn't matter. Nothing mattered except for being released from this absurd job interview. Did she want to work here or not? If she needed to make money they would take her back at ConEd. There was little use for money so no reason for employment. But she must answer the waiting man standing there expectantly.

"I'm not so sure I'd be any good at selling."

His expression changed and so, too, did his appearance. He seemed to be making an appeal. "No, no. Don't worry. Minor part. I have long-established regulars. I'm looking for a person who is interested in all of it. Look… Gems, you see, color, plays of brightness, the things that determine value, rarity, Miss, see, from this quality and source. Not only your diamonds, sapphires, rubies and emeralds, but semi-precious… Thousands of stones. Here. Wait." He whipped away, tore open a drawer beneath a showcase, and hobbled back winded, with a ring in hand. The stone had multicolored bands of burnt umber pierced with streaks of white. "Here. Sardonyx, the chalcedony that in ancient times was associated with the planet Saturn. The sky came down to the earth. Do you see? Look at it and think how fine and beautiful. And, and, have you seen heliport in the white light above the sun?" All at once the old man seemed to be coaxing. She wasn't put off by his extravagance. Perhaps the way she'd been made mad by grief, he'd been made mad by beauty.

Next morning Leah walked through the beveled front door of the jewelry store. Claymore Mandebrote noticed her come in. Yesterday, she'd been hired on the spot. He continued what he was doing before she arrived. Jeweler's glass attached at his forehead, he leaned over his workbench, needle nose pliers twisting a lobster-claw clasp.

"Come here, Miss. You got that application all filled out? " He didn't look up. "What is…" He groaned as a spark of violet-blue seemed to blow out from his knuckles. "God damn arthritis — in my God damned hands… What the hell is your name?"

"Leah Campion." She spelled her last name for him so he wouldn't mix it up with "champion." Often people did. She wasn't put off by his curses, rather they soothed her nervousness.

"Leah. I will teach you my trade."

"I'm no jeweler. I haven't any ambition to be one. Here, it's all in my application. I'm… I don't want to administrate, like…I did at ConEd. I think that working here would suit me. But I don't want you to have any illusions about me. I'm middle-aged, so it's called."

"To me it's called young." He looked at her at last, "I'll just show you a few things," put aside her application for later. "Let's get started before we open up." She followed him out of the back room to the store front. "I never open before ten. Ten to six. Hour for lunch, for you that's at one-thirty. Come on, come on…"

Back from lunch Leah found a frizzy-haired tall young woman in a gray jerkin and blue tee-shirt, shoulders tilted slightly forward, who pranced impatiently at the side counter. She chattered at Mr. Mandebrote whom she repeatedly called, "Clay." Mandebrote emitted bleats of negatives to her volley of requests.

"...Chinese stones. I got back from China a few weeks ago, and since then I've been working fourteen hours a day on them. Rings, and bracelets, some earrings. Come on, Clay, please, take look at what I have…"

"I don't sell commissioned jewelry, Loretta—"

"But you have done, I know."

He shook his head, plucked at his glasses. "Ach, once, twice maybe. Can't do it anymore. I'd have this shop filled to the ceiling with you artists' creations. You have your art fairs, that's where you sell."

The woman's face had set in sullen determination, drawn long, translucent skin unpowered. She pulled her spindly shoulders back, a coat draped open, slid half-off.

"Clay, look at my things, huh? Come on…" Her mouth watered, eyes fried like eggs.

Mandebrote slid his lips into an acquiescent smile. "I'll look. You do beautiful designs. I like, especially, your rings. But go someplace else to sell them. Go to the Jewelry Exchange." She heard the finality in his voice.

"Don't do that. I'll bug off. But you don't have to treat me like an idiot." She brushed past Leah on her way out.

A customer came in, then another. All afternoon she watched Mandebrote and learned the routine. Near time to close, when the store was empty, he showed her gemstones, and began teaching her.

Merry Alice phoned as Leah was making oatmeal.

"You got a new job already!" Almost indecent to be that surprised about it.

"Well, yes… I've been working a couple of days. At least he hasn't fired me yet."

"I should think not. Loved your message, no employee discount. And here I have two sons who will eventually be buying diamonds. Are you his only clerk?"

"Yes, it's a small store."

"Exclusive?"

"Expensive, anyway, if that's what you mean. Mandebrote, the owner, is a gemologist. He seems to want to make me his apprentice. Like something out of Dickens."

A snort of contempt. "How much he paying you, if I can ask?"

"You can ask, but I can't say. I'll find out when I get my first check on Friday."

"You took a job without knowing what you get paid? Leah, honestly—"

"I guess I don't care. Wait a minute, Merry Alice." She lowered her voice, time to quit the sister inquiries. "I did do a Google search. He's been in business forty years." Interesting to find that she had to pretend to be more cautious than she was. She'd done no such search. For whatever reason or for no reason she was satisfied with this particular job. She had to apply a bit of cosmetic treatment so her sister wouldn't get her cocksure dander up.

Merry Alice listened. "Yes, okay. You can always quit if this clerk thing doesn't work out.

"My breakfast is ready. Gotta go…"

She poured her oatmeal into her bowl and collected her buttered toast. Her appetite had begun to return. She wished for something to laugh at, someone there to laugh with. She turned on the television, flipped open her laptop, grabbed the newspaper. Since Tom had left a few years ago, she had gotten used to living without the human voice. Then she stopped eating, and put her head down, sinking into the chair, rubbing her forehead. It was this complete aloneness. If only this total emptiness would abate… She dithered with the idea of taking the pills Dr. Swan had written, a script which she had filled, but left sitting in the cabinet with her good China, never used either.

Then she raised her head and labored to clean her cooking mess, load the dishwasher. A slight lift as she made her kitchen pristine, to its remodeled, spiffed-up state. She felt a bit better, not enough, but the blind gloom dissolved in a hiss of oxygen. At first calm, then lightness.

It was easier to sleep that night. In her mind she rehearsed Mandebrote's criteria: beauty, rarity, durability, desirability, and the gem phenomena lulled her to sleep. So soporific the sounds — adularescence, asterism, aventurescence, chatoyancy, color change, tincture play, iridescence. Shapes like oval, heart, trilling, pear, marquise, baguette — played softly over her disquieted mind.

THREE

SIMON Butler thought it was a good idea. Phone Claymore, an old family friend, at his jewelry store, talk to him. He had to talk to someone. Braden had been no good. Claymore was most likely still there, closing up. He could have rung his cell, but Clay never turned it on. Simon wondered why Clay paid month after month for a device that sat on his kitchen table, useless. And this was the man he had decided to confide in. But Claymore would look at things differently which might help. Simon's anger had toned down. He was regretting his flight from Janey's house. Admitted to himself that he missed her. Maybe Clay could tell him what to do. No answer at the shop. Of course, the answering machine wasn't turned on, which would have done him no good anyway. Clay never listened to his messages.

Simon knew that Claymore often went for dinner to a deli near his store before heading home. A bit of nausea arose at the thought of eating there. He could have a cup of coffee.

At one of the deli's few little tables, Clay Mandebrote, warned by Simon's grim face and cocky stride, sipped his espresso, plunked the tiny cup down on its tiny saucer and steeled himself. Simon had tracked him here to kvetch.

"Jesus Christ…" Out of breath Simon scraped his rickety chair up to the table. "Sex is a trap. 'Erotic combat,'" he said, quoting from a movie review he'd read.

"I have these last couple years given it a wide berth — with a tone of humorous regret to lighten the mood. "Even when the occasion arose. But not all old men do, don't get me wrong."

"I've gotta talk to you, Clay." Interrogate him, it sounded like to Claymore. Simon wondered at his own patience while the old guy babbled. "You know I've been seeing this beautiful chick, Janey Leduc." The name slipped out. He hadn't intended to say it. He plunged on. His own flinty voice sounded off-key. Dolorous angst or melancholy would be better. He dipped his head to hide his calculation. This was too serious to bungle.

"You listening to me, Clay?" He shouted at the counterman. "Get me a Coke."

Claymore watched him slurp the drink splashing over the lip of the glass, making rivulets down its iced flutes. He looked like a peevish child.

"What's bothering you, Simon?" The jittery hands and flushed face were annoying Clay.

"I've been driving myself nuts, just…nuts, over this woman. Janey, my god I don't know how to say this, betrayed me in the worst way—"

"Another man, Simo, you two aren't married."

"No, not that. Something worse."

"Worse? I'm acquainted with the lady and can hardly believe—"

"Well, whatever, it is a betrayal. She lied to me and kept an important thing about her personal life from me. I can't forgive that, I will not."

"My God, Simon, does she have AIDS?"

"You dickhead of course not."

"Either make yourself clear, Simon, or let me go home. I've had a long day. My new employee can tire one. She affects me. A look she can give sometimes like a suffering diva."

Simon wasn't interested in all that stuff. He fiddled with the sticky brown dribbles under his glass. "You can't love someone who keeps secrets from you." Shook his head. "No way."

"I'm going to leave, Simon, time to go home." He grunted as he hitched up from the hard chair.

"Wait. Wait. Will you listen to me? I just want to know if I should fuck it all and tell her to get lost. I don't need this. I do not need this at all."

Claymore felt a wave of disgust at that miserable self-pity. Whatever it was bothering him, the guy was making it worse. He was sure he wouldn't understand Simon's predicament, and he was determined not to have to try.

Simon raced on, made more furious by Clay's disinterest. He'd get some help from the barmy old guy if he had to drag it out of him.

"She — Janey that is — was married once. I learned about it by accident Tuesday at work. And when I confronted her, she laughed it off. No big deal.

"I didn't know that… So what is the big deal? She whack her first husband or something?"

Simon swallowed rising anger, puzzled but persistent. The old man was being ridiculous. "We've been dating for three months, and by God she never told me she had an ex-husband. Even has an eight-year-old son." Indignation lifted his voice a notch.

"Did she drown her son in the river?" Claymore struggled at what horror Simon was alluding to here.

"Are you being dotty on purpose? Oh, go the hell

home, Claymore. I'll figure this out myself."

Perversely, Claymore sat back down. "That's it? That's what's bothering you? Janey Leduc's unforgivable sin?"

Simon exaggerated his pronunciation as if he were speaking to his senile grandmother. "It's a violation of trust. Everything that makes a loving relationship, a real live commitment."

'Well, I do see what you mean, but everything isn't so easy to explain." He tried to make as little of the disclosure as he could. Otherwise he wouldn't get home before the news on television.

"You do understand, then, why I'm so freaked out about this?"

"Sure, Simo. I've known you for a long time. For ages I've known your mother and father…" Good people. Father a little high-strung.

"What should I do? What is there to do? By God, I don't want to quit this relationship. That woman's gotten under my skin." He struggled to collect his wits.

Claymore thought, a rabbi or a priest is what he needs, which he's not gonna get here.

Before Simon could say more, Clay said, "I've got a new person at the shop." Wrong way to go, wholly wrongheaded, he knew as he glimpsed Simon's flushed face, rounded like a child's. A case of misplaced confidence. "I'm no guru. A strange, lovely, sad-faced woman who seems… will listen when I'm instructing her, about the gemstones. Quiet, quiet all the time. I liked her right away."

Simon felt a rebuke. "So, maybe you don't think much of Janey? Maybe you think she's not good enough for me." His anger had swirled in crimson down to his white jaw which he had clenched. Claymore could see highlighted the spots he missed when he had his morning shave.

"No such thing, Simo. I only know Janey a little, but she seems like a nice girl. She has a hard job at the Lutheran Social Services. I know that because my niece is getting help there with this young man she's latched onto, this Edwin guy. Dorrie attracts waifs, since she was a kid. I wish she didn't."

In a temporary truce they left the diner together.

Thinking, that better not be Edwin sitting there. What a long day… Claymore inserted his key and pushed the door open, keeping his eyes averted from the long, angular pale face of the bony young man crouching on his cement steps. Maybe he'd disappear if he could get himself inside real quick. But Edwin sneaked in behind him.

Claymore switched on the table light in his tidy, sparsely furnished living room while Edwin traipsed to one of the twin wingback chairs on either side of the small brick fireplace. An Asham carpet he bought years ago in Damascus covered most of the polished hardwood floor. In a corner under two large windows stood a little desk, green-shaded library lamp on its leather top. Filled bookshelves, a television, a few photos on the fireplace mantle, a number of pictures — abstract oils, Post-Impressionist prints, nothing much else in the room. A sofa faced the twin chairs and there Claymore dumped down in exhaustion. Teaching Leah, okay, but listening to Simon so that he couldn't enjoy his espresso, and now pretending to be interested in whatever Edwin might say, was too much for one day. He was well into his seventies. However, as his mother used to say, no rest for the wicked.

Edwin lifted forward and waved a stapled set of papers at Claymore until he grabbed them. While he looked them over, Edwin talked.

"Will you help me with these forms? Lutheran Social Services. It's for my search for my birth-mother. Dorrie helped me get started, but she's out of town for a few days, went up to the Dells with some friends, and I need advice right now. Did I fill it out all right? It'll only take a minute to check. I want it to be perfect. See if you can figure out what I'm supposed to do with these papers next. Am I supposed to turn them all in to the office there?"

Getting up, Edwin's crumpled papers in hand,

Claymore shrugged out of his jacket and walked back to an old-fashioned wooden coat stand in the tiny hall. He hung it on a hook, then checked the thermostat, clicked it up a notch. It was chilly in the house, empty-feeling, damp for June. He made quick silent promise to get rid of this scruffy young man, then he could go to bed and be warm.

For a couple of weeks Edwin Blake had sought out Clay now and then, to try out his preposterous lies on him. One of Dorrie's waifs, yes, but the least sympathetic of them. Edwin might ask for money on occasion, never for very much, small amounts more to elicit sympathy from Clay or approval in oblique ways. Edwin seemed to know what he was doing. Then always with a wry smile, he seemed to challenge Clay, to try out some outrageous whopper on the old man. Those blatant falsehoods, even the more subtle ones, settled on Edwin's face and would — like secrets from an untrustworthy accomplice — give a hint to his motives.

Claymore slid back onto the sofa and handed Edwin back his papers.

"How is it, Clay?"

"This looks...a lot like a legal document. I'm not a lawyer—"

"No. It's not. I got to get this ready." Edwin went on

talking and talking. He needed it completed by tomorrow morning, some of the questions he didn't understand at all.

While Edwin asseverated, kneading his hands into fist-balls, Claymore became distracted by the young man's lips. Like two smooth guppies they slid over sound shapes as if to help Clay listen like a man hard of hearing would. Edwin had a sharp handsomeness, with chiseled face bones stretched under taut skin.

Clay began to feel sleepy. "Look, Edwin, these blank spaces you're worried about. They need to be filled in by the social worker. Take it there to finish it up in the morning. I'm going to bed now."

Edwin went silent as he walked to the door. With the superiority of youth he was thinking, you, old man, are so friggin' out of it and dumb.

As soon as he let Edwin out, Clay took himself off to bed. He slept the sleep, if not of the just, at least of the worthy.

At the jewelry store Clay Mandebrote, early and well-rested, anticipated the arrival of his remote and sympatica new clerk-cum-student of gemology. A quick study she had been yesterday. He was curious how she'd continue with him today.

He noticed Leah hanging around outside the front

window, sipping from a take-out cup. Mystified, was she timid about bringing her coffee into the store?

As she sipped her coffee, Leah stared at the black, reflective, stenciled lettering: CLAYMORE MANDEBROTE, PROP., CERTIFIED GEMOLOGIST AND APPRAISER, beneath the sign in block lettering, "In-House Bench & Jewelry Service" on the bright, clear, windexed glass. The letters limned the fear she'd felt on awakening this morning. Brought on, perhaps, by the anxiety of a new job, or was it like a new beginning which mimicked death. If she could start again, at her age, almost forty-five, if that signaled a step toward an unknown, then let it come. Better to go toward whatever than linger in this miasma of life without her son. Let it come. Let…it come.

A slow day for customers gave them plenty of time for a gem lesson. Claymore was gratified by the stern attention Leah paid to his tutelage. Her eyes lit up when something he said intrigued her; she saw the beauty he wanted her to see. The polished stones and crystals, radiant metals, shiny offerings created from the composition of the planet, gems judged by Clay not in monetary worth, not in money for god's sake, but for some intrinsic measure of beauty. What that measure was — how a piece of coal under great pressure becomes a gem of immense value — he did not comprehend. Still, although so thoroughly of this earth, a gem burned as from another world for him.

They were examining, as Clay pronounced to her, color play and iridescence in a pair of marquise-shaped aquamarine earrings set in 18 K yellow gold from which hung clustered, green beryl ovals. Clay indicated with a wave of two fingers at its tear-drop how the gems were properly cut. "Check the faceting, that the proportions balance. You don't want to see any shaving. Look for the telltale girdling through its table."

"What is the table?" She asked.

"That is the facet at the top. Flat, you see. If the stone's cut too shallow…"

She learned and he reveled in the teaching. For all his life, no one had wanted, in truth, to know.

But he most liked it when she asked him something he didn't know.

"Where does it come from, the brightness?"

Customers came, were waited on, and went off. In a quiet period mid-afternoon, Claymore called her over to him, brought out a black jeweler's loupe.

"This Chalcedon we call sardonyx, let's take a look at this piece. Look at it, with this eye. Closely. Study it…" He moved his arm slowly. "No, no, no. Bring the gem up to the loupe, never the other way around. We power it to times ten, and if no flaws are revealed at that magnification, then any possible flaw we might miss we don't consider. For our purposes, it's like it's non-existent…even if it might be heavily occluded.

She looked perturbed, *too fast…how can I take all this in…* There was an authority in his words that intimidated her. Claymore rocked back on his worn-down heels and seemed pleased.

"This here, it's an excellent example of 'industrial quality.'"

She contemplated the loupe clutched by his eye. His hand, shaking a bit, moved the jewel up to his face.

"Maybe too many foreign bodies," he said bemused, explaining almost as an afterthought. He went on to explain about crystal shape absorbing light differently at different angles when the bell tingled and a pale young man banged into the store and strode purposefully to the back counter.

"Nothing but consistency of color—" Clay stopped when he spotted Simon Butler coming on.

Simon's voice rang out too loud in the small area, "Oh, there you are, old man, no borax, never doublets or triplets, never simulants or synthetics, haven't I heard that spiel often enough? Only the real thing in your emporium."

"What can I do for you, Simo?" Claymore said, last night's fidgety boy bothering him at work. "I'm busy you see with my new hire."

Simon's eyes flitted past a tallish woman hovering near Clay's stiffened form. Nice looking although middle-aged; he ignored her as if she weren't there.

"I thought I'd drop in on you." He blinked. Over-lit, the shop seemed to show off all the swanky riches. He edged his way down the counter's length and paused to watch what Claymore was doing. Then he at last acknowledged Leah's presence. "You sure you want to work here? Can't believe old Clay would be anything but a hard-ass boss."

Leah said nothing to that. Didn't even wonder how this guy and Mandebrote were connected. These were the kinds of things that didn't matter to her anymore. Popping the loupe into its case, Clay wrapped the jewels in their velvet pockets and tucked them inside a deep drawer in the back wall. "Lesson's over, Leah."

Just as well, since two customers walked in together, claiming Clay's attention. A handsome couple, man and woman talking low and rapidly to each other. Leah stood aside to be unobtrusive but listen to what she would soon be called on to do. Claymore was showing them diamonds, talking to them in his professional mode, the right amount of interest and care, no hint of high pressure.

In the interlude, Simon brushed at his short brown hair and sulked, impatient, head lowered over the vitrine as if enthralled with the fancy timepieces contained there. Leah wondered at the oddity of being in this place, at the reflection of her spare, unremarkable figure in her new, business-looking outfit, her hair molded into chic style by her own talented hand. She had been unconsciously preparing to be back in the workforce these last few days. A good sign of recovering herself, Merry Alice would say. But Leah felt she was giving in, falling into the concavity of what is. From this hollow she had made ready for her new job. An out-of-time disjuncture, a ruptured sequence, mangled reality. It had taken a good deal of courage to proceed.

Claymore left his customers to discuss which of the diamonds and settings they preferred and walked up to Simon who was chumming up to the grandfather clocks in the alcove up front. Seeing Leah's look vacant, he suggested she take a ten-minute break while he finished up with Simon. Not curious, all the same to her, she went to the tiny back hall to make a cup of tea.

Clay thought, I'm old, I eschew crises, Ferris wheel rides, sad movies, why am I plagued with others' hard luck stories, as if I can do anything about them? So Simon wasn't finished venting and came here to disrupt his day.

Ruining his meal last night, and on top of that Edwin, wasn't enough? God's getting a good laugh.

"Simon, what are you hanging around here for? This is a place of business."

Like a soldier prince on the pendulum clock, Simon stood in front of the gold filigreed clock face and jerked to attention at Claymore's sharp words, hurt by the tone. It made him aggressive, belligerent.

"Jesus H. Christ, what's with you, Clay?" His voice lowered so as not to spook the customers. "I've been run aground about this. Janey, I need a little common-sense advice. Janey isn't like she used to be."

"Okay, then listen. She's the same person as she was before you met her ex-husband." A crude way to put it, but effective. Simon cooled down a degree, unstuck his cemented shoulders.

"You haven't seen her like this. She's a different person. Try talking to her sometime. She's someone else."

"Oh, for pity sake, it's you who's changed. Toward her because you see her another way you know that she's been married. Think straight, Simo. You broke it off with her." He spoke cautiously as the best way to handle a fanatic whose focus was aural not logical.

It brought Simon up — something in the jeweler's disinterested assessment made him wary. He pulled away toward the back of the shop, eyes on the opened, walk-in Diebold safe at the far end. In a rush of adrenaline, he resolved to talk to Janey one more time. That was the advice he believed he'd just received from Claymore. He might have been over-reacting.

He turned on his heel and intercepted Claymore who was headed to his waiting customers.

"I haven't changed, Clay."

"Simo, I've got customers."

"I'm the same easy-going guy—"

"I've known Janey since she first came to Chicago." He began to walk Simon to the door. "She didn't intend to stay here long. Then she liked her new job at the Human Services, and liked the city and found a good place to live. For these months she's been testing the waters, so why should she spill her guts to anyone?" At the door he shook Simon off, "Don't bother me at work, Simo."

Simon glared at this furious old goat who like all old men had abandoned love and passion, who could not know what he suffered. But he heard himself thanking the old guy as he left.

After work, Leah felt restless, too much so to go straight home, so she drove to a favorite diner for the first time in months. While she waited for her dinner, unbidden memories came like cold bitter raindrops, in regular, slow plunks. How it had been before Jonathan died — she tried to string out coherent thoughts, live beyond the load of grief that throbbed against her mutinous body, clutching, releasing, but never letting go. In three short years, her mother first had died, then her father, decent man, and her little sister had drowned, swimming out too far. When Jonathan had enlisted, his father took that as a cue to disappear, throwing at her the words that he had never really loved her. So it seemed natural to Leah after bouncing back from all this death and ugliness, that she had reached the edge of her endurance. And then Jonathan had been killed.

Leah ate her chili, reviewing Claymore's lesson of today, what she remembered, what she hadn't absorbed. That bit about testing gems using specific gravity. Finding out if the sapphire is sapphire or topaz.

She paid her bill, left a tip, moved her chair back to rise. She had made her way to living without the rest. And then her boy had died.

As she headed out of the diner, weaving among the tables and counter, the outer door swung open and half-a-dozen mentally disabled people shuffled in. Out of the corner of her eye she watched them straggle past her, happy laughter, empty, brash, or shouted questions at a serious-looking woman leading them. Behind Leah the waitress greeted a small, chubby man, grinning, pink-cheeked, his head lolling sideways.

"Hello, Georgie…coming to eat dinner tonight? Lemme tie your shoestrings before you trip." She bent over heavily, clumsy, her large posterior in egregious display. With a push at the door to open wide as it could go, Leah created a space to slide out while the rest of the group piled in, one after another in ill-fitting, color-mismatched clothes.

Outside, welcoming the dusk and coolness, Leah dimmed her eyes at the horror she felt. "Why were these alive and Jonathan dead?" The religious, the philosophers, the stoics, the sowers of platitudes, fools, all fools. She let out her held breath in shame and anguish.

FOUR

JANEY Leduc didn't hear from Simon for two weeks; however, his nemesis, Arthur Kane, did show up at her doorstep to further his own agenda. Being in the area, he said he came — out of the blue she thought — to inquire about his son whom he hadn't seen in two years. When he called Janey's mother in Toronto, she told him Janey had moved to Chicago, and gave him her office address. But his ex-mother-in-law had neglected, he claimed, to mention that Paulie was in Canada with her.

Aggravated and suspicious, he knew she would put up with him because Paulie was his son. And the boy asked about him and waited for his infrequent phone calls. And Paulie loved his race-car-driving father, so he needed to admire him.

Janey handed him a beer, said little, let him sit and

think about how he was going to handle the fact that Paulie wasn't here. The man had shown up for another reason, and he knew she knew it. Not that Janey could guess what it was, but it was there. Artie never showed up for free.

"Paulie will be moving here in a couple of weeks. I didn't want to disturb him in the middle of a school year." Artie had the grace not to pretend he would come back when his son joined her. Although he seemed worked-up about something, she knew it wasn't Paulie, let alone herself. She continued to give him news about the boy and waited for his next move. She offered him another beer although she knew one was his limit. He never drank to quiet his demons, only drove, fast, and faster, racing in ever faster ovals. His only satisfaction or redemption was in speed. Motor speed, propelling a ton of metal at ridiculous velocity, which atomizes the air with toxic fumes.

He made noises readying to leave soon. She caught the signs.

"Glad the kid's doing good. Don't know who he gets his smarts from."

Janey thought, Simon should see us together now. He wouldn't wonder at her reluctance to admit she married this man. Why should Simon have been spooked by her marriage? Divorce leaves people free; it's adultery that makes people doubt the decency of coupling.

"That guy you're hanging out with… What's his name…"

"Simon, if that's who you mean."

"Yeah, yeah, him, thinks he's a big-shot about cars."

"How'd you find out about him, Artie? If you're snooping in my life, you better quit it."

"When we were in Toronto at the Honda Indy qualifiers, Tassoss said he'd seen Isabelle. You know… idly we got to talking." Janey's adrenaline did a brief spurt. Her sister chatting with Tassos Kyriazes, link by link, Tassos indiscreet in idle talk, yes. If there was another mystery in her life besides why she had married Art Kane, it was why she kept Tassos a friend. One never knew what gossip might pop out of his mouth. And everyone talked carelessly to Tassos. He was garrulous, amiable, genuine. Janey flinched, naive, too, if you gave him the benefit of the doubt. She'd often stopped herself about to tell him something she knew she'd later regret.

"So you're interested in who I'm seeing." That comment might jog him to tell her why he'd come.

He grinned. "Hell, no."

"That I guessed." She couldn't keep the pretense up, was about to ask him outright.

"Hey, hold up, Janey. You left me. Of course, after the first shock of it wore off, I realized it was the best thing for us, that split. Give you credit for having the guts to do it." An alien part of her grimaced, punctured. Although since his entire personal ethos revolved around courage, he might be hiding his malice in a true compliment. But the way he was flicking his eyes here and there negated that kinder interpretation. His attitude swam the self-satisfied river of pride in how they'd each managed since they split up. He earned a lot of money racing, and winning, while she seemed to live at a pace that crawled. She sought out the shadow, he the limelight.

Art Kane at last got around to what had made him come all the way to Chicago to find her. He shook his head. "That Tassos, he's always on the edge of disaster. The guy doesn't get smarter, he gets unluckier. He's in a bad jam right now." He wrinkled his forehead, arched eyebrows raised. Of course she'd be interested. There was always a bond between Janey and Tassos, developed over the years. She liked the Greek sailor who years ago had jumped ship in Canada and turned out to be the master auto mechanic working in Artie's pit. He was clever and canny, ingenious, the most swift and agile of his pit crewmen. When the race was at a critical break, Tassos' hands could intuit and fix a blip in the engine, or any power-driven part in crucial time. But the Greek had bad karma. It was Tassos who had introduced him to Janey.

"What kind of trouble?"

"Remember when Jensen Button won the Canadian Grand Prix?"

"No. Why should I?"

"I had a lot riding on Mark Webber. Then MacPhail on the 37th lap collided with the pole sitter…hell with the contender knocked off the race—"

"Listen, Artie, I need to know why you're here or take your exploits somewhere else. What has happened to Tassos?"

"I'm trying to explain something. They were hydroplaning with all that water and the cars being open-wheeled. We were scheduled to run the qualifying in the afternoon." He would tell her but in his own way in his own time. On he went as it applied to him. Thus was it ever with Arthur Kane. "Up north of you here, the Milwaukee Mile." He smacked his fist into his open palm. "So, if I ever needed Tassos it's now. And he got himself deported."

"No, after all these years? Impossible."

"Things are a little iffy right now. And Joyce, ex-wife number two. First she got him to give her a settlement out of Fort Knox and to top it off, she turns him in to the naturalization department."

"He got a lawyer?"

"He's in Greece. They took no time to ship him out."

"There should have been something he could have done." She was astounded.

"Well there wasn't. So, I got to go to Greece, help find a way to get him back. It's going to cost big bucks. And I won't be racing while I do that. And, and I'll need every cent I've got available."

These details didn't matter to Janey; she was stunned by Tassos' banishment.

"Janey, for a while, I told my accountant (the only way he referred to the man) to hold back my child support payments, only for a few months—" He had meandered in a cunning way, a labyrinth to entrap. She was silent, nothing to be said. "Until I get Tassos back here."

"Artie, this is your son. You're taking this money from your son."

"That guy never let me down. Nothing happened in the pit that he couldn't handle. Once in a race he patched a blown engine, which is impossible. My trophies, I see Tassos' face shadowed in them."

She made a feeble attempt at humor. "It's against the law to hold up child support. But then you'll be in Greece, finding a way to break the law to bring Tassos back."

"Well, nobody will know if you don't tell them."

"I haven't heard from you in months. I thought you were dead."

He looked down, then up, then down again. "Been rough on the circuit lately, no wins. Won't be forever. Last race, Mid-Ohio, I really blew away Buddy Briscoe. Really laid one down."

She stood, at the same time as raising her voice. It meant you better get out of here. "What difference does it make to me? Give your money to what or whoever you want. I will support Paulie myself. But phone him, send him things, don't disappear from his life. And never say I arrogated your place as his father."

Relieved, Artie scooted to the door. "That's fine, Janey. You've always been reasonable, Janey," — going out the door — "A real good sport."

Janey swallowed bile which strobed her chest with burning anger. Then she turned from the door and curled up in the big soft chair, listened to *La Bohème*, bought after her first opera, a visit to the Lyric. She had been overwhelmed by the music even when sung in words she couldn't understand. Maybe, she thought, because she knew they were words but had no idea what they meant. Words can be pure like the music, but they dissemble when you pretend to know their meaning. More than comfort, the opera gave courage.

When Paulie called at eight, as usual, with another day counted down until he would be coming to her, she listened delighted by his childish outpourings, grateful for them.

⁓

First task at work that morning, Janey Leduc reviewed the file of Edwin Blake, her annoying client whom she had sensed from the first moment she wouldn't be able to help. Some cases were like that. She would not have continued at all except for the mystery of Dorothea Pounce.

A few months ago, Edwin Blake had asked for help to find his "real" mother. Evelyn Doss who usually handled birth-mother searches had been on leave so his case had come to Janey. By going through the usual channels, Janey had located the name and present address of the woman who had given Edwin up for adoption. She lived not far from Edwin, a frequent coincidence in these searches. Janey took the preliminary step, before informing him, of making the initial contact with his birthmother, one Dorothea Pounce, to tell her about Edwin. The procedure then was to give Edwin her information and let him decide when and how to approach his birthmother who may or may not want to see him. Almost seventy-five percent of the mothers who put their babies up for adoption do not want to be reunited with them. Some, when found, adamantly refused to see their off-springs. Unless the child did a sneak attack and waylaid them, they never did meet. She had known of some women who in the midst of their off-springs' crying fits and recriminations, relented and began a relationship. All kinds of accusations and denials got batted around. Tearful, happy reunions were rare. There were some successful meetings and bondings. But Janey wasn't surprised when Dorothea made a monumental fuss and caused scads of trouble. However, not at all for the usual reasons.

Dorothea hotly claimed that she was not Edwin's mother. She had never given birth to any baby. She'd been single all her life, if that meant anything. She was vehement, said she had proof that she wasn't the birthmother. She offered to take a DNA test "right now."

In Janey's experience Dorothea's denial wasn't unique. There were babies whose parentage was questionable days after they were born. But Rush Hospital had provided a birth certificate with Dorrie's name on it. This Dorrie shrugged off. "I never signed that. It's not my signature. Along with the DNA test, I'll have my handwriting analyzed. What must have happened was some poor teenager came to the hospital about to deliver and she gave them a phony name. She probably made one up on the spot. Picked any name out of the air and it happened to be mine. A name she'd heard or read somewhere. Maybe then she delivered the kid and bolted out of the hospital as soon as she could stand up. Tell me that some of those girls, scared shitless, don't do that. Check with the maternity nurses. I am not that Edwin kid's mother."

What stuck Janey as odd was that Dorothea Pounce offered to help Edwin find his mother. "Why don't you introduce me, and I'll try to give him some support. It must be god-awful knowing your own flesh and blood didn't want you, just tossed you away…"

Janey had let Edwin meet her; the two flakes, as Janey put it, hit it off right away. Edwin said he "knew" positively that Dorrie wasn't his mother. However, they became fast friends, and Dorrie was kind to him. His adoptive parents, she learned, had abused him, father beat him, mother drank too much, which might be what set Edwin off on his imaginary inner journeys. But he said he loved them, he insisted to Janey, they had been good providers, housed and fed and clothed him. Half the time he referred to them with the "adoptive" tag; the other half simply as Mom and Dad. Now, his parents lived in Florida and had little to do with him. Edwin shrugged off any attempt from Janey to get him to talk about them. Most of the time Edwin preferred to talk about his vague observations, what he thought everything meant. He was redirecting his need, so dire when he was a boy, to make himself important when he told fibs, then made-up stories, eventually out-and-out lies. When he left adolescence and entered adulthood, he tempered his whoppers through exaggerations of what he'd seen or done. Recently he had begun fabricating elaborate fantasies. Janey believed that abuse and abandonment fueled his need to prevaricate. But understanding it didn't make her like him any better. She gave Dorothea credit for having a good heart. Claymore Mandebrote had told her how his niece Dorrie always felt sorry for hard-luck types, ever since she was a little girl. Once she gave a poor classmate her winter coat off her own back.

Janey hadn't been bothered by Edwin in two weeks. Then, along with her recent estrangement from Simon and the repellant visit of Artie, she had managed to up her discontent by running into Edwin the day before her son Paulie was to come from Toronto.

She hurried into Claymore's jewelry store to have a new

battery put in her watch. She had bought some presents for Paulie and wanted to finish up her errands quickly and get home to finish making his room ready. Tasks done, she could enjoy anticipating her son's arrival. In a better mood than she'd been for days she sauntered into the shop, relaxed, ready to spend a few minutes chatting with Clay. There was Edwin loitering in a corner of the shop. He spotted her and danced over to her, grinning. Claymore was dealing with a customer, a tall woman in a loose, filigreed blouse, her eyes downcast at the earrings on the counter. The woman asked Clay a question which was drowned out by the tomahawk yell from Edwin. "Hey, Janey. Long time no see. I've been attending to important stuff so I haven't been able to come to fill you in." He glided over to her, eyes fractating. "You'll want to hear the progress I've made," his voice dropped, "…on my case." The disturbed customer regained her equilibrium and managed to ask her question to Clay who tried to ignore Edwin's outbursts. Like the roof blowing off and the rain pouring in or a madman with a gun, the only sane response for Clay was to deny that Edwin was happening.

"Ah, Janey, a sight for sore eyes. I'll get Mrs. Halbrick's purchase wrapped and be with you in a minute."

Leah sneaked out from behind the heavy Bessarabian

carpet covering the opening to the back room. "I'll take care of it, Mr. Mandebrote."

"Thank you, Leah. My new assistant," he nodded at her as an introduction to Janey. "This is Janey Leduc, helping my niece."

"I know her, too," shouted Edwin."

Clay approached them. "I hear your Paulie's coming soon."

"Word gets around." Janey smiled at him. Edwin stared at her as if she'd grown a horn in the middle of her head.

"Dorrie told me. Lord knows where she picks up things."

"I talked with Dorrie last Thursday." She did like Claymore and wished she found him here alone. Not aware of that before she'd stepped into the place — that she would have liked to have talked with him because he was "sympatico". She did not have a friend, had been in Chicago only a short time so found herself divulging things to the likes of Dorrie and her uncle.

Seeing he had an audience Edwin bloomed into talk. And he talked. And he talked. He had lucked out coming here at this time when not only could he tell Claymore his news, but Janey, too. With the silent clerk thrown in as well. He suffered a moment of distress when a customer drifted through the door but left quick enough, due to, thought Edwin, seeing the prices on Clay's jewelry.

Edwin began his sham story, starting out in the middle of it. A fabulist is what he was — unbeknownst to any of the listeners who considered him a common liar. Although, if she thought about it, Janey would question if there were many really good common liars. Lying is a pathology, a symptom, a disease in the archaic meaning of the word. Ordinary liar Edwin was not. So, perhaps, Edwin could be reckoned a fabulist.

"She's got this antique porch swing and we sat in that. On the porch which is old-fashioned like in a Victorian house, a painted lady, cream and rose-colored and a yellow-green on the trim. Small though. Not a large house like you might see in some places. I had a beer and we just talked away. Once I saw her, I knew she couldn't be my mother. Too old. Not too old, I guess, but old-looking. I suppose she wasn't past fifty which of course my mother could be. But not like that."

Janey stopped him. "Where did you find this woman, Edwin?" What in the hell could he be talking about? His case was still in her bailiwick although marked inactive. There had been nowhere else to look for his mother.

His eyes narrowed at her. "Don't think I'm gonna stop looking just because Lutheran Social Services says it's over." He lifted his chin, "As a matter of fact, it was fate how I found Arlene." His voice dipped, lowered, "Started with a dream I had couple of weeks ago. The Eiffel Tower was all lit-up in a foggy night and there was my mother. I couldn't see her face, but there was a beautiful glowing aura about her. I heard this soft, soft voice saying my name. Not my name of Edwin, but the name she chose for me. It was a French name, she spoke French words that I didn't understand. I wanted to go to her, but when I tried I woke up." His listeners shifted around, bored, but Edwin saw only a mesmerized group caught up in his dream rendition.

So Edwin went on. "Next day, driven by what I'd dreamed, I went over to Columbia College. I was bent on taking a French course so that when I do find my mother, we'll be able to talk to each other." Janey saw the half-smile which altered his face almost to unrecognizable whenever he began to expand a saga — "but I didn't need any class. Before I even stepped into the college, I met Arlene at a coffee shop. When she ordered, I heard her accent, yeah, you bet, French. I went over to her table and, out of nowhere, I asked if I might join her. And it came out in French. Like a bolt outta the blue, I could talk in French." He threw his head back, amazed at himself. "That's how I got invited over to her house, to sit on the porch and jabber away in French. Arlene, you see, will lead me to my mother. She's from Paris. Arlene is. Teaches French Literature at Columbia College." His eyes stabbed at Janey. "You see, I'm close to finding my mother. I told Dorrie I need to go to Paris—"

Claymore bristled, "Well, don't you go asking Dorrie for any money. She doesn't have any. If I find out you tried to get some out of her, I swear Edwin, I'll throttle you."

"Stop being hyper, huh, Clay. I won't ask Dorrie for a dime. She doesn't think my mother's in Paris being French no matter the dream and my suddenly French-speaking. In fact, it went away, the ability…to talk it. Anyhow, I know Dorrie don't have any money."

During this last tussle, Leah had disappeared in her silent way, and Janey had strapped on her watch. She glanced at Claymore; for a moment their eyes met.

Edwin looked distracted. "That Dorrie, she won't say a word. She knows more than she lets on about where my mother is, who she is. Why else is she so damn sure it's not Paris?"

Janey said, "Because, Edwin, it's unlikely. Highly unlikely. Very improbable." She thanked Claymore and turned to leave. Edwin was strutting behind her, repeating how he might want to cross-examine Dorrie some more about why her name showed up on his birth certificate.

Claymore called, "Good-bye, Janey." Then in a mellower tone to his clerk, "Let's get on with the lapidary lesson while there are no customers."

Outside the store, Janey stopped, irritated, shook Edwin's arm in its thin, long-sleeved, blue tee-shirt.

"Listen, Edwin, maybe Dorrie does know more. She's now telling me she may have let this woman use her name, lent her own identification to help her friend out of a…a, what could have been, a tragic situation. If she won't tell you who the woman was or where she is, it's because, maybe because she's protecting her from bad repercussions. Or for some other thing we can't even imagine. I don't know. We have to honor people's privacy. Dorrie has her reasons, so don't badger her anymore. Leave her, and me, the hell alone."

Edwin's eyes began an Irish jig. "Shut up, Janey. You don't know fucking everything. I've got a right to keep on searching. And I can get Dorrie to help me find my birthmother if I want to. I don't need your permission." She watched him forge away, shoulders arched behind, his head thrust forward coyote-like, in authentic anger.

Clay joined Leah behind the back counter at the outer

work table. They talked about the value of a gemstone, a conversation Clay had yearned for in the midst of Edwin's bluster —precise, clarifying words with his new assistant. Impurities, inclusions, shallow-cut, many-faceted, spikes of color, crepeous band, words that mean.

When a customer came in, they halted her lesson, then continued when the store was empty. Leah liked the comfortable unreality of it all, the atmosphere of calm. Late in the afternoon while grading sapphires, Leah called a halt with her sad half-smile. "Enough for today, Mr. Mandebrote. I don't have one of those photographic memories."

"Sure, sure. Go get a cup of tea. It's been slow today. I maybe pushed too hard it being not so busy."

She brought two steaming cupfuls out, one for him. They sat for a moment behind the sales desk.

Claymore shook his head, his dappled hand trembling a little as he sipped the tea. His mind began to dwell on that Edwin's nonsense.

"I had dinner at my niece Dorrie's house on Sunday. She didn't mention any of this Edwin guy's malarkey to me."

Leah hesitated. "You said she likes to help people—"

"Yes, yes, to her detriment. I don't know where she met that one. I don't know where she gets any of them from. She's a good girl, always with the big heart. Naive, and foolish."

Ensconced in her little car, wending her way in the dusk in the early evening traffic, Janey thought about the bizarre goings-on at Claymore's jewelry store. It disturbed her, made her conscious that she wasn't eager to go home to the empty house. With her son still in Canada, everyone she loved in another country, she had been intensely lonely these last few months. Edwin's malady, evidenced so oddly in his story-telling, wasn't unusual. Janey had studied psychology, had seen others with such symptoms of damaged psyches. However, Edwin's manifestations were unique. The way he told his whoppers, the determination he had to convince his listener, got under her skin. Unlike her other clients, Edwin annoyed her.

Even after she got home, so tired she ate a piece of cheese and went to bed half-hungry, her sleep-heavy bits of memory rushed in: her office Dorrie and Edwin… Gotten proof of his mother. That time he had insisted his mother was a famous Chicago personality…in disbelief, then Dorrie had low-voiced tried to turn his persistence, but Edwin's loud claim vehement…television celebrity… face on Skyway billboard, then herself, unprofessional sarcasm, "like Tom Skilling?"… Dorrie's muffled half-chuckle…no…angry Edwin badgered them…his mother at the Goodman, a glamorous…it went on, but not dwelled on all night. For Janey, in aloneness, slept.

At Janey's office in the morning Dorrie called. Janey had her on the line before she thought to check who was calling.

"I heard Edwin cornered you at my uncle's store."

Unfortunately Janey plunged right in, talking without letting Dorrie say why she had called. Her aptitude to jump in and guess what other people mean to say was her stickiest fault which she worked hard to correct. It was a deadly one for a social worker. She always paid for it, like right now. "Yes. He's switched his birthmother from a glamorous celebrity to a *femme de Paris*."

"My uncle called last night. Doesn't want Edwin annoying his customers. That was you. I told him what can I do? I don't control Edwin. He's gotten touchy, short fuse these days, Claymore, not Edwin."

"Edwin got overexcited."

"You said he gave you the French woman story. Oh, God."

"Listen, Dorrie, I'm not counseling Edwin anymore. I will suggest a therapist—"

"Oh, he won't have that—"

"Well, then..." Stymied now. She should have waited to hear Dorrie out before starting in.

"He's driving me a little crazy lately." Dorrie twirled a clump of her red hair.

"Then he has gone a step too far."

"Is there some way?" Dorrie said. "I know you must deal with many adoptees searching for their mothers... Is it always the mother by the way?"

"Yes. Maybe they think the fathers weren't invested much in them—"

"What I've been thinking, is there something I can say to him that will get him to stop?"

"No. He's fixated. I can't ethically, uh patient-counselor confidentiality, I can't say. It's dicey. But you can be sure he won't quit."

"Oh, great. Gee, thanks. Sorry I bothered you." Sounded frustrated, borderline belligerent.

A hasty disconnect. Janey thought, "I am, too."

Claymore Mandebrote watched Leah walk into his store, her thin figure hidden under her London Fog, her shoulders slanted. But she did not slouch, her back was straight although her head held in a slight tilt. Only in puffs interspersed here and there did any gray strands show through her longish dark hair. Long, Clay surmised, not from styling but because she had stopped trimming it of late. She had not told him what sorrow she was hiding, but he had sensed there must be one.

Leah pivoted around the center display table and headed to the workroom. She would hang up her coat and comb her hair. Claymore liked her neatness.

When she came out, there were would-be customers. Unconsciously, she had registered the entrance bell ring as she walked to the back. She was starting to feel at home in this glittery shop. A red-headed, flushed, freckled middle-aged woman, a little short, a little overweight, a few stray hairs clinging to her damp forehead, was hanging over the glass-top covering the counter of gemstone rings, closest to the diamonds. Leah threaded a few steps past where a young couple dawdled. In a hoarse whisper the redhead asked about the stunning cornflower blue stones. Leah pulled out the tray of Ceylon sapphires. The woman's bejeweled hand hovered over the rings.

"Let me see that one," she breathed.

As business accelerated and Clay with great satisfaction was about to sell an eighteen-K gold Calatrava watch, he glanced up to see Leah using the right touch with the redhead and the sapphire. Some of the apprehension he had been feeling began to lift. It was a good move to have hired this neophyte. She seemed comfortable learning the jewelry business which pleased him. And she was becoming an adequate salesperson. Especially at his age it was best not to ignore what puts bread on the table. A familiar voice from the doorway seeped through his thoughts. His good mood drained away.

Dingbat Simon, that idiot, that cretin, that moron — he catalogued an archaic litany of mental aberrations. Yesterday Edwin, today Simon Butler. Claymore got hold of himself, his better self. Simon wasn't any of those things. Simon tended to overreact or get excited sometimes, but he was a good guy. Simon's parents had been his friends. And maybe he, like his niece, was a magnet for the forlorn.

He let Simon wander about self-consciously while he and Leah finished up with their customers and the jewelry store emptied of patrons. Then he approached Simon who was loitering at the oversized fancy clocks.

"What's up, Simo?"

Simon's eyes widened, watered a bit. "Janey was here yesterday."

"Yes. She brings her custom here. Ever since you introduced her when you two started dating."

"I was coming by to see you, and I happened to spot her in here."

"So you didn't come in?" Simon didn't answer. "That was grown-up of you."

"Did she mention me? Did she tell you we've kind of split?"

"She came in for a watch battery. No, she didn't mention anything like that."

"I thought, maybe her coming here… Jesus, Clay, you gotta help me. I don't like this at all. I thought she was, like, the love of my life. I don't know what to do."

"I can't help. I'm no good with things like that. Women troubles. Simo, my wife died twenty years ago." His heart twitched at the words.

"Did Janey say anything at all about me?"

"No, I said no."

"What can I do to get out of this mess? I've got her too much on my mind."

"Talk to her. Take her out to a nice dinner. Pretend it all never happened. Forget the stuff in the past that you two were fighting about."

Simon stroked his well-cut head of hair, perplexed. "She won't return my calls. I tried going over there, but she isn't ever home, or just wouldn't answer the door… I could try calling her at work…"

"That's always risky, Simon."

A few potential customers wandered in, which took

Claymore's attention and sent Simon scurrying out of the jewelry store.

Leah took a walk in the dusk after work. The third time she had done so this week. Maybe it could become a habit. Her appetite seemed better for the exercise. She strolled east into the chill wind off the water. The lake's glassy ripples capped by white furls unleashed a radiant glow beneath the low full moon. A stray thought foundered, part picture, part word. Her son, her Jon, a single thrilled moment, sapphire blue like the ring she'd sold, only incandescent. He was there. Gone. Dissolved in a nanosecond, its track remained. She caught herself smiling. A reprieve at last. She turned to walk home, the wind nudging her back in snappy gusts.

FIVE

PAULIE'S mother trembling inwardly on the platform, waited as the train lurched into Union Station. "Chug-a-lug Toot Toot" — a favorite book when he was a year old. She longed to be holding his hand right now. But soon. Laboring, screeching, the iron cars strained forward. Metallic steam vapor acrid in her nose, she watched the passengers climb off the clanking steps. Her eyes searched as each iron door rattled open and the passengers streamed past. Paulie hopped down, struggled with his worn suitcase — his grandmother had overstuffed it — gripped in both hands in front of his skinny legs, he bumped it step by step. Dwarfed by the myriads crowding around him, he seemed fragile. Behind Paulie, Isabelle's friend Todd, who was accompanying the boy, pushed at the merging people. Janey fast-walked toward the little boy, calling his name. Todd spotted Janey and nodded okay when she grabbed Paulie, then drifted away into the throng of travelers to his own business in Chicago.

Most of his things, his aunt Isabelle had assured him, would be shipped right away. But he insisted on carrying his most valued possessions with him on the train. Hard to make his aunt understand, he could not risk losing them. His grandmother understood the subtlety of such fears and had let him stuff it all in the suitcase at the last minute.

Janey had him in a tight hug. He felt like crying, but didn't know why.

"Paulie, Sweetie, wait till you see what I've got for you at home." They carted his luggage by its handle together into the terminal. Paulie's voice returned to him, and he began to jabber about the train trip. From his pockets the food he'd brought hung out uneaten. He was flushed with delight about railroad travel.

Outside on Jackson, Carol and Braden — who had been driving off and back again around the block waiting — spotted Janey and the little boy. Braden curbed the car among the cab lineup and an excited Carol popped out. She squatted to kiss Paulie, called him "Pet." When he shied away, she poured her affluent excitement over Janey in a flailing half-hug. Then she crouched again to try to entice Paulie into coming near her.

With the resigned patience of childhood, Paulie waited for all the fuss to be over. He thought how like a ballerina the woman, Carol, seemed. Kicking, bouncing, balancing with arms stuck out. Kicking again, bouncing up, spinning with arms brought in. Instinctively, he liked her but kept backing away. Human young don't like being caught any more than a puppy does.

In the car Paulie leaned against his mother with a gust of sheer relief. He was here at last, in a big new town, but safe. Made it this far. They pulled into a restaurant drive-through to collect hamburgers which was fun. His favorite lunch out, he said, which gave Braden a chance to smile at him, tease about root beer mustaches and ask some silly questions that adults always did. But these didn't bother Paulie in the least. He sensed in Braden a tranquility, no foreboding of being pestered or indulged. No good-natured clucking noises, or pretend friendliness. Braden seemed real. Paulie didn't think anything more about Carol in the passenger seat. She was turning around a lot to look back and chatter at his mother. His word-thought was "chatter" like the squirrels his grandmother fed birdseed to in her yard. She grew flowers for butterflies, butterfly bushes — many different species of butterflies landed there. He knew all the species' names.

In a remote chasm of Paulie's psyche, a knot gave

way coincident with the easing of his stomach muscles he hadn't known were clenched. There were things he inchoately felt would be all right now. Streets brightly lit where busy crowds gathered, looked inviting; he could smell the dank lake in the air; the tall buildings seemed like formidable trimmed-out giants, Atlas, Hercules, others he'd read about. They were defenders against any alien invasion. At his new home his mother would have a room prepared for him because she knew what was good. They'd call Grandmother and his auntie who'd make wise cracks — about his riding the train and his reactions to Chicago. What he had been most frightened of he mentioned to no one: the new people he was going to meet. These apparitions still gave him qualms, but he wasn't so worried. The difficulty of making new friends didn't cross his mind. He was missing his old ones too much. The looming threat of a new school he could put off worrying about since that wouldn't come for weeks. A long time away, when you're eight.

After lunch the ride for Paulie grew long, the car stuffy and overheated as they sliced down Lakeshore Drive. Dull and drowsy the boy felt confined in clothes that he'd put on fresh in the morning which seemed tight, sweaty, suffocating. He wanted the trip to be over. As happy as he was about coming to his mother in Chicago, over-excitement and sleepy discomfort was making him anxious. He stared out the window at the glistening lake. Thinking about water…about a documentary of the desert he'd seen on the National Geographic channel. His grandmother liked to watch those programs. He'd been fascinated in a desultory way. Often he took in disparate scenes, stored them for later, and brought one out when he wanted to think about it. In this one, half-naked African children were struggling to fetch water under an intense sun. It looked as if the land sent boiling waves streaming up from the patchy ground. They hauled heavy wooden buckets of water splashing over the rims. That had bothered him, how much water splashed out. Their skinny bodies glittering with sweat they trudged sinking and stumbling ankle-deep through spitting hot sand. Every day, he heard in awe, every single day the children hauled the water. Girls, too, he noticed tiny titties, stick girls grinning in exhaustion, a piece of torn, ragged cloth dropped around their waists. For their mothers, for the village, they labored. This last bit of documentary factoid stymied Paulie. What a burden to bear the water — parched land, skeletal cattle, the distant roar of a famished lion. The lion had sunk deep into his consciousness. He labored with the vision like the children toiled under their water loads. How long would each water trek take every day, to walk sizzling in a blanket of heat, to strain the very insides of yourself, to burn feet, ankles, to stretch arms like rubber bands. If he had been an African boy…dingo dogs…nipping lion cubs… But this need to bring water, without him doing it they would all die of thirst.

Paulie's mother brought him out of his trance-like thoughts. She hugged him and whispered it wouldn't be long now and they'd be home. He looked into his mother's eyes. She had been watching him gaze out the side window. But she had no idea where he'd been. Yes, home soon. He sighed.

"It's a big city, Paulie. Like Toronto when we go into town. But where I live, it's a house like we've lived in before. Like Grandma's." She gave him a nudge for acquiescence.

"I sure could use a glass of water."

Braden laughed. "You've had a long trip today." He slowed the car down and made a left turn. "There. Here we are at your street."

Shortly after she got Paulie to bed, Janey answered her phone's ring without looking and felt a little shaken when she heard Simon's voice. Still, she wasn't put off by his call. The pressure of the arrival of her son, she would later decide, combined with the recent reappearance of Edwin, lend a credence to Simon's familiar voice. For months she had enjoyed their uncomplicated, undemanding relationship. At least she'd pictured it that way. But everything had turned topsy-turvy.

Simon's voice came low and confident; they wasted a few minutes speaking in noncommittal phrases that it was safe to talk.

"Claymore, you know, Dorrie's uncle, he just got out of the hospital. Refused to stay more than overnight."

"What happened to him?"

"He had a slight heart attack."

"Slight?"

"Well, I mean, not the big one. They kept him to do tests. Must be okay. I didn't talk to Dorrie. Got it from Edwin. Only have met the guy twice and he comes poking into the dealership, bopping around, pretending he wanted to buy a new car. Asking if I can get him a good deal. Brass balls."

"Not possible. He doesn't have a driver's license. Lost it on points last year." They made knowing sounds companionably.

"Edwin kept calling it Claymore's 'ticker.'"

She waited, not sure what to say, nor why he called. To let her know about Claymore was a weak reason as they both knew.

"How you been?"

"…My son came today. I…" Don't say more, wrong subject. But why the hell should it be? Still she knew better than to make this talk personal.

"I wouldn't care, would I?" Simon countered. The next move should have been his, but she'd swiped it from him and spoiled the moment. But, he wanted Janey back, so he smothered his ire. Phone conversations got awkward often for him; why people text. He plunged on, gave a nervous, tickly cough.

"Janey, hey…maybe we can go out, huh, for a drink after work? Things between us have gotten all mixed up…and I've been thinking about…you. What about it?"

It seemed reasonable. She wasn't angry with Simon's outburst anymore. What Carol had said made sense. She'd hurt him by not considering their relationship as seriously as he had. An ex-husband, a young son, catalysts.

"Okay, then. But not until Saturday. We can celebrate the weekend—"

"How about Boleo in the Loop? I'll meet you there about six-thirty." He was looking to romance her. She didn't know much about Chicago nightlife and would be pleased and impressed by his choice. If he could push aside for now the problem of her betrayal, he could get her back. Simple as that.

Feeling more himself, Simon Butler again enjoyed being service manager at the dealership. All the shiny new models, compacts, subcompacts, SUVs, enormous trucks, sports cars, minivans, in the showroom and in the giant lot, sparkled again, sang to him once more when he arrived at work in the morning. Call them wheels, call them your ride, what one drives into the service bay we fix up no matter what the problems, we keep them all on the road, America rolling. He could once again be smug. Janey judged right; he wasn't Artie. The hard arrogance was missing from Simon. But she had, as so many do, chosen a type like the last. In this case Simon became a recognizable slice of Artie.

Simon would have liked to stuff Janey's betrayal deep beneath the traces of other rotting memories, but he couldn't do that. His anger stayed submerged, but not far from the surface. The hurt she had caused him set deep. His irrational desire for Janey, if that's what it was, had wetted down the burning treachery into embers of disquiet. But the ashes still smoldered.

The kid, though, could become a problem, could disturb his balance, could end up being a drawback. The boy would be an unpleasant reminder standing there between them, shoving Janey's betrayal every day in Simon's face. Was he supposed to play games with this kid? He'd never been interested in playing sports, preferring taking things apart and putting them back together. Mechanical aptitude it had been called. He supposed, for Janey's kid, he could get outside more. Simon did enjoy watching football. He wondered if this kid liked the Bears.

Late on Friday afternoon, Janey and Paulie waltzed into Claymore Mandebrote's jewelry store, both laughing at a silly joke Paulie had told which he found hilarious. A hot late August day they were swept in on the cooling breeze off the lake. Clay looked up from behind the back counter when the bell tinkled. Only one customer stood talking to the new clerk. Clay seemed downcast and melancholic to Janey, but then she thought he often had a woebegone air. He'd been sitting on a high wooden stool, a loupe clenched in his eye, holding up in his skinny fingers a gemstone in an old-fashioned Tiffany setting. He'd lost weight since his heart episode, a grey cardigan sagged over his shoulders, cheek bones protruded, flesh drawn in, peaked.

The clerk, Leah, was informing a stocky, sandy-haired man with a high, freckled forehead, about a blue Topaz, how it starts out its gem life pure white.

Paulie stared at the displays around the shop, kid-curious. He wandered over to the little alcove that housed a few grandfather clocks ticking in counterpoint rhythm. Ticking clocks being novel to this electronic born generation, the little boy watched, a bit hypnotized.

As Claymore reached Janey at the central glass showcase, she thought he seemed startled a little.

"Janey, it's you. Have you had second thoughts about the watch?" Then as if to clarify, he added, "a nice birthday present."

"Yes. I owe a fancy watch at least for my sister who did most of the heavy work taking care of Paulie in Toronto… You had a stay in the hospital—"

"Only overnight. Yeah. It was a scare. There in that white room I said to myself, "if I die, I don't believe it's time. And I'm all right." He nodded at Leah, as he pulled out a tray of ladies' watches. "She kept the shop open the last few days all by herself. She doesn't dink around. Doesn't get tedious about my heart. Steady and unemotional. What a relief compared to Dorrie." He stared at her a moment. "You neither…don't seem to me to be the kind that'd put up with a lot of nonsense." He was thinking of Simon.

"I can't. Every day I deal with delinquents, addicts, prostitutes, ex-cons, abused wives, the slow-witted, unlucky, and insane. How long would I last if I didn't secrete a shell? This way, I'll be burned out for a year before I notice." She watched this old-handsome man adjust to her last words, become amused. "Come here, Paulie. This is my son."

Paulie's eyes widened under the fall of his tousled yellow hair. "Awesome big clocks. You gotta wind them all one by one?"

Claymore's expression turned solemn. "Oh, yes. Each one."

"They'll never be synchronized then."

Claymore stretched his bottom lip over his teeth. Big word for a little guy. "No, not ever."

"Funny that, isn't it?" Something in a glass counter further on caught his eye, and the boy skipped away.

Claymore's attention riveted on Janey. "You might as well know that Simon Butler came to me in a state about you. I didn't interfere and I'm not interfering now. But if you do start seeing him again, it will save the sanity of all his friends and acquaintances." They were grinning at each other which felt good to Janey. This cranky old shopkeeper understood some things tacitly.

The shop's other customer sauntered out. Leah walked over to Clay.

"Says he's coming back with his fiancée. I think he will."

Clay introduced Janey as his niece's friend, which she thought she strictly wasn't, and also a good customer, which she would be if she bought the watch. With a yell, Paulie ran over to them.

"Come here, Mom, I've gotta show you something. It's totally awesome." He grabbed her sleeve and tried to drag her to the counter. Once there he pushed his finger onto the glass, leaving smudges. "Look at that."

It was a butterfly pin, cloisonné with tiny jewels that sparkled conspicuously.

Without looking up Paulie said, "It's like a real butterfly, not a pin. It has all the parts in miniature. I can tell you what kind, too. Exactly. The other pins aren't like real butterflies. But this one is. It's a swallowtail, a pipe vine swallowtail."

The bell tinkled and Claymore traipsed off to help the new customer. Janey smiled at the surprise in Leah's voice. "How do you know that?"

Still without moving his head, "I like butterflies. This one is dark blue and blue metallic green, the forewing is iridescent blackish purple. See the lighter purple sheen on top? Then the big orange spots and then the splashes of green. Wow, oh wow. Even the clubbed antenna. It could be a real butterfly."

"I suppose it could be," said Leah, "there's not much to butterflies."

Paulie jerked his head up, indignant. "What d'you

mean? Butterflies have brains and hearts, long-chambered hearts." Leah stepped away from the counter.

As usual, Janey felt like apologizing for her precocious kid. Did they all think he was a mouthy brat? "Well, let's go, Paulie."

"Wait. I want to buy that butterfly."

"Oh, not now. Did you forget? Your grandmother and auntie are coming tonight to stay for the weekend."

She got him away. Might come back and buy the watch. But the butterfly pin, wasn't something for Paulie.

In the evening, a moment to herself, Janey read the *Trib*. An article on the sports page: Art Kane had won his third straight Sonoma. So he hadn't gone to Greece to rescue Tassos.

⁓☉

Simon Butler sauntered into the Kimpton Gray Hotel and rode up the elevator to Boleo at the top. Rich blue satin striped decor, open skylight, the brilliance of the Loop spreading out before the diners, this was the place to reunite with Janey in a classy way.

Down below in the street while Janey waited for the light to cross Monroe, she felt the awkwardness of the time. Did she mean to start up again with Simon? If she did not, she ought to question the wisdom of seeing him tonight. Then again, she had once enjoyed dating him… The rest of that thought dissolved in slight discomfort. Since her son's arrival the structure of her days had changed and her priorities, too. Before Paulie came, she'd led a less-confined, impulsive pattern of going where her days took her. Simon might drop over and bring Chinese food. A client might mention a new exhibit which she would go view unplanned after work. Perhaps a spontaneous dinner, Indonesian say, with Simon, then they would meet up with Carol and Braden for a night of truly smooth jazz. Or Simon would talk her into going to that stupid comedy club he loved. Mitzi at work would give her an extra ticket for the Lyric Opera, and she'd go, spur of the moment. It had been dizzying but now it was back to normal, which she much preferred. Future plans, anticipation, considering what she wanted to do. Once late at night Simon demanded they all eat at Gage's. Feeling dragged, she had met Braden's bemused eye, and he'd made a sympathetic face at her. And he didn't know the half of it.

There was a richness in the sculpture of a life that included Paulie's needs. Registering him for school, an ordeal for both, following his interests — those butterflies, picking out planets among the stars, baseball ever since they'd gone with Braden and Carol to a Cubs game. Paulie was thrilled to live so near Wrigley Field, and to have found two neighborhood kids to play ball with. It's a subtle, formless choice, when life asks us to decide on a pattern, an abstract calculus. It will make all the difference.

A doorman swept her into the hotel. She located the elevators and up at the restaurant drifted with the maître d' who held out her chair at Simon's table. Simon ordered an array of Peruvian bar food, the specialty empanadas. They ate, drank wine, while he discussed the usual, his job, mechanical quirks, Chicago politics. Her mind wandered, but she plugged in when she heard he was sending his parents to Hawaii as an anniversary gift.

"That's thoughtful and generous of you," she said.

It irked him, her saying that. "You surprised? I'm a thoughtful, generous person."

"You are." She had never thought otherwise.

Although he had been satisfied with the way the evening was heading — Janey seemed relaxed, normal — he wanted to push. He had warned himself not to try to clear up everything with Janey this time out together. But the normalcy of her words and attitude bothered him.

By the end of dinner, Simon suggested a club for

some dancing. But exhaustion began to sink Janey. After work she'd made a critical stop at a busy post office for a client and smoothed over Paulie's fussing with what he thought was a too-early bedtime chosen by the imperious babysitter. But the tediousness of Simon's talking, the realization that she didn't have anything to say to him, deadened her spirit. He had his good points: he kept his fingernails clean, never drove under the influence, and hadn't hung her up in a smashed car precariously swaying over a thousand-foot ravine.

"Let's skip the dancing, Simon. I enjoyed dinner but I'm bushed—"

"Evening's still young, as they say. If you're tired, let's go back to my place for coffee." He stopped, gave the waiter his signed credit card slip. Janey felt trapped.

"I need sleep more than coffee—"

"You know I've got a big welcoming bed."

She stared at him stupefied. Maybe she hadn't heard him right.

"I need to go home, Simon. My son's there with a sitter who's expecting me—"

"Oh, your son, that son." Rancor returned in a flood. She had a nerve using the kid as an excuse.

"Yes. We had a dinner date—"

"Oh come off it, Janey. You know I want a chance to

explain. Make things right. I deserve it. I listened to your story."

"You did, and you explained your feelings, too Simon, as far as I could tell."

"It was bullshit, your excuse for hiding him from me."

"If you say so."

"You were married, had a kid, didn't tell me about it. Then you explained, if you want to call it that, the divorce because he got you in an accident. Crazy. It isn't like you at all, Janey. I know you, Janey, something else must have happened. But you kept it all from me."

"From everybody here in Chicago. I didn't want to bring that all up—"

"Oh yeah, sure. I know you Janey. You love to talk. It's what you do best." The injury, the betrayal contorted his face, his posture, the tone of his voice. "And I tried to accept it and start again." He had denied his own feelings, that had been his concession. Recognizing that now fueled his anger.

"There's so little you know about me. You've got this flat, black and white photo in your mind that looks like me. That's how much you know." She pushed at her chair and sprang up.

"Wait, I've got my car—" He reached out to grab her arm.

"I'll get a cab. Let me be, Simon."

Astounded by her abrupt retreat, something he wouldn't have guessed any woman would do in this environment, he didn't follow her. Infuriated, he insisted he would take some care before his next move.

Summer was ending in a heat wave. Janey had cancelled her morning appointments to take Paulie to his new school's orientation at ten. She was drowning him in assurances and oatmeal. He didn't feel like listening or eating, but there's wasn't much chance of avoiding either. His mother's cheerfulness increased his anxiety, but she didn't notice. Yes, he nodded, he was aware that both his new friends Rex and Lydia were, as luck would have it, enrolled at the same school he was. He wouldn't have to wear a uniform as he'd had at his Toronto school. And he probably wouldn't have to take French. At last she stopped while she read the paper, crunching her toast. He looked up at her. She was too quiet.

"What, Mum?"

"Well, here, your dad's in the paper again." Rarely did the boy ask about his father, but he always showed interest in a languid way about Artie's races. Today he lifted his eyebrows at some escaping thought. She plopped the *Trib* sports page in front of him. "Here, read for yourself, your father's won on the circuit again. He's famous like that."

She knew better than to say a critical thing about Artie. Though Art rarely called Paulie, she wanted her son to be proud of his dad. She hoped, knowing Art's fearlessness, it would help him develop his father's physical courage. She was relieved Paulie preferred riding his bike, chasing butterflies, memorizing constellations to playing with cars. Even with Art's genes, Paulie ignored speed which had dazzled and intrigued Art from a toddler. Still they were blood. Did she not want Paulie to inherit her own strength, her endurance? She never thought of that as she might have with a daughter. A hodgepodge of strange ideas developed out of the nurturing and cultural differences between genders. Now universities recognize many gender identities. And still there was no understanding. None whatsoever. Janey took her son off to school. Her little boy ran ahead and joined Rex and met up with Lydia. A difference, some said, too great to be reconciled.

Whatever had happened before, Simon could not stop himself from wanting badly to take Janey out again. And again and again until things started to be right. No matter what, he couldn't shake loose from his desire. Distraught in the first stage of loss he denied that this relationship was no longer working. Of course, it was working, only stuck in a trying period. The intensity of his emotions proved that. The next date would be less tense. He planned a foursome. His good friend, the amiable Braden, and Carol would make everything normal. Janey acquiesced because a movie and a pizza on Friday sounded good after a hard week. She had hesitated when he called, give her credit. However, for a professional in the field of the human mind, she wasn't able to see her own missteps or recognize her misplaced sympathies. Or perhaps she agreed to the date because Braden and Carol would be with them. She liked looking at Braden, exchanging an inkling with only a glance. His eyes were motile, reflexive, unearthly. She easily met Braden's eyes. She averted hers from Carol often.

Waiting at the table for Simon and Janey to arrive, Braden poked Carol with his breadstick. "Come on, don't be negative. You agreed to help Simo same as I did."

"Give him some support, yeah. But hang out with him and Janey all evening, that I didn't sign up for."

"You and Janey used to be friends—"

"We still are, sort of. Nobody sees her much since her son came… Braden, I think Janey's going to break it off with Simon for good. I've got a feeling."

Braden was coming around to the same belief. "I know Simo, he's persistent. That day we played golf with those jerks from Springfield… I mean, I see how other people see him. The back nine mix-up set him off and he refused to finish the round. He won't give up his point. Won't budge, not a word, not a step if he thinks he's right. He won't give up on her easily."

"He's too friggin' needy—"

"Don't go there, okay? I've known the guy since junior high, and he's stood the test of time."

She laughed, "Oh, that's what it takes, huh, longevity? No love at first sight for you."

"I'm not talking about love, I'm talking about friendship. Different bond." He stuck the breadstick in his mouth. His angular, slightly agitated features morphed back to normal composure mode. Not ruffled for long, almost too unexcitable for her. It didn't seem he could be pushed too far. Didn't have a too far. Could that be good, she wondered for a moment?

The restaurant door opened, held wide. In scooted Simon with Janey behind him. Night dazzled, contrasted with the indoor bright ambiance, a black dark, shining sparkled oval, layer upon layer of ebony lacquer. Braden smiled at the couple as they approached, Janey looking refreshed in the little Italian place, warm moist odor of herbs and oil, melted cheese. Nothing was more beautiful than the night.

Simon took Janey's hand which stayed held inside his damp grip. Something was getting through from Janey's message center at last. We're like those orangutans she'd visited at the apery in the Brookfield Zoo. Captured, behind reinforced glass, enduring their confinement, not knowing at any simian level why they were held prisoners there. The male orangutan, it became clear to Janey, seemed to have a glimmer of why they were captives. He futzed around with a sharp stick at the corner where the glass fit into the wall of his enclosure, while the female sat lost and quizzical — as if the way to freedom meant something else to her.

The three old friends seemed to do most of the talking and kidding around. Simon loosened up with Braden there. Janey listened, distant, apprehensive, drank three glasses of wine, instead of stopping at two.

The informality and comfort of the pizza joint could have reconciled Janey to Simon, but it didn't. When he took her home, Simon's feverish kisses, heavy breathing, muttered rhapsodies didn't stop her from bolting out of his car as soon as she could unentangle herself from his arms and legs.

About Janey, later Carol confined to Braden, the double date had restored their friendship. Braden felt an inchoate uneasiness about the whole evening.

Quiet in the house when she got in. Mrs. Gallop was sleeping on the sofa and had to be wakened.

Before going to bed Janey crept into Paulie's room to check on him. She thought nothing, didn't approach his bed, never considered a movement which might wake him. She stood inside the doorway and let the end of the night expire.

Alone in the jewelry store, Leah Campion watched her sole customer exit and glanced at the wall clock. Middle of the afternoon. What a long day. Only September and already damp winds bit and harassed, kept people at home or at indoor malls. Later in the year the bitter cold, much fiercer weather and driving snow, will not deter the shoppers. But that state of mind had to be built up to. For the last six months of moderate, mild or hot weather had determined Chicagoans' activities. Later it would be different; twenty degrees would feel fairly balmy. Musings like these, loose and detached, kept Leah from falling into the hollow of grief. Best to keep thinking on the thin surface, like gliding on the first ice over a deep inland lake.

Claymore had left for lunch and to do a few errands.

He used never to leave the shop until closing; however, Leah had won his trust, so he felt comfortable doing so. He had said he'd be back in no time.

But Clay didn't make it back before the robbery. Gloomy lowering clouds shaded the jeweler's front windows. Dressed in a black hoodie, low-slung jeans, and a green windbreaker, his beat-up torn running shoes silent creeping in, he drifted through the doorway like a ghost so that when she looked up at the bell's tinkle, she didn't see him at first. Tall, young, skinny young man, face covered in a dark ski mask, eye holes trimmed in red. Menacing as he slid his cocked legs across the floor, a hand up, pointing at the ceiling, the other hand bunched in his jacket pocket, suggesting a gun there.

He said nothing. Swaggered across the carpet to where she stood behind the glass counter next to the computer and cash register. Strange she felt no automatic adrenaline alarm. Almost as if she was not sure even with his mask that he meant to rob them. No fear rumbled in her, only the stray thought — it hadn't been a soldier with a rifle pointing at Jonathan. A bomb in the road — an IED. This covered human form, this shape with his hand in his pocket, shivering, pointing, menacing…it could not be that she wasn't afraid, but she felt nothing. A wet, fetid rush at the bottom of her throat, the taste of gall.

He waved his red-gloved hand. Likely trying to hide his true voice, he rasped an order at her. Through her distilled reality, Leah heard his threat, but didn't move. He repeated his demands, assuming she was shocked and muddled. If she moved even an eyelid or showed any anger, he would have pulled out the gun and shot her.

She heard him, "Go, Bitch, dig out all them jewels, the diamonds. Hurry up, them diamonds, huh, faster or you gonna die."

Leah moved in slow motion, said, "Only the diamonds," as if waiting on an impatient customer.

"Red ones, too." He was breathing heavily. Rubies. "Hurry up, Bitch." Another ripple inside his jacket pocket, slither of intimidation. His voice again pseudo-gravel, like scraped knee-caps. Scooping out of the display cases what he pointed at, she flung the gems onto the counter where the robber swept them into his jacket pocket. He dove around, bent sideways over his gun pocket, and ran out of the store. Jackrabbit fast. She hadn't even seen him open the door.

Claymore returned, muttered "goddamit, goddamit, pressed the button to alert the police, and tried to comfort Leah until they arrived. With revolvers drawn, two uniformed cops plunged through the doorway. Leah heard them scuffling, clattering, questioning, as if the air were compressed. She told what happened. Claymore held her hand which was freezing cold and seemed to shrink from his touch. All he said after the policemen left was that he had not shown her how to activate the alarm. But then, if he had, she might be dead. Claymore sent her home and began to assess how much he had lost.

In her car Leah started for home then pulled over to the curb and stopped, her body uncontrollably trembling. Waited until she steadied herself, slowed her rapid breathing and was able to drive home. Standing on shaky legs in her kitchen she drank strong tea, began to think. This was violence, not like a movie scene or television program which she didn't watch much. Not at all like the words in a book. No connection to the display put on by convicted killers for the cameras. Once she had broken up a fight her young son had stumbled into over stolen cub scout money. There had been recent videos of people being killed, shot, through open car windows, in the back when running away. Not like what she experienced today. No. A pain sliced through her chest. She bent sideways against the sink and sobbed.

Janey Leduc received another invitation from Simon Butler, the relentless suitor. Although the pizza double date had been awful, this offer intrigued her enough to consider it. Never mind that she was determined not to see him again and that she would have to ignore her scruples and go out with Simon in spite of them. Braden would come along, Carol as well, to this offbeat cabaret show. He'd left a phone message to check her calendar.

On a whim after she retrieved Paulie from school, she drove to Simon's dealership to give him her answer in person. Paulie had seemed overwhelmed by his first few days at school, so she thought a treat — looking at shiny new cars — would help relax him.

Paulie inferred that this man Simon had once gone out on dates with his mother, even though they didn't seem to go places often anymore. When his mother had first introduced Simon, he had sensed uncomfortable tendrils in the air. So Paulie had snubbed him to his satisfaction. He had done it so well that he felt a twinge of guilt. He was being mean like that bully Mike at his school in Toronto. He had felt angry when Simon held his mother's coat for her. In spikes of vexed confusion, he recognized a falsity, a spooked look on the man's face. Now they were going to see the shifty guy at his job. One thing the boy was firm about: those new cars were not going to impress him at all.

Janey left Paulie in the showroom with a chipper

salesman to show him fancy automobiles while she went through the opened service door where she had spotted Simon.

"Hey." He was both pleased and dumbstruck to see her there. "You got my message, then?" The man had no finesse, only determination.

"Yes, I did." He came around the high desk to get her answer. If it turned out he had to talk her into going, he could work it better close up.

Overanxious for a positive answer, he rushed to sell his plan. "Sounds great, right? Like I said, kind of what you'd call avant-garde, or New Age." He didn't know what to call it. "At the Haymarket Pub in Ravenswood. This group called the Moth Story Slam has a gig where the customers come up one at a time, and you tell your five-minute story, but with no notes." He added, "There's going to be music late. It's called cathartic cabaret."

"Yeah, I googled it. It might be fun, something different."

"So, we're going." He grinned. "I might ask Braden and Carol if they want to come with. That okay with you?"

"Yes, of course." She had hoped for that. "I'll let you get back to work." She glanced behind her. Paulie tired of sauntering among the cars had walked up to them. He stared at Simon. "This is where Simon runs the service area, Paulie."

He wanted to diss the guy with a real spitter-like, so what my dad races Formula Cars, in a snarky drawl, but it didn't come out. Nothing did.

It's going to be all right, Simon thought later. Janey brought her kid to see where I work.

Walking through Haymarket Pub, Simon followed the maître d' to their table and behind him Janey snaked around milling groups of people. Braden, his hand on Carol's shoulder, leaned against Janey and whispered, "What this place? Simo gets some nutty ideas."

"Comedy club plus." She watched Carol snuggle up to him.

"Geez, what a crowd. Look at him ducking left and right, the man in charge." Carol grabbed onto Braden's arm as if she might get lost.

"A hoard of the curious," Janey said. An odd envy welled in her chest. She pushed through faster to keep up with Simon who was almost sprinting. They were seated near the stage which Simon mentioned to Braden with a man-to-man mojo nod.

They drank martinis, and talked, ate the pub's famous hamburgers with Brie and grilled vidalia onions, and talked, laughed loud and talked some more. Most of the conversation blew past Janey, sliding off her consciousness like a breeze off her warm skin in summer. Idle words, gossip, daily goings-on, nothing stuck. Carol and Simon had gotten into one of their frequent tiffs.

"Hey, Simo," she said, a new assault from another angle, "when's your big improv show starting? You going up there with something to kill 'em with?"

Braden no longer noticed Carol's glib taunts. Always she made fun of everything. She wasn't cynical, but could be hostile, like a comedian who believes nothing is out of bounds for a laugh. They had been tourists in Italy in a tiny old town whose church was built in the Middle Ages and claimed a relic of sacred significance. Roped off near the altar, lay a cast of Jesus' naked foot. Before anyone could stop her, Carol stepped over the rope, and slinging her sandal off, put her foot in the holy footprint. She had grinned at Braden, "Same size as mine. Jesus wore a size nine in men's." Braden had ignored the looks of horror on the faces of the faithful.

On the other hand, Carol made fun of what was intentionally comic, laughing at the people laughing. Not with, at. She was being her usual self. However, this evening Braden had felt under a cloudy gloom for no perceptible reason since they had arrived. Janey wouldn't look at him.

Simon kept on the defense. "Wait until you see this

program. Not like the usual stuff. It turns weird they say. Funny weird. The way people carry on with crazy stories."

"Oh, crap, like sob-stories, blubbering on TV reality shows—" Janey started.

"No. Not like that." Simon flared up, always took her bait. "Those are pathetic and ordinary. These here are creative, original skits."

"You've seen it then?" Carol said.

"I read a review about it. Just shut up, Carol. You never know what you're talking about."

Carol howled, "Oh, right. So I would be great when I got up on that stage."

"You wouldn't have the guts, no guts."

Braden plucked at his tie, stretched one arm up, flicked a wayward onion onto his empty plate.

Janey said, "I'm going to the bathroom where it might be quieter. I want to phone the sitter. Paulie was feverish and sneezing when I left."

"Oh, it's a cold, Janey. Kids are prone to getting them." Simon said. He left off listening to Carol insist on her aptitude for parody.

"You don't know how mothers are," Carol said.

"Like you do, Carol?"

"Oh, ouch," she gagged at him.

"Anyway, why would Janey be that worried about him now? She wouldn't even have known he was sick all the time she left him dumped in Canada," Simon snorted.

Janey had been half-way up; she sat back down. Heat baked perspiration between her shoulder blades.

"If you go now, Janey," Braden said, "bathrooms shouldn't be so crowded. Looks like the performance is starting." Braden was chastened, alarmed by his repugnance of Simon. He had reacted directly to Simon's insult, but Janey read more in his words. He knew the fury in her when she fell back into her chair. At that moment her submerged attraction to Braden surfaced in sprays of longing. When she'd first met Braden she thought his eyes were beautiful, strands of white and cobalt shards all lit in a glow of pale blue. They were agates stuck among sharp uplifts of cheekbones and jutting nose. With his round eyes, his veiled words, half-smile, she saw for her a beautiful man. Fission of magnetic field, pitch of gravity, two protons collide when it is said, and such as this time gripped Braden.

With smashing drum rolls Moth Story Slam got started. A skinny man in a hard, white mask punctured with holes, wearing a suit striped yellow and peach and a blood red tie pounced on the garishly lit stage, waving a mike. First a few professional comics led off the improvisations.

Obviously, these improvs, rehearsed in advanced, came off polished and funny. Then a scattered few extroverts who try anything once, told crippled reminiscences and shaggy dog stories, eliciting titters from the crowd. After which a couple of drunks meandered on incoherently until coaxed off the stage amid a few catcalls. Janey sank further and further back in minuscule motions until her spine pressed against the chair.

A dolled-up matronly woman rambled on about black garters, lacy frilly boost bras… She seemed to be showing how she tried them on at Victoria's Secret. Janey's eyes began to swim. Simon and Carol were laughing at everything. She swiveled around. Braden had disappeared somewhere.

As the night wore on, the more mundane and uninspired the five-minute monologues became. Not intrinsically dull stories, not comic sketches, but labored admissions, like forced confessions about accidental drownings, dysfunctional families, mysterious goings on, hinted at, of chicanery, vice, illicit conduct, all with undertones of unloving betrayal. A hundred shades of self-deluded mockery. Too like a grotesque therapy session at the office. Her head began to ache, from the nape of her neck upward over her head to a pounding over her eyes. She wondered how this crowd of customers kept giggling and encouraging this pathetic behavior. Or was she the only one who was appalled? She sent her painful head panning: apparently she was. Where had Braden gone off to?

At the music interlude, Braden reappeared. Said he'd been outside getting some fresh air. Simon asked him if he'd started smoking again. Carol twirled around spiking him with her eyes. No, he assured them, he hadn't and took his seat. Janey glanced at Braden her face hurting.

Janey waited appalled, and thought, I'm going up there and tell them.

Voices clamored for the show to go on. Simon winced at Janey's thinned-lipped look of disapproval that he so disliked. The madcap white mask like a cartoon bubble loomed toward her, its boney arms waved her up.

A bevy of putty dancers cavorted behind Janey who found herself on the stage. But she paid them no mind as she grabbed the mike and spoke out.

"People, performers, masked guy, everybody, listen to me. None of you understand…what you are doing up here on the stage and what you are sitting down there listening to. Those things you told about yourself — obliquely or starkly — or what you down at the tables heard, none of you recognize it, the woeful soulless misery, with no, none of the insight which if you had any would make your words, such things, unspeakable, unhearable. It isn't right to go on like this. Stop this. Everybody go home." Someone threw a plate of spaghetti onto the stage. It splattered on her shoes.

The audience began to boo at her, shout ugly insults. The holey masked MC raced up and marched her off the stage, amid ridicule and laughter, a tittering of mock applause.

Outside, Janey breathed in the frigid, non-saline watery wind outside the Haymarket Pub, blowing against her face from the east off the lake. Braden and Carol had ducked off in the opposite direction.

Simon stuttered at her. "That was the most…em, embarrassing, fucking ex, excruciating few minutes…of my life. Why, why did you do that?"

"I don't know." Random ideas scampered through her mind. She stared in front of her, an image of Paulie this morning sitting at the kitchen table in the patch of sunlight from the window over the kitchen sink playing with the new animal figures she'd bought him.

"What the hell happened up there, Janey? You humiliated yourself, you know that?"

She was astounded. "I did? You say I did?"

"It was like you told them all off."

"That wasn't my intention." But, it niggled at her,

maybe… "You didn't go up there…?"

"I don't have any good stories. Nothing dramatic happens to me. Not like your hanging for your life in a crashed car over a fucking ravine. With that race car driver husband of yours. I thought the worst you were going to do was tell that drivel. But this topped it. Really topped it. By a mile."

"Oh, all right, okay. I'm sorry. Forget it. So what I said didn't suit you. Leave it at that."

"You got fucking booed off the stage."

As they crept into his car, she heard what sounded like an honest thought. "I wanted it to be fun, different, you complain about our dates being all the same. This would be good fun, a riot, something new."

She waited until he was settled, had gotten the car started. "It was a good idea, Simon. Not your fault it started to remind me of my clients. Movies and TV shows have that effect on me, too. Even bestsellers just like case studies. Although I think sometimes that's the way the authors want them to sound…"

The sitter was in the hall when Janey got in, anxious to go home. Janey sighed at her. "Everything fine, Mrs. Gallop?"

"Oh, yes." She glanced to where Janey's purse stood on the side table. Then she heard Janey continue.

"It might have been an enjoyable, kind of creative evening. Where people could act out funny skits… You know, Mrs. Gallop, I am a social worker, for my sins…"

The sitter nodded, shrugged into her coat, disheartened. She could just leave the half-tipsy woman to her blather, but to go home without her pay? "Yes, I know."

"But sitting in that pub, was like a continuation of work. Wrenching stories to laugh at, make fun of, self-mockery."

"Ah, Ms. Leduc, it's getting late…"

"…I might as well have stayed in my office. Lear was playing at…that Shakespeare playhouse…at Navy Pier, I could've gone there. Don't you see the difference? You don't. I'm so tired."

"I better go…"

Janey reached for her purse, "Oh, I'm sorry. Here," and shoved the money from a side compartment. "Good night, Mrs. Gallop." The door closed behind the hustling matronly woman's broad back.

Janey perseverated, sitting on the kitchen chair, coat dropped behind her, shoes kicked under the table, not able to go to bed. She had planned a clever story while they ate dinner, if she'd gotten up the nerve, but as the audience began trotting on stage, with their miseries of self-loathing, she became jittery. Something else had to be said. It was inexplicable. Only a few words, like haiku. Bad idea, but I hung on to it until it was done. Said and done.

She drank a glass of ice water from the refrigerator, then padded into the living room and slumped on the sofa, too discouraged to undress and go to bed. She had after-images of thick-headed Simon in the darkened car, Braden and Carol disappearing into the night. It was simple. Don't do it. The ineffable is what we cannot say. Do not even try. Not in that manner. Whatever makes us think that we can conjure up a way to close the gap because we want to so badly. She had meant to relay a narrative she had concocted out of an inviolable childhood memory. She closed her eyes retracing the evening. She had meant to tell a story hidden in a regular design, to the sub-rhythmic scaffolding beneath a holding pattern, not for control which is in fact an effect of regularity. But to discern what lies beneath. She was so tired of case histories. They are all alike. It shouldn't be that way in a story.

Tufts of sweet-smelling air, and the prickly grass and soil beneath her. Green to the horizon and the tennis court, and the school building beyond, and the blue, ever mysterious blue sky, a few small puffs of white clouds. Herself, a child, with the sense of the earth felt beneath her hips and shoulders, and the warm sun on her bare arms, of the soft fuzz on her skinny brown legs stuck out of Bermuda shorts. Big violet cone flowers on a cotton shirt, yellow trimmed in red, scuffed white sneakers, cling of gym socks. Somehow she had made an impress of the infinity of blue, how she'd seen the clouds ride high above, the sky inconceivably higher above them. Moment of perfect stillness forever. There must have been noise from the tennis players, shouts, speedy steps scurrying at an angle to smash yellow balls, gull cries from blocks away barely heard. Time stretched out to eternity. And then, a glimpse.

Janey, smiling, looked in on Paulie and went to bed. A crest of happiness crashed over her. Only for a moment, but that is always enough. She had slipped into an absolute stillness. If only she had conveyed the opening she sighted, not the thing itself, the sighting. Instead she had sounded like a parrot.

No matter. In the morning all that occurred this night will be past. Paulie will fuss about the oatmeal she cooked him, wanting the sugary cereal his grandmother bought. Then she would hug him, and he would eat the mush with a put-upon air that was his kid's way of handling her.

SIX

AFTER the basketball game Braden laid it flat out to Simon. He was tired of hearing about Simon's blighted relationship with Janey. Over a pitcher of beer at the Publican on Fulton, the two friends at first carried on as always, dissecting the Bull's win, chatting, ribbing, until Simon like a tedious pedagogue turned the talk to Janey. He hadn't called her after the fiasco the other night because she had gone too far. He always liked her spunk and independent spirit, but getting booed like that had been mortifying. It showed up her arrogance.

"Like she's better than other people. I think that's why she didn't tell us about her being married. She didn't want us to look down on her."

"For what?"

"Being divorced."

"Simo, you better run a check. I think your brain's been hacked and malware's frying your synapses."

"She went up there with a smile on her face to tell them off. Holy crap it was like I couldn't find a big enough hole to crawl in—"

"Well, that was how you saw it. I bet you Janey didn't mean it that way. That's what you're missing."

"Braden, they threw wet coasters when we were walking out."

"So what?" Braden hadn't seen anything flying. "That's despicable."

"It was pitiful—"

"Jesus, Simo, can't you just forget about it? For a fucking month now, you've been going on about Janey. It gets old, Simo. Give yourself a break, and me, too."

Simon looked down at the floor, grimaced. "Braden… Jesus, why rip on me? What do you know about women… people? You prefer computers."

"You're wrong there. I work on computers because it's an easy way to make a living. Computers are gadgets, intricate, useful, elaborate, yeah, but gadgets. Tools. Clever invention, but still, no more than a data-gathering tool. Not even as useful as a wrench, in a way. A…gadget." He felt uncomfortable in the heat of the overcrowded bar. Around his neck a ring of sweat prickled.

"Yeah, yeah sure, but face it, you're no good with understanding people's feelings."

"And you are? Let's get out of here, Simo. Place got packed in the last half hour."

As Simon followed on his heels, Braden heard him muttering, "I think Janey lost it when she climbed up on that stage. Didn't care how it affected me, she was going to spew no matter what." He insisted on making Braden see his point.

∽

Amid the magnificence of science is where Martha Gibson wallowed gloriously like the hippos in the old song. And as a staff member at the Field Museum she asked everyone to follow her into all the glories of the universe contained there. She loved her job, her only one since she graduated from Boston College and came back to Chicago to live. Her long-time romantic relationship had attenuated with distance, but at the Field she chose to stay. When she went to Boston or Benjamin came to Chicago they became lovers again. But there was no frenetic desire to push either of them to live together. Benjamin wouldn't leave the Boston Symphony, who in their right mind would? And Martha didn't want to leave the best job in the world at the Field. So there they were. They did talk daily and texted, of course. Each time after a few months apart, they both realized they were bonded more tightly than either had thought when apart. They took their vacations together and went to exotic locales, Bali and Kuala Lumpur, Mumbai, Kyoto, places where Martha said she must find out about life. For Benjamin they went to Jerusalem. Martha Gibson was searching for her soul's light in far-off parts of the world. She was soon to find intimations of it in Chicago.

The first time Janey took Paulie to the Field Museum it had been to see the Herman Strecker Moth and Butterfly collection. They had spent all of their time on that display. But when they returned a few Saturdays later, he discovered other fascinating exhibits and collections especially Neanderthals, comets and planets, and the SUE The T. Rex. This week Janey brought Paulie to Meet-a-Scientist Day at the Grainger Science Hub. He'd been apprehensive and glum lately with the stress of his new school and thoughts of how much better he had liked living in Toronto. With his mother, of course, before she'd move to Chicago. His grandmother from Saskatchewan preferred to live in Canada — Toronto where his aunt had settled a long time ago. It was confusing why people moved anywhere. He was homesick and he had no idea for what.

The first scientist they met happened to be Martha Gibson, also feeling homesick she had no idea for what. Benjamin's phone call early that morning had been dispiriting. Mundane, joyless. Perhaps Ben was worried about his oboe solo this evening.

Paulie had begun grousing when Janey had nixed his signing-up for the overnight "Dozin' with the Dinos." Then he whined — this really did hurt — for being too late for the live Lepidoptera display, a transparent plastic bubble filled with growing flora and myriads of flittering butterflies. He had been captivated by the promo video: hundreds of species, shifting sparks of vivid colors and intricate patterns. But they hadn't made it to the museum before the show ended.

Martha Gibson overheard his bewildered lament, the young boy with loads of curly hair falling in old-fashioned blond ringlets, mouth in an "0" of crushed hopes. Martha Gibson loved the live butterfly display which although closed hadn't been taken apart yet. She introduced herself to the adult with the articulate child.

"I can get you in the display right now, if you want. There won't even be other people there." Paulie looked up at her as if she were the archangel Michael, sword and all.

Janey said, "You may be saving him from being put up for adoption." They walked off to the butterfly conservatory, laughing, while Paulie tugged at his mother's arm to hurry them up. He sneaked peeks back at the little woman, inches shorter than his mother, who belonged to the wonderful museum.

When they got to the butterfly enclosure, Paulie said to the scientist woman, "I used to catch butterflies, but I don't anymore."

Inside, the butterflies swarmed, gracefully and gently. At first, Paulie named the ones he could identify, then his excitement settled into the warm sense of beauty around him. Martha Gibson and Paulie whispered facts about the different kinds floating past them. Occasionally, a butterfly would land, on Paulie's shoulder, on Janey's head. Martha put out her hand and a Monarch lit on her finger. To Paulie, Martha merged with the flocks of intricate sparkly tinctures of butterfly. She became their medium. He was magicked.

After the butterfly visit, Martha took them to lunch in the cafeteria. Paulie knelt on his chair, sitting on his heels, talking to this grownup who treated him like a person.

Paulie kneeled on his chair, sending Martha shy smiles. "I never thought I would see anything like that."

Janey picked up his sandwich and handed it to him. "Here, eat up, you goofy goofy boy."

Martha Gibson tapped the table top. A tangible clarity

came like a phantom, that she wasn't being another self, like the scientist self, kind-friendly-person self, girlfriend-of-Ben self. Nor was she in work mode, no mode, no edge, no posture; as if there were no need to do anything but be. Lost but not unfamiliar feeling, not new. Akin to when as a girl she'd sat in the decrepit kitchen of an old Armenian woman, a friend of her grandmother's, who had fled from the Turks after they beheaded her husband in front of her. She ran with her infant son hidden under her peasant skirts. Young Martha had been listening to the old woman's story, but not apart from it. She became that half-crazed mother. Truth meant for her to be there. But she wasn't recalling that long-ago incident. Not alive in her mind now, only there floated a thought lingering between unconsciousness and subconsciousness. Being in the moment that the guru teaches which means an ineffable place of comfort.

Sandwich and milk consumed, the boy rattled on, still in delight.

"...You know Monarch caterpillars are poisonous so birds don't eat 'em. And Monarchs migrate to Mexico and California and it takes 'em six months to get there. And Mourning Cloak and Anglewings can travel for a year. I painted in Art class the most colored one—"

Janey held up her hand. "Paulie, have to get home and

Martha has to go back to work."

Martha Gibson leaned across the table, sketching something on his napkin with a pen she'd dug out of her work coat's deep pocket. "Did you know, Paulie, have you seen a fish butterfly?"

"A butterfly that's a fish?"

"Yes."

In front of them, with expert strokes she drew the Mosaic butterfly. With its folded wings, an angelfish appeared. Paulie snorted in delight. "A Mosaic. Hey, I never saw it like that before."

"There're lots of strange and mysterious connections. Fascinating, unpredictable links, relations and correlations." The boy wasn't sure of meanings, but the words intrigued him.

"Like your mom," Martha Gibson continued, "has the look of the folksinger Joan Baez when she was young."

Janey guffawed, "Oh, come on," both women giggled, "that's hilarious," and Paulie joined in because it sounded very funny and his beloved mother was here with him forever.

Not long after the visit to the Field Museum Janey dropped into Claymore's jewelry store to buy a watch at last for her sister. Without Isabelle's help with Paulie,

Janey would not have been able to start her new job at Lutheran Social Services immediately last winter. Maybe not a watch after all, but a bracelet or earrings. Nothing ostentatious, she directed Claymore and, God, nothing sentimental. All jewelry, Clayton admonished her, every piece in his store had emotive energy, undertones, depth.

"Well, okay, something jazzy, with color."

"Here's the thing—"

"Very…nice." The exquisiteness of the bracelet made it totally unfit for Isabelle.

Clay spit out, "Nice?"

"I mean beautiful. But not for my sister who's more…pedestrian."

"It's you who's got pedestrian taste… Here's something I don't often get in." A shimmery bracelet, its indigo stones on a fox gold chain. The subtle play of deep blues fascinated her. Then, it might be something that Isabelle — after all the total genetic package from the same parents — would like.

She picked up the slender bracelet to get a closer look. "Beautiful shade of…"

"Phylo blue," said Claymore, satisfied with her reaction to the sapphire.

Janey dangled the stones in front of her eyes, a little mesmerized.

"I took Paulie to the Field Museum Saturday. Have you seen their jewel and gem collections?"

"I haven't been there in decades. But yes, I remember well some of the exhibits." Clay leaned over the glass counter to relieve the sciatica pain raging through his right hip.

"There was this incredible colored stone from Australia, a sharp bright turquoise—"

"Chrysoprase," Claymore said.

"I didn't know sapphires came in pink and white."

"You have little to no acquaintance with gemstones."

Janey was used to crabby clients. She ignored him, and switched topics. "Last Saturday we went back and Paulie got to go inside the live butterfly exhibit. He hasn't stopped talking about it."

In the event, she purchased the pricey bracelet for Isabelle and, pleased with herself, started to head out when she felt a gloomy ambience. The windows had darkened with the evening. Claymore's assistant had slipped out and gone home. He had begun to limp toward the back of the store. Enough for today of peoples' moods spilling over onto her.

Janey next drove to fetch Paulie at his friend Rex's house and take him for tacos. He wasn't there. Rex said the Cub Scout den mother didn't take Paulie with them when she took the boys home. Rex thought Paulie was still at the school or maybe trying to walk home.

He doesn't know the way home. She sped to the school, found the doors were locked, no one around and Paulie nowhere to be seen. Intense worry scrabbled at her gut.

He should have called her cell. He had. She had switched it off and after the session with her last client had neglected to turn it back on. He had left a few sparse words on it, come and get him at school.

Commanding herself not to panic, unaware that her time flying home would have qualified for the Daytona 500, she stumbled up the steps, when out the door ran Paulie shouting, "Mom, here's Gibby, she brought me home, can she come out to get tacos with us?"

Gibby said, coming up behind him, "He called the museum, got them to give him my extension… He sounded panicked."

"I knew what to do, huh. 'Cross the street, the lady at the candy store let me use her phone. But your phone wasn't working—" His face — the fear he must have felt.

Blood began to return to Janey's circulatory system. "Thank you, Martha, I can't thank you enough."

"I'm glad he thought to call me."

"I used the telephone book."

"I thought this den mother was going to—" Janey began.

"She said there wasn't room for me in her car. She had other kids." Paulie dashed off to the kitchen.

"Oh, good god. How could she leave him standing there?"

"I'll go punch her face." Martha Gibson lifted her fist. They grinned at each other. Paulie ran back from the kitchen with a cookie."

"You did good calling Martha, Paulie."

"Gibby, Mom, everybody calls her Gibby. Can Gibby come eat tacos with us, huh, Mom?"

Curious point about the new friend her son had foisted on Janey was the easy way the two women got along. Janey sensed a need on Gibby's part to talk freely. And Gibby seemed, if it wasn't too highfalutin a word, authentic. She didn't strain to be friendly, scientific, regular. Their talk felt real to Janey who disengaged her normal caution around strangers, strangers being anyone she hadn't known well for many years. Since Simon had shaken her confidence in her people-judgement, and Edwin in her professional judgement, her trust in Martha Gibson would end up being crucial. Some people get shook when they make mistakes. If Janey misjudged Martha Gibson, all hell would break lose in her psyche.

After her rescue of Paulie whenever Gibby had time, she would show up at Janey's office and the two would pick up sandwiches and talk. One evening Gibby took them to the planetarium show, a night that adult Paul said had given direction to his life. He had seen clearly, at age eight, what he truly loved. All things are a long time coming to fruition. There is no past, no future, only the infinite present. As there is no time. Because everything is fated — but not determined.

∽

A few minutes after four by the office clock, Janey closed her laptop and pushed it aside among the papers deposited across her desk. She fiddled on her smart phone, checking on train schedules, before she called her mother. Both her mother and her sister where coming for Thanksgiving, American not Canadian, and she wanted to check their arrival time. They would stay at her house even though both would be squashed together in the guest bedroom. No answer. She left a message. Since she had no more clients and had worked through lunch, she thought about leaving early.

In strolled Dorothea Pounce, big grin, colorful skirt draped down to her black ankle boots, bangle bracelets on both bare arms. Over the skirt floated a black and red cape decorated with tiny gold and silver threads.

This was Dorrie's way, show up with no appointment, unannounced, when least expected, but at a good moment when her popping-in found no one with Janey. Uncanny how Dorrie managed these things.

Janey squinted, turned her head away, said nothing.

"I'm not busting in on anything, am I? The receptionist wasn't at the front desk." Of course not.

Dorrie sat herself down on the low sofa at the window where the glowing sun split by the white blinds made an aureole around her frizzy red hair. She was almost a silhouette. Janey swiveled her chair to right angle to the window.

"I was planning to leave early."

"I won't take long. It's just…I haven't done well by Edwin…and I need your advice."

"Hunting-his-mother thing?"

"If I had only pretended it was me since my name did show up on his birth certificate. I could've kept the masquerade going, pretended to be his actual birth mom. Then he would have been satisfied. He wouldn't be this hounding avenger, a goddamn pest to everybody."

Janey swallowed her words half-way, choked a bit. "Dorrie, don't you think you did enough damage when you claimed, illegally, fraudulently, unethically that you were the baby's mother to the adoption agency? Never mind how you concocted to get his birth certificate compromised."

"It wasn't unethical," voice heavy on the last word.

"Want to argue that?" She would. But not right now.

"Water under the bridge…"

"If you say so… But Edwin, whose grip on reality is tenuous at best, won't stop his dogged searches. Seems to me putting up with that is a small price to pay for your… deception."

"Quit with the goddamn self-righteousness. You shrinks are supposed to be non-judgmental."

"I'm not a shrink. And the only true non-judgmental people are brain dead."

"Well, I'm beyond that guilt shit. I did a favor I owed a very good friend. Big time owed."

"A favor!" Janey about flung herself out of her chair at the effrontery. "You broke half-a-dozen laws—"

"It didn't seem like it at the time. Now listen, Edwin's gotten this peculiar idea that he insists I gave him a hint or clue. He said I hinted that his true mother is a local celebrity."

"That's old news. He hasn't told you he's got a better candidate now? At the jewelry store Edwin was spilling it to your uncle. She's a French woman. Edwin wants to go find his mother in France."

"Oh my God, a new assault on me. Opening up an attack on another front. He thinks he can squeeze out of me the name of his mother. No one, no one ever will, I told him. Whatever he does, or anyone else, I'll take that secret to the grave with me. I swore to it. And I will."

"What if she dies, the birthmother?"

"Dorrie looked taken aback. "How do you know she's not dead already?"

"Is she?"

"No. My God. How do I get him to go on with his life? It does no good to chase after someone who wants nothing to do with you. In France, Jesus."

For a moment Janey thought how they all use the same worn-out words. Empty words. Empty like her stomach right now since she'd skipped lunch. And at least three more people with words that have exhausted meanings will come tomorrow. If she could say to them all, these are vacuums, these words the way you're using them. Think what they mean to yourself, if not to me. There sat Dorrie split in two parts, defiant warrior and wounded mendicant.

"I can't do anything with Edwin, Dorrie."

"Yes, yes you can. Find me some way to help him. So he will let it be. Go on with his life instead of harping on what's done and gone. Not dwell in the past. Those people who adopted him are to blame. Didn't have to be such mean bastards to him. Edwin might have been satisfied with them and not insist on a real mother."

"Can you give her a first name?"

"Hell, no."

"I mean an alias, so we don't have to keep calling her 'the birthmother.'"

"No, I can't. I was sworn to secrecy."

"An alias, Dorrie."

'I said no."

"Well, never mind. But I can't help you. I'm not that certain Edwin isn't your son." Janey said in her best confrontational mode. Simply good therapy, but this time she enjoyed it.

"I'm not the kind of woman that would deny my own. Abort the fetus if I had to, but not give up my kid to someone else. Look at what misery doing that caused Edwin."

"I suppose… Okay. I haven't got him on my client list anymore. I've told you that. But, unofficially, I'll get Edwin in here at least to dissuade him from going to France."

"I'll bet the little shit doesn't even have a passport."

Dorrie stood up, darted to the door so fast it startled Janey.

Janey called after her, "By the way, his mother might be Marine Le Pen."

"You think?" Dorrie's harsh chortle hung in the air behind her like the challenge it was.

SEVEN

FOR the last month, Leah had slept through the night. At dawn she woke without dread. As she went through her morning routine, she no longer moved fugue-like, but with intent. Time had begun its heartless healing.

She had been startled by her lack of fear during the jewelry robbery. No bright limned vision, no rush of blood or palpitating heart, no wet palms or slowing of time. Normal fear had been ripped off the caul of her stillborn grief, and revealed her despair. So calm and easy when menaced by the gunman, she felt not courage but indifference to her fate which acted like bravery. She could face the gun-wielding thug. If he had shot her dead she would not have cared. To admit that to herself had shocked her. This is what her devastating sorrow had done. When I begin to fear again, she thought, that will signal that I'm resigned to his death. But her stomach-grinding sorrow did not let her believe it could ever happen.

Yet, this morning, at breakfast her eyes caught the sun's rays through the gray sheen of morning rain, and she had felt a drift of well-being, like the flavor recalled of her normal self, shunted far away for months. She could be glad of it.

At the jewelry store, Leah walked into a shouting match between Claymore and a redheaded woman. It appeared a half-comical exchange, but the — she supposed — dissatisfied customer spewed language which froze Clay. When the fiery-headed woman whooped, Clay flinched. Leah approached in slow-motion. Claymore waved her to them.

"Come here, Leah. This is my niece. She's all noise, no bite. We're having a discussion here."

The niece tossed off an ironic smile with lips half-cocked, eyes blinking. "We're having a little disagreement, my uncle and me." She stepped back from almost in his face. "Didn't mean to scare the wits out of the paying trade."

"No, no, she's my new assistant, Mrs. Campion. Leah, I'm going to finish polishing the stones that get custom settings. Cover in the store, will you? Not too many people on Wednesdays…" He headed behind the Persian door hanging. "Buzz off, Dorrie. Think about what I said."

"Hey wait, just hold up a minute Clay…"

Leah held her breath while she hung her coat and turned to face this woman. Like an intruder, she thought. Dorrie had not moved. Her eyes followed Leah as she rearranged diamond ring trays under a glass case.

"You haven't been working here long?"

"Almost three months." Her hands lapped a pearl necklace onto a velvet bust piece.

"Like it here?"

"It's interesting." Not to be baited into a conversation, immune to another's curiosity.

"He tried to teach me the business years ago, but I resisted."

"I like learning about the gems—"

"Yeah, Clay designs beauteous settings. Intricate. Almost too ethereal to be worked into jewelry."

The door buzzed. In strolled Edwin Blake, angular, lanky, neatly dressed. Edwin charged at Dorrie as soon as his near-sighted eyes spotted her hovering at the side counter.

"Did you ask him?" His head swiveled. "Where'd he go?"

Dorrie pushed his arm, shifted him to the ornate clocks

alcove. Needn't have bothered; Leah had no interest in what they were saying.

Soon a customer arrived. Relieved, Leah showed a slim, older woman a pink gold pendant and a necklace of teardrop diamonds cut in triangular facets. Better to work and avoid overhearing conversations. The woman picked up one necklace at a time, dangled it in her long fingers. She contemplated in silence as she decided between them. And so the gist of the hushed talk between Dorrie and Edwin floated back to Leah anyway.

"Doesn't he want to help me?" Edwin dashed his hand across his forehead, disarranging his long brown hair.

"It's not exactly that, Edwin. He's tired of finding you jobs. Why did you quit the florist shop? Delivering plants. You liked driving their van."

"I lost my driver's license. My boss found out. I've gotta make some money right away." "Unless you're planning a robbery, it doesn't work that way. Edwin, you're twenty-eight. People are going to get tired of finding you jobs you don't keep. Your friends, you abuse them with your—" Here it got tricky. He'd fly off the handle if she mentioned his penchant for lying. She'd accused him of telling tall tales once, and he'd carried on as if she'd stabbed him in the throat. Gagged and flailed his arms. Foolish and ludicrous melodramatic posing. "There was that scholarship we worked on, and you got it. Then in a month you dropped out—"

"I got sick."

"Last year, I co-signed for a car, but you don't make one damn payment."

"Okay, bring up all my so-called faults. Dump on me, everybody always has. It's the world's favorite hobby."

"Oh, for Christ's sake, Edwin."

"I'm going to disappear outta the lives of all you perfect people. Never bother you again. I'm leaving as soon as I get the cash, for Paris. You dropped me the hint, gave away not on purpose, a clue to where my mother is. So, keep on hounding me about trivial shit. Actually, I've got two, two excellent plans for finding her. And you don't know it but you are responsible, by chance. You give away things, unconsciously. It's Freudian."

"I give up." But she didn't. "Edwin, I want you to understand how things are. Realistically. In real life."

"Shut up, I get it. You never tried to help find her. You think this is all a game…" He flung his head back. "If you would just tell me who she is, and stop antagonizing me, I might leave you alone."

"I will not ever break the promise that I made to her. End of discussion. I got places to go. See you later." She made for the door. He stepped in front of her.

"You must hate me, Dorrie." Teary, inky eyes glistened.

"Go down to Lutheran Social Services. Talk to Janey Leduc. Seriously this time."

"What for? She's as much help as a bullet through the head."

"There's some things she can explain better than me." She shook her frizzy curls off her hot forehead. Claymore's new clerk seemed to be closing on a sale. Uncle Clay, who was never coming out as long as she stayed, kept the store too warm.

"Dammit go see her. Come on, I'll drop you off there now. Maybe she's available or you can find out when she will be."

He sent a glance crawling around the jewelry store. "I'm not inclined to follow your advice when you've been so rude."

"If I start being nice to you, it'll mean I've written you off." She got tired of humoring him.

Leah handed the customer her wrapped purchase. She watched the niece and young man — a strange pair — leave the shop together. It was not only the customers that were bizarre in this place. Claymore rousted himself out of the back room.

"Gone, I see. You must've gotten an earful. Why my niece bothers, why anybody bothers, is a mystery to me."

She smiled. "Well, I like it when I make a sale." The smile brightened her eyes.

"Such is the power of the purse to ignore distraction." He thought he'd said something wise. She had puzzled him with her remoteness. But she was warming to him. "My niece is…a good woman, and smart most of the time. Trouble with her is, she's loyal to a fault. Proud of it. Too proud. Know what I mean?"

"I think so." Too proud was easy to see. Loyalty depended on a lot of things.

While he huffed back to his work bench, business returned as the entry bell announced customer after customer. Clay never stirred out. His eyes and hands fixated on the intricate dance before him, a pair of woven rose-gold and amethyst loops made to dangle on soft lobes and air music below the threshold of hearing to accompany their brush and sweep. The earrings will float, expand, and the vision they create will transpose the ocular angles and mosaics in orbits of beauty. It will be the reason for his art.

Exasperation snaked like ground fog around Janey Leduc's tiny office. She'd been provoked by events to feel clammy and irritated. She'd seen in the *Trib*'s sports section that Artie Kane had been stripped of his points, but she hadn't had time to read the article. He had not gone to Greece to bail out Tassos, obviously. All morning she'd encountered a parade of clients each with a litany of betrayal. Some had taken bad advice, others had good intentions overturned. Small wonder that therapists have a high burn-out rate.

Pulling back her hair until her roots stung, she felt a blister of tears in the corners of her eyes. There was in the end, maybe, no improving the human race. But, hell, she was only trying to help a few miserables.

Elbows on her desktop, she glanced up out the window, birds, cardinals they were, hiding in the arborvitae. Why so beautiful today?

Edwin Blake barreled through the doorway, slouched against her desk like a guilty wraith.

"She told me to come right in." She never did, but Janey let it pass.

"I have only a few minutes, Edwin. Sit down if you want." He had already dropped into the client's chair.

"I didn't get to talk to Claymore. He hid in his back room." Then he guffawed, not crazy-like but off-putting.

Janey refrained asking him to start from the beginning. If he did it would be more incoherent and long-winded.

"What did you want with Dorrie's uncle?"

"I thought I could get him to help…" Edwin enjoyed

pregnant pauses.

"Help with what?"

"I needed to get some money fast. But forget that. I think Dorrie has plans for me. Not her own plans, but from my birthmother. She's using Dorrie to send me messages." He blinked fast. "Sometimes."

"Dorrie has told us both, emphatically, she has not been in touch with your mother in twenty-five years."

"And you believe her?"

Janey bit her lip. "Why not? Edwin, what, specifically, did you come here to talk to me about? I haven't any idea what Dorrie said or what Mr. Mandebrote did… Why you're telling me this?"

"Dorrie hinted that my birthmother is in the field of entertainment—"

"In France?" She cussed to herself. Hadn't meant to say that.

"Forget France. That didn't work out anyway. You see, Dorrie hinted my mother's right here in Chicago. Got to be. See, Janey, Dorrie let slip who my mother is." He swung his long limbs up around his hips and a wide, satisfied grin appeared from under his sideways glance. He waited, like an elephant with a trunkful of spray.

"Don't fool around. Dorrie did not hint who your birthmother is. She won't tell anyone, ever."

"Did I say she had?" He smeared the words, scoffing. "I figured it out by myself. Pamela Crawford, on the radio in the evenings. She is my birthmother." He unscrambled his legs, defiantly.

"Pamela Craw — Why on earth? Edwin, what gave you that idea? Pa—"

"Yes. It's her. Has to be. Pamela Crawford, 'the Voice of Chicagoland,'" he trumpeted.

"I know who she is. She can't be old enough—"

"How would you know?"

"Her picture all over the billboards—"

"Yeah, well, they touch those up."

Useless to go on. Finally, she understood the meaning of the word flabbergasted. To ask Edwin why his vanished mother has to be this particular radio personality, rather than another celebrity, even, say, Oprah Winfrey, would elicit a skein of intricate, fantastic lies. Anyway, eventually he would let go of this one as he did his French mother. When Edwin latched onto a potential birthmother, he stayed with that woman until another woman tempted him away. Logic, reason, even emotion seemed not to have anything to do with the woman chosen nor why he dropped her.

Janey said nothing, waited for Edwin to leave. He seemed to be decamping from his chair. Marie, her coworker down the hall, an overworked canny black woman with street cred had cautioned Janey not to take destructive defensive reactions away from some clients unless she had replacements. You don't want to leave someone out on the street with no defenses. Marie perceived do-know-harm like a subtle Buddha. If Edwin tells lies to keep his life from crashing, best to let it be until you can find something else to replace the symptom. It should be so simple…

Edwin had unwound and gotten up to leave. Still there was something else.

"I'm going to talk to Pamela during her call-in hour."

Surely he wouldn't get past the screener.

"Edwin, is that a good idea? Would she want to have her personal life broadcast to the world—"

"Sure. They all do, all these celebrities." He had a point.

"All right, leave that aside. Hypothetically, say you get through to her and accuse — tell her she's your long-lost birthmother."

"Great." He sank back down in the chair. He loved hypotheticals. "I announce, 'I found you!'"

"What if she flat out denies it?"

He gave her a you're hopeless shake of his head. "She won't because she is." Then he popped around to the doorway. "You should've seen Dorrie's face when I told her. I've fallen onto the truth. Family bonds, blood will out, a link with those who share our genes. It was only a matter of time before I ferreted it from Dorrie. Instinct. Forget Dorrie's secret. That belongs to me and the woman who gave me birth. She's talking on the radio all the time knowing I'll find her out."

He was stumbling over his own fantasies. "Edwin? Listen, Edwin. Whoever your mother is she doesn't want you to know. It's hard to accept, but you have got to."

His face locked in defiance. "You shitting me?" Some concepts are so odious the mind blocks them in entirety. Everything was determined in Edwin's mind ahead of time. "Dorrie thinks I should take a class or something in the evenings. Get my mind off things. It's friggin' boring at this job, and I've only been there three days. Christ sake, working in a factory that makes shoelace aglets. She says then go out and expand my mind. Yeah. A drama class at Columbia College is going to let me stretch. Whatever. It's another ploy of hers. Trying to distract me now that I'm closing in."

"Dorrie's been your friend. She thinks, as I do, that you shouldn't dwell on the past. You need to look ahead. As I said…your birthmother, wherever she is, she wants to remain anonymous. Many do, for various reasons."

"Well, in my case, she's waiting for me to find her. It's

the way she wants it."

"Edwin, don't go all dramatic on me." She wanted to laugh, to throw a humorous towel over a too-zealous dunking.

"I'm fine. I'm good. At last the unveiling. When I talk to Pamela Crawford."

"Before you discuss motherhood with…Pamela," or Oprah, "at least find out if she's old enough. If she's thirty-five she's not your mother—" Maybe put him off until he latches onto another victim.

"Know something, Janey, you don't have a tactful way of talking to people."

"Why pursue Pamela Crawford if she's too young?" Polite enough?

"She's in her forties," Edwin insisted.

"Well, find out." She stood, leaned her palms on the edge of her desk. "I've got a client coming." Her eyes narrowed. Edwin left with barely a nod. "I will not see that bastard again," she said out loud. Not in a polite tone, not at all.

After collecting her son from school, Janey started chicken baking, warned Paulie not to stray too far, took a hot shower, then felt ready to tackle the article about her ex-husband. Arthur Kane had won the race, but then had been disqualified for purposely impeding another racer ahead of him. The other racer's car had spun out, allowing Art to overtake him. There was more. The car Art bumped belonged to a teammate Artie had been slated to help win. That was the gist of the story. Rules and background details, what was at stake… She didn't grasp how bad it was. Maybe some kind of betrayal, it appeared. He was quoted as apologizing. That was all.

Janey called Paulie in, and while he washed up, thought she should throw the newspaper out. Often the boy scanned the sports section, keeping track of the Cubs, or now in frigid January, the Bulls. He knew his father's races made the paper. If he'd already seen the article, she should mention it. Artie is Paulie's father.

Paulie slid into his chair, chatting, grinning, his hands clean but face still dirty. He seemed happy. For a while after his grandmother and aunt left, without all the noise, frenetic holiday activity, he had been subdued. But he'd been buoyed-up quick enough, glad that they had gone and not taken him away. Gibby kept him busy. With her museum connections, she turned gloomy grey winter days exciting. She helped keep his mother fresh, too. Gibby was not ordinary, in some ways unique. A simple errand, say to buy face cream, ended up in an adventure at Macy's. She'd questioned the natural ingredients labeled on the multi-colored globe at Chanel's boutique. Ouzo on Halstead Street, lordy, the woman could speak Greek.

What would Paulie say if he saw what Artie had done? Our defensive reactions can tear at our children opposite from pelicans who tear at their own breasts to feed their young. She watched Paulie chew his chicken leg, jabbering about dodgeball at recess. A quick decision, she would not throw away the paper, nor show it to him. Let it be. If Paulie saw the article, they would talk about it.

In the event, Paulie spotted his father's name and read about the NASCAR race. All his life the word NASCAR shouted from a page; he would stare at it the rest of his life. However, he didn't mention it to his mother. When she heard him fussing, she crept into his room to check why he wasn't asleep. Vague apprehensions assaulted him. Free-floating anxiety wrestled him like Jacob with the angel. Something significant was out of joint.

He put his face in the pillow and mumbled, "I saw about Dad in the paper…"

She put a hand on his back, more to steady herself. "Yes. Such a deal… I was going to talk to you about it."

"That's okay."

"I thought you might be hurt by it."

"Really it's okay." He squiggled around and pushed

himself up against the headboard. "Only, I don't understand what they said he did…" He expected her to tell him the truth. Children always do, and continue to expect it way after they know better. He needed this adult action to be cleared up. Grown-ups' motivations alarmed him.

"Even if it doesn't matter, you need to know what's going on."

She wasn't getting it. "I mean I just don't get what he did."

"What he did?" She shivered like a wet animal. Suddenly, felt better. Kids, they're resilient, doesn't the research say? Not fragile as she'd always feared.

"They made it sound like he cheated." His voice slithered.

"He broke a rule, Paulie. If you impede — get in the way of — another driver's car, you get disqualified. That's what your father did, sorta bumped him. Against the rules, not like in ice hockey." That got a smile.

"Like basketball. Is it a block or a charge?"

"Yes, Smarty. They called a foul on him."

"A catcher can block the plate—"

"Yup, rules are different for different sports."

"A batter gets to go to first if he's hit by the pitch, but if a kid throws the ball and hits the runner, the runner is out. Rex always argues about that and Lydia swears she's not throwing at him on purpose." He was tired and whispered, had slipped down in his bed.

"Those are some rules. In sports people make up the rules."

"But, Mom," his eyelids closed, he propped them open, they dipped back down. "It said he cut off his own teammate. Must've been a accident. He apologized."

"I watched a lot of your dad's races, but I never followed all the details…" He had fallen asleep, constructing an acceptable trope.

Simon trotted into Clay Mandebrote's shop, renewed hope in his springy step. He crossed to the back counter where Clay appeared from his workroom. Not a customer had bothered him yet this morning.

"Can I do for you, Simo?" He'd given Leah the morning off to visit her lawyer, she didn't say why. Here was Simon dragging him away from a diamond ring setting, a design formed in rose gold. He'd been almost mesmerized by the intricacy of the gem balance.

"I want a little gift for Janey."

"What kind of piece you looking for?"

His eyes flew along the glass counter, measuring the wares. "I think…tonight…Janey and me are going to dinner, a pretty bauble—"

"I don't sell baubles." He moved to where Simon's gazed had stopped. "Something like these bracelets? I sell a lot of bracelet watches. They aren't as costly…"

"I want something really pretty…looks expensive." He pressed his index finger against the glass. "That." Clay drew it out, a silver Ziegfeld daisy locket with an oval link chain. He laid the piece before Simon.

"Two seventy-five," said Claymore.

Simon's head jerked up, "A little pricey, say what." He whistled, played with the links between his fingers.

"It's evocative, lovely." Waited. Claymore surprised himself that he didn't care whether Simon bought the locket or not.

"Yeah, I recognize value. Like why a guy looks at a Mercedes in our dealership, even if he doesn't have the dough. It's pretty all right, but maybe too much for now."

"I think we're talking at cross-purposes," Claymore said. Always the out-there response he'd come to expect from Simon.

"I want to show her I'm a man that appreciates quality. Nothing crass in me." Forget flying coasters.

"How about these pearls?" He flipped the tiny price tag hanging off the clasp. Better priced for Simon. He didn't want any dilly-dallying. His arthritic hands had been soothed by working the diamond's setting."

Simon became distracted. "Yeah…but the other one I like better. When Janey and I get back together. Soon… All right, I'll take the pearl bracelet. It'll surprise her to get a pretty gift."

Clay stared at the man, then went to finish the sale. Simon's optimism amazed him.

Against her better judgement, ominous premonitions and Gibby's quibbling, Janey accepted Simon's offer to take her to dinner, no strings attached. He had said he had missed her. She remembered when dates with him had been exciting. So, she missed the excitement, if that wasn't wrong, she would go.

Yes, Simon had been angling for a relationship revival. When he had called he implied he craved more than sporadic dating. She was finding closure. Closing the door. Whether from controlling passion, or something else, we fool ourselves to get what we think we want — even the trivial stuff.

Simon refused to see what Janey's few casual dates with him signified. The lack of her earlier desire he saw, yes, but the emotional void, no. About Janey he'd developed a particular diplopia, a mental double vision obscuring reality. He was giving everything he had to reestablishing a former love affair which he himself had shattered by insisting on having been betrayed. But betrayal is not wiped away.

At dinner Saturday night Simon slid the package wrapped in glittery silver paper across the table to Janey. As she opened it he watched her face, felt confused, exasperated, let down. Hardly the reaction he had expected.

"You like it?" he said. She hesitated, brief nano-second when she appeared about to push the pearl bracelet away. Gave a brief, faint smile and thanked him. Had it been some trinket she could accept…

She stared at the pearls. Withering swirls…mistaken seeds…recognized too late. "It's lovely, Simon, but not my birthday." Looked up at him. "I'm not going to accept it." Gifts are objects, nothing, no fuss. Pearls not her thing — how could he know, but it must have set him back a few bucks. In return for what? She didn't want to guess. Mistake, the word drummed in her subconscious ear. Didn't want it, didn't want him to have given it to her, didn't want to be shoved into this position. For a dozen reasons she would not take it. She rejected this set-up.

Simon scowled at her, his anger and humiliation clear. "You don't like it?"

"Sure I do. But I don't want any gift." She left it at that. Would say only that. A weird time distortion tried to confuse her. No one uses gifts as bait, or bribes, ornaments of conquest anymore. Sure they do. Only fools think that nothing is what it once was.

"You can't mean that." His voice grew edgy. He slid his hand across his forehead and fidgeted with his chair. "It isn't a big deal. Just something of my…that says I'm glad we're hooking up again."

"No, we aren't. I've tried to tell you, Simon. It's obvious, these last couple of dates, we can't go back, can't restart a relationship. Too much hanging over us."

"We can fix things." Anger burned his humiliation into his throat.

"I'm going now, Simon." He sat in silence while she left him.

In a moment of non-reflection, he foundered with the words to get himself through this impasse.

The arrogant bitch. He wouldn't bother with her anymore. Gotten over her at last. Good deal if he was. She wasn't his type anyway.

For lunch Janey and Martha Gibson liked to hit various cafés and diners in and around Michigan Avenue, Martha not too far from work, Janey far away from hers. Janey's recent caseload weighted heavier than usual, a glut of messy problems trudging into her office.

On the surface the two new friends did not have much in common, but both had similar temperaments, outlooks, attitudes. Both wanted time spent with other people to mean something. Past the stage of hanging out, and not at that awful last part of life when so few people you can say you loved are left. You never know if each meeting is the last. Janey made friends easily and shed them easier. Martha had solid, long-standing friends — most of them living far away — she heard from sporadically. With Ben in Boston she texted or phoned every day, otherwise she was in daily contact with no one. Except for her mother in a nearby assisted living home, recovering from a small stroke. At first she took to Janey's company because of her attachment to Paulie. The precocious boy was warm and appreciative, he touched her heart. But later she came to depend on outings with Janey to juice up life's routineness. Janey was used to going out to lunch in rough times as a reward to herself. Many reasons to find comforts of late, at work and Simon. She told herself she wasn't burning out. Things were just nutso. The two women weren't given to many confidences yet.

Today the talk turned job-related which was normally not the case. Janey felt prodded, tentatively, to let a private complaint leak out.

"I'm tired of being a lone opinion at work these days.

The cases are tough… I'm always on the other side, the side of one. Maybe I work from a different set of parameters."

"I," said Gibby, "work with disinterested people, scientists. We have lots to say to each other. But we argue with theories, empirically you could say. If they disagree with me, they wiggle their noses." She wrestled with a drippy Reuben which took up most of her attention. Janey who had finished a tuna sandwich had an impulse to vent. An urge she couldn't jar loose from.

"Wouldn't matter if I wiggled my nose. Nobody looks at me. All day I cope with what my clients can't cope with. Always distant…" She felt a heavy pressure to tell about the disastrous date with Simon but sensed they hadn't reached that level of comfort with each other. She needed to be sure how Gibby would react. The invidious pearl bracelet she might have been able to joke about, but it didn't seem right.

They chatted idly over second cups of coffee until the time to head back to work approached. Janey grew frantic to tell Gibby about Simon, Gibby not anyone else.

As if she had conjured him, into the diner walked Simon Butler, with Braden O'Neill behind him. They took the table nearby, there being none other available. Simon wouldn't look their way. Braden waved at Janey. Gibby had met Simon but did not know the other man. Janey could hear their talk, mostly Braden with a stream of computer gabble, neologisms, opaque analogs, although language, words.

When Simon's grim gaze landed on her she nodded at him. He raised his voice to Braden, "Look who's over there, the winter witch." Braden moved the angle of his shoulder, ran his fingers through his thick, gray-tinged hair. His eyes so silver-blue they struck like astral points. He was Simon's nemesis, her discomfort. He smiled uneasily at Janey as the two women walked past.

Braden muttered almost to himself…he'd never before seen Simon be purposely rude. "You don't know what she is. I think she's a man-eater. Don't you see how I got taken in by that two-faced chick? I have to defend myself."

Leah had noticed first that the drive to work took less effort, the flow of traffic in harmony with her speed, not impeding, compliant with her direction, in league with her need to get to work. And, Claymore seemed less abstracted, almost attentive, coming close to charming although charm wasn't in his character. These were changes in her perceptions due to a subtle lift of grieving. She resented feeling better, but there was nothing she could do about it. Anticipation had sneaked in for Claymore's tutoring. Claymore thought she might like to learn to repair watches and clocks. Almost imperceptibly the air had lightened around Leah. She even began to enjoy talking with customers.

While Claymore was eating his lunch in the back room, Janey Leduc and her small, curly-haired son came into the store. Leah was gift-wrapping an English hand-enameled box for a customer. Janey whisked up to the clerk, wanted quick to get over this onerous chore.

"Claymore here?" Already half-way around the counter. She'd come with some of Simon's belongings left at her house. Let Clay deal with Simon's detritus. He, at least, was a neutral entity unlike the others she met who were Simon's old friends. She didn't care to have dealings with Simon again.

"He's having his lunch in the back—"

Lifting the box and balancing the bags, she strode to the workroom. "Paulie, wait right here for me." Paulie's eyes were transfixed at something intriguing under the glass. He barely heard her.

When Leah came near, the boy jerked his head up. "These are some cool butterflies. They're shaped like butterflies, under here." He felt chary of speaking to an adult with his mother not right there. When they ran into the candy shop, he and his friends only pointed at what they wanted.

"I'll get them out so you can look at them up close." They were cloisonné, bright enamel colored, aubergine, saffron, cyan blue. She put a few in front of Paulie who caressed them with his fingertips.

"They're not rough like this."

"What aren't?"

"Real live ones."

"No. These aren't copies from nature. They're designed."

He wasn't sure what that meant. His forehead creased in a frown.

"You wouldn't find butterflies like these flying around. They're made up."

He balked, insulted. "Some," poked on the glass. "See here… like this one."

"They're not toys. They're decorative, pretty jewelry."

He fussed to himself, "Colors like Monarchs. Or you know? Have you seen an Eastern Tiger Swallowtail?"

Leah felt her face heating up. "No. No, these are pins, not like the real ones."

He mused…" How much would it cost, that butterfly?'

He mumbled the words into his jacket collar.

"It's seventy-five—"

"Dollars?" His eyes grew wide.

"Yes. But, if you don't have that much now, I can keep it for you. Then when you've saved up enough—"

"For my mother."

"You can come back and buy it for her." She saw his eyes light up. It might take a while, but he had money saved from Christmas. Leah flinched and sidled away as if at some irregular noises behind her.

Paulie caught sight of his mother darting from the back room. With a clipped thank you to Leah, Janey grabbed her son's hand and whisked out the door. A shroud of despair engulfed Leah, smothered her under nihilistic panic.

Clay returned, smacking his hands together. "I'm gonna make that guy come here and collect his chattel. I'm not delivering it to him. What the hell do people think this place is anyway, a train station?" A quizzical look at his pale assistant replacing some cloisonné butterfly pins.

EIGHT

BRADEN phoned Janey the day after seeing her at lunch with Martha Gibson. Janey had heard about Braden's breakup with Carol Quinn. She assumed the call was to get Martha's number. Friends didn't poach their friends' ex-lovers. But Braden talked in his affable way about almost nothing and then after an awkward pause, asked her to go to dinner. He was nonchalant about the invitation, even suggesting she bring along Paulie.

"Can we meet at your computer place? I'm thinking about getting him an iPad. They use those in elementary school now."

"Hey, good idea. We can look at what's there. He like computers?"

"Not as much as butterflies. But I suppose he does. Uses mine to run kids' apps."

"Great…so… I'll see you guys Friday, about six."

She was thrilled. Had long felt an attraction to Braden, but she was good at not letting that kind of thing surface. The kind of thing that involved people who so-called belonged to other people. They were best left as daydreams.

But here was Braden available and interested.

∽

Claymore stretched his neck which had tightened while he was studying a book of diamond ring settings, and replaced the heavy catalog in the slot under the counter. Damned if Simon Butler wasn't pushing through the door, with annoying disapproval written all over him.

"Hey, Clay," he strode up to the old man. "I got a rude text to come pick up my stuff here. Guess Janey's not up to facing me yet."

" I stashed them in back."

They hauled the carton and athletic bag to the front. Claymore wrapped his scarf around his neck and settled his coat on.

"You closing up?"

"As you can see."

"Are you going to that deli…for your dinner? Mind if I tag along?"

Sitting back in a booth while Claymore finished sopping up his meatloaf gravy, Simon dragged on and on with his load of self-pity. Claymore wished he had the wherewithal to stop him. Simon had learned that Braden was seeing Janey.

"The way I found out," he repeated, "was from Mickey who spotted them together at the Bull's game. The kid, too. Braden told Mick he'd scored some half-court tickets. Like that would be easy to do. Braden would ask me to a game like that. I'm never gonna trust him again. I swear. Braden. Behind my back."

Claymore waved his cup at the passing waitress and got a refill on his coffee. He bet that the meatloaf would come up on him tonight.

"Yeah, Braden probably could've told you. I might've, in his shoes, but then I might not have. You gotta admit, Simo, he's got a reason to avoid letting that out to you. You make a bigger deal out of things than God himself. And look, here you are. Hissy fit my niece would call it."

"What is it with people always hiding things from me?"

"Don't put this on the level of Janey's ex-husband. It isn't the same."

"Maybe not. But it bites."

"Has Braden called you since Mickey blabbed?"

"No."

"So he's waiting to explain when he sees you next."

"I called him and told him off, ripped on him but good."

"That helps."

"What'd you want me to do? Suck it up? Well, this sucks."

"Enough with the sucks. Be a man, use 'fuck' when annoyed."

Simon snapped his arm across the table as to grab Claymore by the shirt and shake him. "You think this is funny, old guy? You make a joke outta everything. I wish I was dead." He slid sideways in the booth and glared out the window.

"All right, enough. You ruined my dinner. I think I'll go home." Claymore scrunched along the booth seat.

"I see it now. I've been a damn fool. This isn't Braden's doing. Janey did this. She finagled him into a date. Poor chump fell for it."

"You're not making any sense." He had managed to pull out of the booth, was grappling in his baggy rear trousers for his wallet.

"Janey is the woman I wanted to marry, and she's filled with deceit."

"Simon, you're overwrought. You've been like that since you latched onto the fact that Janey married that car-racer husband. Go home." He watched Simon drop his head into his hands; felt some pity for him. "Some things we just can't have."

Simon snarled, "Oh, go to hell."

"I'm not a good one to confide in…with personal problems. So sue me." Claymore shrugged. No one who isn't a Jew would use that so well.

Simon sat staring at the air. Stupid old fart implied it was finished with Janey. Gone for good. Simon found no fault in himself. Only in the stars.

○

Gibby waited ensconced in a tall, old-fashioned wooden booth. Paulie ran up, heralding himself with a loud yelp. Janey meandered after him, joined in the jabber. Something about their get-togethers provoked horse-play.

"So, this place will deliver the goods, Reuben-wise?" Janey said.

"Yes, and anything-else-wise." Janey left them to use the bathroom.

Paulie bounced on one leg tucked under his rear end to raise himself up. "Gibby, I hope they get married. Mom and Braden."

"Yes?" She'd been hearing about Braden from both mother and son a good deal lately.

"Is it good if they do?" He felt his future in the balance, all of it at a critical mass. The diner, and even what he was eating, dipped into the ground fog of memory. Here the answer hid in the umbra of fear. Everything had felt as if it depended on what Gibby would answer.

She spoke a language of science, talked with him, not exactly as if he were an adult, but as one does to a whole person. Gibby had no child. That may be why. Never saw childishness…but, she had seen him be infantile. He had his moments. They all do now and then. But Gibby held steady.

"I think, yes, it would be good. It would be very good."

In full-blown, legitimate chemical attraction Braden had come on strong. Janey had in Braden sensed the potential from the beginning. Through those early electrical first dates with Braden, Gibby had kept her grounded. Not by comments or advice or anything stupid, but with stability, symmetry. Like now, in the midst of an aroused and excitable state — going to meet Braden later — Janey felt released, listening to Paulie and Gibby, the blue moth and planetary talk. Braden had taken them to a Bull's game; Gibby knew about butterflies. In Paulie's mind Gibby and Braden were parts of a whole. Janey shivered.

"You think you can eat a whole Reuben sandwich?" she heard Gibby ask him.

"Why not?" said the boy, more like taking a dare.

"I don't think he knows what a Reuben is," Janey laughed.

"I do, too," Paulie affronted.

"You'd better order grilled cheese."

They were off that Saturday, Gibby and Paulie, to the Audubon Butterfly and Insect Garden at the Brookfield Zoo.

Janey joined Braden at his work from where they went to a matinee, ate at a bistro, walked in the chill clear night to Braden's apartment over his computer store, and made strong, sweet love with more passion than either had ever envisioned in or out of movie sex scenes. It's not to read about, but to remember or to experience. Words, images, oils or other media, the bold beauty of art, are only approximate. What Janey and Braden experienced that night was the fruit of love.

Late that night, in her own bed, Janey thought over the love making, picturing what she could as if outside her body, watched the intimately entwined bodies, pulsating throats, fragrances of lust, and yet, so close, so melded, as to feel together at a deep level of consciousness. Had Braden felt it? She hadn't spoken, hidden in contentment, humbled, almost disquieted by self-swallowing desire. What she didn't know was that he was at that moment alone in his bed, swearing to himself that he would keep her by him forever.

And Janey determined that, soon, she would go to Braden and pour out the story of the car accident on the mountain, hanging with Artie over oblivion. When she later told Braden, she cried and cried until he stroked her face and whispered it was all right. Cold, freezing cold for a long time.

At dawn Janey slid out of her bed and crept to Paulie's room. Beyond the half-closed door, in the weak slash of setting moonlight, she watched him sleeping. A plan formed as she put on water for tea in the kitchen. A true father for Paulie. It seemed as if Braden might do. She had to turn her heavy load of emotion toward motherhood immediately. Her cynical side foisted itself on her. Nothing's perfect, nothing's forever, if Braden hadn't been moved last night as she had been… Not a thing in life so far had turned out as she had thought it would.

She would try to keep Gibby, although friends had

slipped away or slunk away, or been too overbearing, those she had distanced herself from. Some had disappeared, a mystery to her, each time she had moved. Even in Toronto where her mother and sister had inexplicably chosen to stay, new people had been shallow imitations of remembered easy friends. If it worked, like with Braden, she would give Gibby as a gift to Paulie, too. The steamy aroma of tea she breathed in, and drank the liquid in wonder. After which she pitched forward on bare feet, and trundled off to wake Paulie for breakfast.

༄

Leah Campion had tumbled hard flat against the earth in her wrestle with the oily sumo of grief. Months after she took the job in the jewelry store, she had been startled herself when she could find pleasure in everyday tasks again, to feel a sense of accomplishment, the smile in her response repertory had returned. Work, learning with Claymore, gave her focus, took her some distance away from the tragedy of Jon's death. Even her sister, Merry Alice, on her last visit, admitted Leah's mood had lightened — as Merry put it, getting that clerk job with that old guy hadn't been a total mistake.

But now, a slippage. Something had gotten in the

way of such progress as there'd been: the small boy at Clay's shop, his fascination with the cloisonné butterfly. A setback caused by a whim of the universe. Some kid making noise. Janey Leduc, she knew the mother. There were people who came in, like this Leduc woman, who were friends of Claymore, or his niece. Customers, hangers-on in some cases. She'd given in, only momentarily. But it had been enough. If she had been shut off, she would have contended with it, the memory of the butterfly boy would have dissolved. Instead the encounter had fostered a myth. Jonathan might not truly be dead. The immediacy of the belief would devastate her, when she realized. As yet she had not wept in front of anyone.

A well-dressed man was stationed in the store when Leah arrived on a dreary Monday morning. The rejected suitor Simon, involved with Janey the boy's mother, was chatting up Clay. In the back room where she walked to hang up her coat, Claymore had left his radio on low. "Some broken hearrrrts will never mend," the twangy tenor sang. Leah cursed at the voice, so smug in its unthinking prophecy. Those who truly suffer can't sing about it.

Simon glanced at Leah as she walked by; his mouth hadn't stopped running. "So, I'm admitting, Clay, so I'm not…okay, you were right. I didn't want to see it at first.

Braden, my best friend, gone off with my woman. Shit, how common is that. Make a stale movie, huh? And like I said, I won't take it. For one thing, I'm finished with that bitch. And Braden is a loser. Scavenging, picking up leftovers—"

"Shut up, Simon." He barked and turned to Leah, "Watch the store. I've got to make a run to the bank."

"Come on, I'll drop you off. I'm on my way to work."

Clay went to the workroom to pick up his jacket. Those long minutes Clay was gone, Simon locked onto where he'd disappeared and ignored Leah's presence. In a reluctant shuffle the old man followed Simon out.

For a time the store stood empty and silent. Then, the buzzer. In walked a man and a little boy. Leah stiffened as she looked down at the child. Did the fates find it amusing to torment her because she'd been feeling better? Janey Leduc's son clung to the hand of a good-looking guy who sent an awkward glance her way. Hoodie under a lined trench coat, long dark untrimmed hair, but clean-shaven classic jawline, brave angular nose tipped to one side, he had an open countenance on which Leah read self-conscious unease. The boy tugged on the man's hand. Leah asked, as usual, how she could help, meeting eyes of topaz clarity. Diamonds that were valuable scattered no color.

"He dragged me in here," Braden smiled, "to show me something special—" Letting go of Braden's hand, Paulie scampered to where he'd found the butterfly pin.

"Here, Braden, come and see. It's for Mama." He stabbed at the glass as if the cloisonné butterfly might any second fly away.

"Hey, Paulie." Braden leaned over the case, nodded his approval. "Very pretty."

The boy sputtered in excitement. "Oh, cool. Look at the other ones, Braden. Their colors, real butterflies don't have these. But I like them."

He grinned at the boy, slid down the counter to where something under the glass case had caught his eye, a sparkling ruddy-orange gem. The boy tagged after him, carrying on about moth blends.

He said to Leah, "There's something here I'd like to see."

"This…it's a jacinth ring." She drew it out of the case and handed to him. "A jacinth stone, striking, isn't it?" The gem split refracted light into a stream of iridescent flame, colors of ephemeral fire.

Paulie, objective obtained, asked to go home. "One minute more, buddy, I think I have to buy this ring for your mother." Paulie watched envious that the man could pull out his wallet and so easily make the purchase. When he became a man, with credit cards and power, that's what he would do. Not put a beautiful thing aside for his mother, but buy it right away. It made him begrudge Braden. But not for long. As an adult he wouldn't remember the incident when Braden bought his mother the ring. He had no awareness at that moment that Braden was about to ask her to marry him. The feeling of powerlessness, of being small would come back to him whenever he exercised self-discipline. In the future. Until he became a man.

Janey lifted the lid off the pot of spaghetti sauce, fragrant steam rising. She stoked it slowly with a big wooden spoon and mused over the soft plopping bubbles. Before the sauce condensed from its herbs, tomato, and oil into the perfect fusion of taste, it needed thirty more minutes of undulant simmer.

Janey could make out her son's shouts amid the other shrill voices of his friends as they rode their bicycles up and down the sidewalk. She daydreamed while the sauce cooked down, not hearing Braden let himself in the house. He'd gone after fresh bread at the bakery. Fresh bread a necessity of life for him. He came into the kitchen with the winter cold clinging to him.

They sat in the living room, sipping red wine. Outside the light faded and Janey went to turn on the porch light,

Paulie's signal to come in. When she opened the door she heard his boyish treble telling about fireflies.

Braden waited until she sat down next to him again.

He lifted his wine glass, "Let's clink 'em."

"To celebrate?"

"This was a fine day." She smiled. No answer to that. "Your Paulie's got the energy of a race horse. Listen to him out there, top of his voice."

She took Braden's hand, held it simply in her lap. He fought an urge to give her the ring, but knew it would be better after dinner when Paulie would go to bed. Braden didn't live there; didn't often spend the night. Was away by the time Paulie got up in the morning. Janey had seen to that. Some fusty old-fashioned ideas she clung to. Because he was going to marry her, he didn't mind.

Paulie came in, trailing his excitement behind him. He launched himself to the bathroom to wash his hands. Janey came back from putting the pasta to boil.

"He doesn't play games on the new tablet much. It's fine but…he does use it, looks up his science stuff, talks on Skype to his grandma and aunt, at school they—"

"He's not that into computers. Paulie prefers to see with his own eyes not with pixels. I'm not myself, either, even though it's my business. They're simple, for simpletons. It's not generally known, that. I make a living doing something that's always come easy to me." His eyes grew wary. "Not what you do."

She kissed him, like a soft promise. "Meaning computers ain't people?"

"That's what I mean."

"Wish someone would tell the world that."

"Just so."

Later that night after Paulie was in bed asleep, Braden finally gave her the jacinth ring. She felt overwhelmed with doubt, without an answer, while her thumping heart beat out the long seconds.

"Are you sure, Braden?"

"I love you." His face turned colorless, and he seemed stricken.

"Oh, and I do so very much love you." The words almost adhering to her dry mouth. "I want you to be so, so sure, before you entangle your life with mine."

He smiled a bit. "I'm sure. I am."

"It isn't just because it's what I want."

"My reason," he began. They were sitting close, entwined, and she felt the vibration of his voice coming from a deep well inside him. "I'm happy with you and not happy without you." Simple lad, a man who suited her. But he didn't stop there. "We can be happy… Contented, satisfied, together."

"We can't make each other happy, you know." Her heart began its normal rhythm again.

"Why not?" He could barely hold her as tightly as he wanted to.

"You," she said, "are my darling simpleton, and, of course, we should get married." Somewhere among those words lay a gossamer of fine truth.

A sound sleep. Flits of dreams odds and ends of disconnected fractured images, at slashed angles one scene knocked against another, some still, some passing, then gone. All linear dreams of a boy's solid sleeping. Paulie's limp body turned and stretched. His arm re-curled under his ear. Soft, non-invasive sound, indistinct and far away, heard above the remnants of a fog horn, deep below conscious threshold. The boy for a moment came awake, then fell back into slumber. From down the hall had floated in that moment of waking, his mother's, then Braden's voices from afar.

∽

Janey peered over the laptop on her desk. Sounded as if Dorrie were towing Edwin into the office by his hair. By the collar, by the scruff of the neck? Both dumped themselves into the two chairs recently vacated by a divorcing couple with eight children. Janey couldn't hide her annoyance — body language and facial expression, all lost on Dorrie and Edwin anyway. How the hell had Dorrie muscled past Laverne LeFleur — the flower was thistle-like when it came to keeping clients from barging in? Between Laverne and Dorrie maybe it was a toss-up.

Edwin let out a crude half-cry, half-laugh. Keeping still, Dorrie seemed to challenge Janey to deny them. She had on a soft cloche hat which she pulled off, letting loose her insufficiently combed red silvery hair. Strands flew in the staticky dry air.

"I was at," she said in a low voice as if pressed to speak, "my uncle Clay's, you know, his jewelry store yesterday. He told me about your break-up with Simon. He said you dumped a bunch of Simon's stuff on him—"

"Yes," Janey prompted. "Why have you brought Edwin here?" She met Edwin's scowl with one of her own.

Dorrie's hackles went up. Edwin, after all, had been Janey's client. She did, however, ignore Janey's tone.

"He's gotten this email from his parents, adoptive parents. Show it to her, Edwin. They live in Florida now—"

"I know." She took his cell from Edwin's hand, scanned the missive. Edwin remained quiet, out of character for him, wordless in fact. He allowed himself a knowing smile. A sly smile, Janey assessed it. Edwin had a specious charm which she had fought against when he'd first come to her. She was generally good at keeping the requisite distance from her clients. Edwin, she had thought, was manipulative enough to trip up or even sabotage her clinical work with him. To strengthen her resolve, she avoided any compassion about this execrable letter. Something odd was going on right now. Odd even for Edwin's case.

Edwin's parents, whichever one had typed the thing — it was signed "Mom and Dad" — had written him a harangue. They taunted him, in nasty innuendo hurled damaging insults. A litany of his past mistakes and humiliations. They called him ungrateful, spiteful, and mean. They said that everyone saw through his lies and despised him for them. He was a freeloader who misused his friends, and that he had no friends. As a child he constantly let them down. They were ashamed of him. And weren't going to send him money or help him in anyway, anymore. In fact, he wasn't to contact them again.

Janey stopped reading and studied Edwin's face. His defenses lay in a puddle of ashen misery. She pulled her lips between her teeth to keep herself from consoling him.

Looked down a moment to stop pity leaking through her eyes.

"They don't know who I am," Edwin said, "How could they? They're not my flesh and blood." Dorrie leaned over and gripped one of his dangling hands. "Doesn't matter what they say."

"Edwin," said Janey in a confident voice, "this email is meant only to hurt you. I hope you'll delete it from your phone. I want to assure you these people…your parents are sick. All the hate inside of them they've chosen to pour out on you. I can't say why they're so hate-filled or why they want to take it out on you, but it's…not you. It's something else, not anything you've done that's made them attack you like this. They've been sick a long time considering how they treated you as a child. Nothing you can say or do will change them." She caught her breath. Of course, she would fail Edwin. There was no way not to, not in circumstances like this, there never is. This is the tragedy. Maybe Dorrie in warm-hearted instinctual words could offer him some solace. Her job, a therapist, was to get him around to seeing his parents in a healthier way.

Dorrie's flushed skin blended into her tinted hairline. She sent Edwin a mute appeal. "Listen to Janey, Edwin. They were both abusive drunks, those jerks who raised you. So forget it. You will find out who you really belong to… Maybe I should tell you who your mother is." She waved a fist, "Like right now. I'd betray a sacred trust. But I didn't foresee this. It's tearing you apart. Maybe I should give you her name."

"Dorrie, wait," Janey said. "You aren't helping."

"All right. Yes. Finally, at last." Edwin's head popped up, his eyes slid back and forth from one woman to the other, one to the other. For a moment elated, then irrationally, his mood changed. "What if I don't want to find her anymore? Like Janey said this birth woman didn't want her baby. Too bad for me it had to be me." He stood up, pushing back on his chair and announced he was getting outta there. Dorrie who still clung to his hand, grappled to hang onto him, to lift herself from her chair.

"Should I break my vow, tell you who she is, about everything?"

He shook his hand free. "If you do, I swear I'll never speak to you again." A few long steps and he was gone.

Dorrie dropped back down on the chair, eyes glazed. Janey's heart rate slowed back to normal. Close call.

"Are you his mother, Dorrie? You have a strong concern for him. And that elaborate birth certificate story is pretty unbelievable."

"No, I'm not. Ask him. I had DNA testing months ago

to satisfy Edwin." Tears floated beneath her lashes. "He desperately didn't want her to be me." Defeated, Dorrie didn't want to say more. She clamped her mouth shut and made ready to leave, heaving out of the chair, fumbling with her big handbag.

Janey said, "Edwin thinks he's better off with a make-believe birthmother. In a few days, maybe less, given time to digest this assault, he'll restart his search in another direction again. Now his fears and anger are too near the surface. I hope you will someday tell him what you know. Truth is better. Have you been in touch with Edwin's mother lately?"

"Not for years. I don't know where she is. Maybe not even in Chicago."

"When you're ready to tell him, let me take it from there. This sacred oath has been a gross burden on you."

Dorrie recovered her spirit, with some verve said, "I screwed it up, didn't I? I've been punished, though, all these years I helped out a good friend." Janey stayed quiet.

NINE

HIS longish curls blown every which way Paul Kane slammed the brakes of his bicycle in front of Claymore's jewelry store and set off the buzzer as he burst through the door. He shuffled the bike in with him since he didn't have a lock yet, and leaned it against the outer window's half-wall. He was on a mission. As soon as Claymore came across the floor, the boy extracted a small camera from his polar jacket and announced that he'd come to take a picture of his color-dappled butterfly pin. His eyes darted, sending sparks around the shop as if he half-expected the inanimate pin to come flittering to him like the butterflies at the exhibit in Gibby's museum.

He wanted to show Rex. When Paulie had told his buddy Rex — "your buddy" is what Braden had taken to calling him— about the butterfly double, Rex had rolled his eyes and said don't be stupid. But Rex was always calling kids bad names, and defying the teacher, and spitting gum wads on the playground, so Paulie paid no attention to his opinions. Which Paulie did not realize made Rex all the more friendly to him. But he needed to prove the similarity with the pin to Rex. His butterfly wasn't in its regular place when he rushed up to the glass counter to look.

Old man Mandebrote had come over in his gimpy walk and tried to draw a smile from his tired face muscles. That only worked to make him look macabre.

"You're Janey Leduc's boy, right?"

Paulie blinked in suspicion, with a formless misgiving at the old man's words. Paul Kane, son of Janey Leduc and Arthur Kane — he'd learned long ago about "married", and he took "Kane" because he was a male, and so was Arthur Kane, his father. It made sense to him that way. Rex was Sanchez like his father. But then there was Lydia, his other best friend, a girl, who was Lydia Demos like her father, although that was maybe because her mother was Mrs. Demos. So, Paulie had reasoned that Lydia's mother's last name and her father's last name before they got married, must have been the same — Demos. Some of the kids had last names different from either of their parents. He hadn't wanted to get into explaining that.

Maybe he'd be able to ask Gibby who knew how all the butterflies and dinosaurs got their long names and would be able to give him a scientific answer.

Here was Mr. Mandebrote waiting for him to say something. He held up his little camera. "I came to take a picture of my butterfly. But it's not here."

"Kept on hold for you, right, boy? Maybe my shop assistant took it in the back…"

That explanation worried him. Paulie was hesitant about hidden things which when concealed often disappeared for good.

"But she's not here today, only works on weekdays." He raised his voice to clarify. "I'm alone in the store on Saturdays."

Paulie felt he had to explain further. He held up his camera and fiddled until he had in the viewer a picture he'd taken at the butterfly exhibit. "Look, I took this. If this isn't the coolest… At Gibby's museum there were live butterflies." Clay felt the camera shoved at his waist, his leg muscles gave a little from standing still too long. "And it's pretty much exactly like the pin here I'm buying for my mom. Really real colors, but the one made of jewels here is shinier."

Claymore squinted at the little screen. "Not jewels, cloisonné, which is enamel set in wires." It's like a hard, glossy coating, he wanted to add. As if it would matter to this kid.

"I wanted to compare the cloi…c…" — stumbling over the word — "pin with the real live butterfly in my picture."

"Well, okay. I'll look around for it." He shuffled toward his back alcove. "We don't carry many brooches anymore. They don't sell… She might've put it back where I work." On the wall, next to the big safe, hung a few documents. Paulie scrutinized them. One in gilded raised letters, CMW, said that Claymore Mandebrote was a certified master watchmaker. Another, a licensed gem appraiser. The third was a diploma from the School of the Art Institute. The streak of artist in Clay, atrophied from little use, still a part of him, had made him want to teach Leah if she had artistic sensibilities.

He searched his back-room studio, but did not find the pin. He even looked through little used drawers and in odd corners. No cloisonné butterfly.

When he returned to the counter empty-handed, the boy's eyes turned up from his little camera, hope dashed. Clay shook his head. Paulie spun around on his sneakers and began his retreat.

"Well, thanks for looking," he squeezed out, for politeness' sake.

"Wait a minute. I'll call my clerk and ask her where it is." He dug out his cell, phoned her. Paulie trotted back, deep in disappointment, call it premonition. He knew his beautiful butterfly double was irretrievably gone. Never mind how or why, that didn't matter. To kids things appear and disappear for no reason, as if at the whim of an unknowable deity. He could have left the store then in his certainty and never returned. However, he waited while Clay called for the dreadful satisfaction of being right. He heard only Clay's half of the conversation, enough to understand. His butterfly was lost to him. Clay sounded evasive, using short words going back and forth. Clicked off and turned his attention to Paulie.

"My clerk, Mrs. Campion, she says..." The old man leaned way over. Paulie could smell peppermint, maybe his toothpaste, or a piece of hard candy residue. "She thinks she accidentally sold that very pin to a customer. She felt hurried by the customer so bad that only when he was gone did she realize she had sold him the very pin she was saving for you." The boy looked away, a stone of silence. "She says to tell you she's very sorry." Leah had not said that. Had been too embarrassed, Claymore imagined.

It was absurd to feel badly for this kid. In the face of the world's sorrows, children in misery, his was small time, easy to make better.

"Look here, kid, since it was our mistake, you can choose another pin, for free. You won't have to pay for it ever. And you can take it home with you right now. There's some other beautiful butterfly pins under this glass. Come and look at 'em. Pick out the prettiest one for your mother."

The boy's face contorted as if he'd been slapped. He shook his head, speechless, retrieved his bicycle and jammed it out the door.

Paulie peddled the dozen blocks home heartbroken. He was too confused to tell his mother or Braden or anyone but Gibby about the lost butterfly pin, baffled about his anger which had oozed from a wound scabbed-over that he never in his long life brought to the surface and came to terms with. When an old man, he could sniff out similar anger leaking from the distant past which ever only caused blips he hardly noticed. This insult, however, had hit a nerve for keeps. Gibby was in Boston this weekend, far away. Calling his grandmother to tell her about his loss, if he could get it out over the phone, would soothe his mind. But neither she nor his indignant aunt would take his sense of personal injury in the right way. He'd be up to his ears in sympathy and love, and the insult would dissipate. He didn't want it to go away. He needed this outrage to be admitted. In the event, it was Braden who had to tackle Paulie's anger.

When he pedaled furiously home and burst into the house, Braden was sprawled out on the sofa, reading a book, all warm and cozy.

"Where's Mom?"

"She stepped out for a few things she needs for supper. Where you been?"

Paulie flung his jacket on the floor and bristled at the inquisition.

"Hang it up." The boy did, his face and hands fiery red. "What's the matter, Paulie?" He straightened his posture and stuck a scrap of paper in his book to mark the place.

"That stupid lady at the jewelry store, she sold my butterfly pin, the one for Mom, right out from under me." The words fueled his smoking ire.

"Monstrous." Paulie glared at him. At once Braden regretted his trivializing tone. Shouldn't use irony with a frightened eight-year-old. He knew little about kids.

"Sit down, huh. Quit standing there as if you're about to bust open your shirt like the Incredible Hulk." He didn't get it at all about angry kids.

Paulie dragged over to the sofa and plopped himself down. Braden saw the boy was unhappy. He feels cheated. "The owner, this old guy, called her and she said she accidentally sold it. To someone else. Why would she do that?" He slid to the floor, held back tears. "Then the old guy said he'd give me another one. I wouldn't need any money." Paulie stared up at Braden. "How stupid. Like it would make it okay." He puffed his cheeks out, straining not to cry.

"Well, that was nice of Mr. Mandebrote. Don't go getting on your high horse. It wasn't his mistake."

"So what!"

A side of Paulie that Braden hadn't seen, obstinacy or belligerence. Little chip on the skinny shoulder? Janey should be handling this. "It was to make amends, you know what that means, Paulie? To make something better we did bad. So the old guy offered to give you a pin which would mean he was sorry. Chink, no sale."

Heavy silence, such silence which clogged good feelings between them, stopped up all understanding.

"It was a mistake, Paulie. The pin got sold by accident."

"Yeah, sure." Spit the words out like Rex would.

"Come on. Do some deep Yogic breathing. It'll be okay. What's done can't be undone." Braden winced. It is what it is, he was telling a kid, and he hated that facile, meaningless excuse for every wickedness.

"Stupid." Why had he bothered telling anybody about it? He peeled off the floor and was about to creep away. The outside door clanked open. Janey pushed in shivering, put down grocery-loaded cloth bags.

"Hey you guys."

Paulie scrambled to her, flung his arms around her waist, hung on for dear life.

When he lay in bed that night, let down by Braden who'd never failed him before, Paulie with all his child's strength yearned to talk to Gibby. Nothing was the way it should be, he sniffled, at the border of sleep. He would wait, wait, to clear the whole problem up in a scientific way with Gibby.

∽

Janey slid her car forward in the line of vehicles waiting for their star-gazers to disgorge from the Adler Planetarium. She spotted Gibby flushed with cold and Paulie spinning along beside her, still excited, head filled with the blue-green, saffron, and blood red planets, the thrilling views of the Milky Way and the most distant stars. They crawled into the car both chattering like indoor cats through the window at taunting chipmunks.

"So, it was wonderful," Janey said. The car seemed to fill with outer space.

"Awesome, Mom."

Gibby was chuckling, "I can never have my own son, now. If I did and he proved to be less excited about the universe as this one here is, I wouldn't be able to hide my disappointment. I'd ruin the kid's life."

"Idiot," she said to Gibby. All the science things Paulie loved and she had thought he only wanted to chase butterflies. Her son hung over her shoulder, words piling up in his hurry to tell her. "Seat belt on…" She heard a click.

"You won't believe, I got to meet a real, live astronaut. Gibby knows him so we got to go right up to him and he talked to me… One show Skywatch about what's up in the sky now, the constellations, and the next one Welcome to the Universe, the secrets of the stars, where stars came from, and then there was Destination Solar System. They had live pictures from the space probes… You won't believe what I saw!" Finally, he quieted. He was looking out the window at the first two stars flipping on over Lake Michigan in the early winter dusk. Or was one a planet? "It's not blinking," they heard him say to himself, "It must be Venus."

Out of the corner of her eye, Janey caught Gibby tilting her head into the headrest. "Tired?"

"Exhausted."

"You stayed for all three programs."

"They're only thirty minutes each. I couldn't have dragged him away."

"Thanks." She smiled at the oncoming cars forging ahead down Lakeside Drive. "You did good."

"I like this stuff myself, you know." She found herself thinking he never will be my son. Never my son. My son. Odd to have that thought come. She wanted him to be Janey's son.

"I wonder where he got his smarts from? Maybe fairies switched him at birth."

"Oh, shut up. His resemblance to you is uncanny. And I expect I'll see it when I meet your mother."

"Lordy. Don't start with her."

"Paulie," Gibby called to the backseat. The car was warm, traffic light, there was an obscuring comfortableness keeping the boy safe in his capsule. He would be dozing except for the adrenaline residue. "Can I… Is it all right if we tell your mother now what we talked about at lunch? Before I get dropped off…"

"I don't think so."

"If you've changed your mind."

"I didn't change my mind. You tell her later."

"What?" Janey felt a chill. Was it necessary for every fine moment to be tainted?

"I can't explain it the way you could."

"What? What is it, Paulie?"

"No big deal."

Gibby said, "You'll feel better."

"Oh… alright… It's that awesome present I was going to buy you, Mommy. The lady at the jewelry store said she'd keep it for me and she sold it to some other person. It's okay, but it's okay…" It was not at all as he had told it to Gibby at lunch.

Gibby wondered, the power of the stars. "He was pretty upset about it." She said.

They drove on in silence. They thought he had fallen asleep.

Gibby said, "He thinks he let you down."

"Oh, it's not that. He went to the person who could explain it to him. He's bothered if something doesn't add up."

"What nonsense."

"You know bugs and the planets. I know a little about human motivation." She reached over and took her friend's hand. "When a human is somewhere in or near the normal range I can't give advice. I'm better with the nutsos. I'm glad you found us looking for the butterflies."

In a hazy way Paulie overheard words that comforted. A filter of meaning, encrusted with part of his light sleep's reverie. What makes jewels? The boy in foggy half-sleep mused. What makes a beautiful butterfly?

⁓◯

Leah Campion registered no distress over selling the pin she was to hold for the little boy. She wasn't sure she had. In a moment of confusion when she had been surprised by Claymore's phone call, she said she may have sold it although she didn't recall doing it. Perhaps, Clay himself had sold it, not knowing it was promised. It should have been in the glass case, and if she hadn't replaced it there, well, that was odd. However, in a busy day, with distractions…she may have sold it… Although, so might Clay have.

She had only one qualm. After she said she would save the pin, she should have put it aside. Or not promised to hold it for the boy at all. Never make promises to children or simpletons, her grandmother used to say. It made no difference to Claymore. She heard an undertone in his questions to her. Awkward with the boy beside him. If someone had bought the pin and other items, she might have bagged up the brooch along with the rest. Maybe that happened. Such a lot of fuss. And she knew he would hate her for it. A ping of regret that she'd let him down.

Even though she knew it she never used the boy's name. Her Jonathan, now been dead twelve months and six days. He couldn't be dead. It was a mistake.

༄

Edwin's mind was a circus warehouse: fabrications, delusions, inventions, defenses, mixed with half-truths, beliefs and facts about his life colored by perception and misapprehension. What he saw of the world honestly and truly were the everyday events. Nothing in him was phantom. He did not hallucinate. He was not a psychotic, nor a sociopath. Edwin saw what went on around him with clear eyes and took in the occurrences as they happened. But his mind bent things as they are, not with his imagination, which involves discernment. Another part of his mind began to mold reality, form it into his liking. Then out popped his lies. Subtle lies, sometimes white lies, tiny lies, whoppers, but lies. And so it went.

Some days Edwin simply told the truth, like today while having lunch with Dorrie who hadn't seen him since the blowup in Janey Leduc's office. She had invited him to meet her at Potbelly Sandwich Works. She liked their homemade sub roll and wanted to treat herself because she'd been put on temp work at Marina Rinaldi.

She took any job which would supplement her chintzy pension check, but was never happy about it. Squeezed into early retirement at Morton Salt, she had been managing to eke out a living.

He jabbered on about wanting a motorcycle while Dorrie did her part by nodding and listening. It was normal talk which lulled Dorrie into thinking that something in the awful email from his parents had shocked Edwin into good sense. But, when his sandwich got eaten, his comments became more Edwin-esque.

"I got lost in Milwaukee, took the Metro there," he began, then stopped. Here she was supposed to ask what he'd gone to Milwaukee for. She didn't. "I was following a great tipoff about my biological mother." She would not ask about that tip. She knew asking would set him off. No more would she try to winnow out any element of truth from his fabrications. She swore she wasn't going that route again. Stymied, she sat numbed as he forged ahead.

"And on my way home on the train I saw a monkey sitting all alone eating a Snickers."

That un-numbed her. It was true Edwin had probably gone on this hunt for his mother, probably, to Milwaukee, probably. What had come of it intrigued her, true. No monkey eating a candy bar, however.

"I thought you gave up looking? I said I'd tell—"

"I knew you wouldn't. Your damned sacred vow, your oath, your friggin' pledge never to betray her. I knew you didn't mean it. You'd never unmask her."

"Don't go there, Edwin."

"Ever been to Milwaukee, Dorrie? It's easy to get lost in that place. You get off the train and whammy it hits you. You don't know where you're going. Unless it's to the Lake. Our lake."

"Of course, you hadn't been there before…" Did he look on his Google map or take a fold-up paper one? Lost because he didn't know what he was looking for.

"No taxi in sight." Edwin didn't trust Uber. "So I started walking north, what I thought was north but turned out to be west, dirty factories, and then I wandered some empty streets. Then, I found some guy and asked where I was, he pointed one way and said, 'downtown' then swung his finger the opposite direction and said, 'Potawatomi.'" Casinos were, also, anathema to Edwin.

"I hid inside my coat best I could and soldiered on. I was in nowhere land. People talking outside a tavern, I heard them say Jeffrey Dahmer had lived nearby. It's getting overcast and I'm walking on the street where Jeffrey Dahmer had lived." This could have happened. Dorrie's eyes widened. "I'm thinking, what if I get whacked and eaten?"

Dorrie put down the tail end of her sub sandwich. "Dahmer's dead, been dead for years." Left the best bits of the sub on her plate.

"Did they execute him?"

"He died in prison. Another convict killed him while they were supposed to be mopping the floor." Dare she ask? "Well what tipoff sent you to Milwaukee anyway?" She drawled. Knew better than to sound interested.

Edwin scrunched forward, tipping his empty coffee mug over, retrieved it, set it aside. His excitement was palpable. "I asked again at a bar, ratty place, how to get to Marquette University, 'Marquette,' I kept saying to this dodgy-looking guy, 'Marquette.' The dude came outside and told me go straight, then turn left then right. Long friggin' walk it was, colder than a witch's tit." He shivered, adding a bit of animation to his narrative.

"Okay, okay, you went over to Marquette's campus…" Move this along, she urged.

"Yeah. I warmed up in one of the halls. Tried the little chapel but the doors were locked. Tons of frozen students walking around. You know, I should have gone to college. I got full scholarships to Loyola, U of C, and DePaul. But then, I couldn't decide which school to take, so—"

"Edwin! What were you doing at Marquette? What did you go there for?" Cut to the chase. "I can't sit here much longer. My knees are stiffening up on me. They hurt like hell then."

"Oh. Well, see, I got this clue from Janey that my birthmother might have been a student there when I was born. Makes sense. Not wanting to quit school, she gave me up, but it was supposed to be only for a little while. While she got her degree…a good job, professional…"

Dorrie shook her head, sad now. "Janey never told you any of that. She doesn't know anything."

"No, not directly, but I got that hint from what Janey said in a report. A dead giveaway, unconscious. She didn't outright say a name, of course, she doesn't know who." he huffed, glared at Dorrie as if she had jumped to an absurd conclusion.

Dorrie waited. Try to humor him once more, bring this craziness to an end. There had been nothing to his hunt at all. Naturally there wouldn't have been. What had she been thinking to let Edwin ramble on this long? He had fabricated a story about a collegiate birthmother out of whole cloth. On some impulse he had gone to Milwaukee, and to Marquette, a submerged craving to go to college? To learn from Jesuits? A fierce longing to tell her uncle flooded her. She hid a smile. Often when she tried to follow the labyrinthine logic of Edwin's thoughts and his devious lies, she disliked him the way her uncle did. Claymore considered Edwin a phony and a pest.

"Okay, so you got this hint, or tip, or clue, but since you don't have her name, it wouldn't have gotten you anywhere." Said kindly because she had almost taken against him a few minutes before.

She rustled in her purse to retrieve her wallet. Where was the damn chit? She'd pay for his lunch, too, rather than wait until he dug money out of his pocket.

Edwin wasn't about to let her off the hook. "It was a good clue, even without a name. In the report Janey wrote about me, she recommended Catholic Social Services. Maybe I could find help there. She must've meant I should search outside Chicago. Wisconsin... I felt my birthmother wouldn't go far away from me. Then, the Catholic thingy. Put one and one together and there you are."

Hard to believe what Edwin make up out of what Janey had written. It astounded her as very little did anymore. What a hoot people could be. "Let's get outta here while I can still get up and walk." She had spent over thirty years at jobs that took a toll on her legs. Things like that catch up to you.

༄

Janey Leduc hesitated to label it, but there it was. Simon Butler had begun stalking her. Lately she had spotted him outside her office building, as if loitering on the sidewalk. He'd quick turned away when he saw her. She had the feeling he'd been there other times when she hadn't seen him. And she had begun to rethink the couple of times she'd caught sight of him in her neighborhood. He had no legitimate reason for being that far north. He seemed to swagger as he walked to his car. Another time she had come home and recognized his car driving off. Once when she had shouted out the door for Paulie, she'd caught the back of Simon scurrying down the street. Those incidents taken together made her uncomfortable. Did these sightings fall under the meaning of the word "stalking"? It was hard for her to concentrate. What would she have advised a client?

Loading the dishwasher, mindless bending and straightening, freed her to think about stalking. These Simon apparitions seemed ominous. She would have warned a client not to ignore them.

On the sofa Paulie messed with a digital gadget Braden had given him. The TV glowed, sound on low, and the lamp shade's color mixed white light to ambient rosy-yellow-peace-like clarity. No, Simon was neither addled nor vicious. But so the client might have said about her stalker. Professionally, and in her gut Janey knew, stalking is done not just to annoy. The client refuses to go to the police. He hasn't done anything. And, and…her answer…the stalker evokes fear. Not nothing.

Tomorrow, then, talk to Jack who had the most experience with that aberrant behavior. Sensible and professional he'd be. She couldn't convince herself no matter how hard she tried that her circumstance was different from the harassed women who came scared out of their wits. Of course Simon was stalking her.

In the office, Jack Larsen normally exuded empathy. Today his dimpled smile and pleasant demeanor had morphed into the manner of a prosecutor. Even his tenor voice fell an octave.

"Hard to believe Simon Butler is stalking you. You can handle that turd."

"Come on, Jack. Say what you think. I'm overreacting."

"That's not how I'd put it. Listen, he's a… I never liked him. But it's hard to imagine that guy bothering you."

"How come you never let on you didn't like him?"

"Good would that have done?"

The conversation had made a subtle turn. "Nevertheless, he is bothering me. It's irritating." She felt as if she'd sucked too much air. Intricate red shifts, gravity tremors, such as to signify descending, shifts impalpable, refracting-off waves across the universe infinite.

Knowledgeable, trained social workers didn't respond like Jack did. She had a sudden intuition of what happened here. She felt Jack's response sink, leaving concentric rings in a noxious pond.

"You don't know, Jack, what Simon might be capable of doing."

"Don't rip on me, Ms. Leduc." He was blowing her off, as if she were wasting his time.

By the end of the afternoon, having reviewed some stalking research, Janey decided to inform the police. To have a paper trail might not be needed, but was an essential step. On her way out of work, Jack passed by her, sporting a chagrined smile. "'Night, Janey."

"Thanks for your help," heavy sarcasm layered on each word. "If I'm found bludgeoned to death, don't feel too guilty or anything."

He took a hesitant step toward her. "There is stalking… and then there's…stalking."

Then crab-like he scuttled away.

At the police station she asked for Sergeant Pivik and filed a complaint on Simon. To be fair she would call Simon from home to warn him off. Paulie would be collected today at school by Gibby. He was staying late to work on a science project. Paulie had arranged by himself to have Gibby pick him up so that he could show off his project and his "real" scientist friend. So Janey didn't need to worry Paulie would overhear her. Talking to Simon from the car in this instance had seemed tacky. She needed to rid herself formally of this incubus. Simon had gone on long enough.

Simon answered on the first ring while she was settling her first words.

"Janey," he said her name out plain and unadorned.

"Yes, Simon—"

"This is a surprise, a shock y' might say."

"The reason I'm calling—"

"Braden dump you?"

Her jaw stiffened. Chose her words with wary precision. "The last week I've noticed your car or you, in my neighborhood, or near Social Services, and even at Paulie's school. If you're trying to get my attention, I wish you'd stop."

"Don't go hyper. I get around. Chances are I went past those places by pure accident."

"So many times—"

"Maybe you're hoping to see me, or making this all up. Forget it. If you spot me, I'm on business or pleasure elsewhere."

"Past my office three or four times in a week?"

"What're you doing, flattering yourself? Like I'm so heartbroken, boo hoo. Get over yourself."

"I don't make guesses how people feel."

"What is this? You throwing around false accusations?"

"Stop it. Stop it." She let out her breath. "If I see you anymore…where I am liable to be—"

"It'll be a coincidence."

"Listen to me. I signed a complaint at the police department." She heard his disbelieving cry. "It's stalking what you're doing. Stop it."

"Jesus Christ, Janey, you didn't do that."

"Yes I did."

"You fuckin' crazy—"

She hung up.

Gibby and Paulie barreled through the back door, shouting and laughing about planets and moons. Janey slunk into the kitchen, pretended nothing had happened out of the ordinary. She would talk with Gibby, later, when Paulie was sleeping.

Simon squeezed his phone in a death grip. She'd hung up on him, the bitch. He flew from his manager's station in the service bays, crossed the showroom, crimson flashes ran along his cheeks. A salesman friend, squint-eyed, dark haired, husky guy, saw Simon's scowl, eyes red-rimmed, and called out his name. Simon snarled that he was going to bring in the Caddy for brake work.

Simon shut himself up in the Cadillac, felt a sharp sting as if his face had been slapped. He trembled with indignant fury. Guilt knelt behind his anger. He had let his desire to run into Janey force him into this ludicrous position. It had at first seemed romantic, trying to get her back again. If he'd gone over some line, it wasn't his fault. Anyway, she should be flattered he didn't want to give her up. It was love that had propelled him to pursue Janey. She really wasn't worth it. Wasn't worth this fuss. Errant thought — he must be too hung up on her. She didn't understand him. Didn't get him at all.

Simon pulled the Caddy into the service garage and went on with his work day. His confrontation with Janey left a fading mark on his mind. His specious repentance dissolved as the afternoon wore on until by evening he was convinced that Janey had harassed him. Catholics have Imperfect Act of Contrition, Protestants have Grace, Muslims have remorse as a pillar of faith, and the Hindi,

Karma. The Jews, well, their thoughts about heaven and hell have been equivocal from the beginning; nevertheless they will take a few more thousands of years to study it. God may not expect much contrition from His flock. But will He look around after the end of time, shake his Godhead, a wavy nimbus, white floating aureole of divinity, and wonder where everybody is?

In defiance of it all, Simon Butler planned to drive past Janey's office to satisfy himself that he had nothing to be ashamed of. Then he would go out and look for a new girlfriend. He had his eye on the newly divorced receptionist with the soft brown hair. More important, he would get his buddy Braden back which would be the one thing that would tick off Janey most. He would get revenge for her ugly slander.

Gibby took Paulie to the Brookfield Zoo to watch pup seals frolic, set up by a friend, a CZS staff member who promised them an inside look. That outing allowed Braden to take Janey to the Japanese Cultural Center. He had long wanted to go to the Buddhist tea ceremony, but not alone. Unfortunately, he had never been able to convince anyone to go with him. Janey, different from everyone, said she was delighted to go. And he believed she was.

After the elegantly simple ceremony they found a new way to use words. It broke a code of silence — that inviolate silence kept in order to hide from the other what each feels most strongly about. These new words branded the emotions and created ineffable bonds which lasted the rest of their lives. When in a whirligig of passion and full-throated desire lovers can forge in flesh, the weak atomic force. That day at tea the nuclear force annealed, without which love does not exist. A bare-knuckled reality, as real as an idea began the afternoon of tea when they chose new words as they talked.

The day Paulie went with Gibby to see the fur seals remained an early memory within his reach. His mother — Paul remembered when he was an old man well after her death — had been home. He had run into the house, sat in front of her on the floor and told her all about the fur seals. As usual she listened, asked him the proper things. She knew what would have been important to him. In memory none of what she said had stuck, but the image and the joy conveyed what he wanted to keep forever. Memories are tricky. They leave assorted mirages, disparate, partial, very like dreams which tell a different truth, or tell of the truth in a different way. But then some textures of his boyhood remained firm and irrepressive.

His mother even as a weary old woman, lifted her eyes above the crowd. That night after the fur seals…

He was reading a butterfly book when she checked on him before she headed to bed.

"Paulie, lights out."

"Know where the Monarch butterflies are right now?" he said.

"South, I should hope."

"They're in Mexico. Millions of them… By the millions they land on acres and acres of the Oyamel fir trees. They like milkweed plants." His eyes sparkled with excitement, almost feverish. "They sip nectar and rest."

She swallowed her heart which had slipped up into her throat, and fought tears.

"You rest now, huh. Go to sleep."

Paul Kane, a mission specialist on his way to the space station, had thoughts unfettered by gravity. He had been dogged by accusations since his second marriage failed, that he did not know what love was. Both of his wives had said it in one way or another. But he knew he did. It was what his mother felt fiercely for him, what she felt wholly for Braden, and with the reach of his eyes when in space he looked at the unfiltered stars he thought it was what she felt for Gibby. He had loved Gibby and Braden. And his mother. He knew what love is.

When after Braden's death at sixty-eight, a foreshortened span, Janey had talked about grief, and leaned on him and Gibby to find some relief. Her voice later in old age, maybe a voice inside himself, she had told him, you needed Braden, I needed Braden. There were desires only a man could fulfill for me. What you and I got from Braden's goodness. Our home. Your little friends who have grown up with you. And I needed Gibby for what I could get from no one else.

TEN

LEAH Campion had kept the jewelry store open all week alone while Claymore was home with the flu. What could he do but trust her to run his business? In truth he worried more that she might be set upon again by robbers than that she might not be up to the job. It never entered the old man's mind that she might steal from him. He had taught her enough to handle any transactions. She was honest.

The normal flow of customers that week had been broken only twice: once by Simon Butler who hovered in the alcove tiffed when he learned Clay wasn't there; and once by Clay's niece, Dorrie, and the daft young man, Edwin, who had clamped onto her when he found out she was keeping his birthmother's identity a secret. It made no sense to Leah. Nor much to Clay, who had his doubts about what shenanigans Dorrie might be engaging in. His niece was a decent, reasonable, thoughtful woman, although over-sensitive. If she knew Edwin's mother's name, Clay was mystified why she tormented the young man by keeping it from him. Might she be threatened by the Mafia if she let the name out? What hold over her had this woman who gave up her baby son?

Like Simon, Dorrie and Edwin hung around the shop after being told Claymore was home sick. Although Leah was not friendly she was always polite. She stood near them wondering what she could say to make them all leave.

Dorrie seemed to enjoy sweeping around the store, choosing a Madeira citrine ring — dark cherry colored —, trying on a looped bangle in sterling silver, calling out a created-emerald, generally showing off. Dorrie had been well taught by Claymore, also. Edwin put up with her, of course, because she held the key to his happiness. This all was annoying on some level to Leah. They played off against each other — Dorrie must feel remorse for being adamant in her decision to withhold what Edwin demanded. An odd relationship, a friendship distorted by misunderstanding, on purpose, and it perplexed Leah. All three people were dissembling which did not allow a bit of self-awareness to sneak through to them.

Leah watched the skittish young man pluck a Rolex from a glass display case and slip it on his arm. He made admiring sounds and rotated his uplifted wrist at Dorrie.

"A movie director gifted me one of these puppies, Dorrie. They were filming a street scene in the Loop and I was in a throng of extras. This big-time director — can't remember his name — he pulled me aside. He was impressed by, his exact words, my innate acting ability showcased by the riveting way I crossed Michigan Avenue. In appreciation, he sent me an expensive Rolex watch."

"Yeah? Why don't you ever wear it?" said Dorrie.

"I lost it in a poker game."

"Too bad." Dorrie seemed amused that her uncle's new clerk didn't like her humoring Edwin or suffering his playacting. Leah had come up a few feet behind them, frowning. Usually, Dorrie would shut him up. But this lie reminded her of a braying donkey.

Leah had heard Clay's stories about the mendacious Edwin Blake, and she had drifted on the periphery of encounters between her boss and his niece about Edwin. Here she was seeing him in action. Once Janey Leduc who had a Masters in Social Work, said under her breath that Edwin had a borderline personality disorder. But Leah didn't buy that as an excuse for constant storytelling.

And there he stood proudly waving a Rolex, the living, breathing liar.

Edwin replaced the watch. As they started to exit the store at last, the buzzer blared and in walked a man Leah recognized as Braden, right behind him Janey Leduc and the little boy.

A small group of disparate lives overlap marginally, their outer edges leaking like the narrow runnels in pockets of wet sand near the bright ocean. They stand in the pattern of the flow. Each life absorbs energy from and will influence the circular waves of the other lives. Everything in the universe exerts a pull, creates a dynamic on all, violent or subtle, always real. This state only in imagination can be understood.

Braden knew Dorrie, Clay's niece, and as Dorrie smiled at him, Simon stepped forward from the alcove, a mass of aggression. Simon eyed the newcomer with the blatant hatred of a child. Stepping around the counter away from Dorrie, Leah asked who'd like some help. In an opaque reflection, she saw the boy behind Braden who had come in with him last time, and in the periphery of her eye she caught Janey Leduc. The butterfly pin. A momentary clutch of distaste, like acid stomach.

Dorrie swooped on Janey, Edwin hung back, Braden unseeing told Leah they had come to look at matching wedding bands. Leah placing bands of gold and silver in front of the couple, spoke hushed like a priest after communion. Edwin scuttled to Dorrie who had ambushed Janey. Dorrie cried out muddled words, something about Janey knowing why they had come to the jeweler's to question her uncle. Something, something, something. Edwin reached Dorrie and his voice rose in self-righteousness, a pose. With Edwin everything seemed a pose, was a pose.

"They aren't interested in me, Dorrie," Edwin said. "I told you. We're wasting our time with your uncle and especially with…" he swiveled and pointed at Janey, "…with her. She has her priorities and helping me was never one of them. Isn't it a happy chance we ran into you here, Janey? We can tell you off to your face and be done with it."

Paulie trained his eyes on Edwin insulting his mother. They were blank and frightened and amazed. He half-expected Braden to go up and punch Edwin in the nose, but Braden didn't pay attention to the ruckus. At that moment, Simon fastened his smug-looking eyes on Janey, riveted on her, sensing the others, but like a tracer bullet, sought out his victim exclusively. Braden pounced at Simon, shielding Janey.

Paulie became disoriented in the confusion. Did no one understand that the traitorous clerk who had lost him his dazzling little butterfly was tip-toeing around here guilty as could be? For the first time since he was a tiny kid, Paulie grabbed his mother's hand squeezing it hard. The sparkly colored butterfly — he gave a quick glimpse over the glass counter —, is it there? Had it flown back?

Like an ersatz avenging super villain, Simon had upstaged the others with his enormous indignation. He slashed among them then stopped short as if he'd seen them surround him, threatening him. This spate of familiar people stood against him like a hostile wall. Under his arm he had carried in a box of cigars for Claymore, as a peace gesture. There next to Braden stood Janey with her son, Janey who had crushed his dream into millions of shards. Claymore's ditzy niece and that indistinct hanger-on of hers with the long face banked up against the counter with the silent clerk. Silent. Silent. It had become quiet after his shouting.

Simon peered at Braden, tried to pull him away from the bunch. His boyhood pal, grown up together, in and out of mischief, harangued by parents, the girls they had chased, women they had caught. Men entering mid-life mostly satisfied. What right did fate have to rip Braden from him? Janey didn't count. Women didn't have friends like men do. Distressful, Janey had left him, he could do something about it, already had asked Tiffany out. But Braden was not replaceable. It did not enter his mind standing there that he had dumped Braden because his manhood had demanded it. He could blame Braden, Janey, fate, maybe God, but never rapacious manliness. And manhood's clamor for itself would not end here. But no matter the inviable necessity, he slumped a bit when the scene faded out.

When Paul was as old as Claymore was now, he could still bring back the cacophony at the jeweler's and the dislocation that made him grip his mother's hand and bury his cheek against her hip. He'd been ashamed at almost nine years old to be clutching at his mother, to let fear make him hide his face. The crisscross of ugly emotions at that juncture had been palpable.

Simon went into attack mode, shuffled his feet like a boxer. "Who the hell you think you are, Braden? Messing with my leavings."

Janey circled the men, still clutching her son's hand, waved off Dorrie, avoided Edwin gap-mouthed standing in her way, pushed him aside and barged through the door, out and away. Braden could handle himself. Dorrie and Edwin would probably enjoy the confrontation.

The clerk had scurried to the back. And Janey would be damned if she subjected Paulie or herself to any more of this theater of the absurd.

"Shut up, Simo, you're making a fool of yourself." Braden, at last.

"What's happened to you, Braden, you're a changed man. That bitch got you by the short hairs." He gave out a strange cackle. "You'll find out what she is, and don't come crying to me when you do, when she ruins your fucking life. You friggin' loser."

Half-way out of the shop Braden whipped around and glared at the frothy man. "You're all worked up. Better go cool-off before you hurt yourself." It was harder to walk out than Braden made it look.

Edwin was frozen to the floor beside Dorrie.

"Good god," Dorrie said. "What's got into you?"

Simon's voice wavered. "Where's your uncle?"

"Home sick — in bed I hope."

"Here. I brought him some cigars because of the fuss I made last time I was here."

"Good thing he didn't see the fuss you just made. He shouldn't smoke those things anymore. Not good for him."

He shoved the package at her. "Take the stinking things. I'm outta here."

Edwin gave a sarcastic chortle. Dorrie joined in with her brash guffaws. Leah crept out from the back, cell phone raised. "I don't have to call the police, do I?"

Dorrie's eyes followed Simon's disappearing figure. "All hell broke loose… It's over."

The strange duo out the door, Leah fumbled with the luxury timepieces Edwin had toyed with. She needed to get things straightened out.

On the sidewalk, a glance back through the glass front window Dorrie said to her unnaturally silent companion, "A bit of a kick-up is good for that Janey."

Leah might agree, but only for a moment did she feel better. She had too much pressure on her heart.

For both Janey and Braden, the confrontation at the jeweler's pricked a sliver of distrust between them. Janey wanted to examine what had happened while Braden thought they would do better by dumping the Simo ordeal in the trash. Swoosh, like a computer. They relied on the arousal and love-making that offered closure and came often after excitement of any kind. Along with satiety and exhaustion, they talked in post-sex intimacy, relaxed, concerns allayed, unguarded, almost lulled to sleep. And that talk was useless, ending with Braden's solemn words, "Simo will get over this."

The world proceeded in discreet increments of assumed time. One chilly Saturday morning in spring, Janey stirred pancake batter at the kitchen window while straining to track a Magnolia warbler come to the feeder when up poked Gibby's fist knocking on the pane. Owl-eyed Lydia sat on the front porch steps with Paulie playing checkers. Hovering over them knelt Rex shouting unwanted advice to Paulie who seemed more interested in keeping all his checkers on the board than jumping Lydia's off it. From the open door, the kids' banter and challenges floated into Braden fussing with his laptop and on the new sofa.

"Come in, you idiot," Janey called to Gibby. "You're chasing the warbler away." Gibby flipped her another kind of bird. Janey laughed. It was the way Gibby did not-so-clever things that made them funny.

After they had devoured all the pancakes, Braden, who had promised, took the kids to the park, riding along on their bicycles. The two women sat at the square parquet table, drinking hot coffee Janey had brewed up fresh. This was an ordinary morning that no one ever remembers. Yet it is a pivotal moment. Countless of these moments have passed us and we are content not to relive them in memory or therapy or at the times of our deaths. Yet they survive.

Janey wiggled on the chair seat, a sure sign of some mental discomfort. Gibby had come to talk seriously. Janey tried to put her off.

"I told you about that big hullabaloo at Claymore's store when Braden and I went for rings?"

"You touched on it. No details. Simon went off—"

"I think he may be starting to stalk again. When I went out with Braden once, I saw him hanging around. And now that Braden's moving in… He knows we're getting married in a few weeks… He found out. He even shows up when Braden is here. Braden read him the riot act, but I doubt if Simon registered a word."

Gibby seemed unconcerned. "Can't see Braden being fierce. Not in his nature—"

"He's not a push-over."

"I meant he doesn't fly off the handle…"

"That's how it works. Braden yells and it's over. Simon doesn't care."

Still avoiding Gibby, she shifted topics. "The other night Paulie was going on about a butterfly caught in glass. Damn that stupid pin. I don't want him obsessing on it."

"Paulie said 'caught in glass?'"

"Yeah, why?"

"He's talking about something he saw at the Art Institute, a French Baccarat. A paperweight, a twinkling, jeweled butterfly enclosed in a glass globe. That kid's so observant. We were waiting to leave. He wandered into a room off the lobby. There were hundreds of them exhibited in illuminated cases."

It was like both women were wool-gathering, distracting themselves to avoid some sensitive point.

"Inside each little globe was a different butterfly. I had to drag him away. I don't think he liked the whole roomful… It was art, not science."

"You hope he prefers science?" Barely following Gibby's train of thought.

"I don't trust art, entirely." Gibby winked at her. "Outside the Institute Paulie stood in front of a skinny black guy playing the one-string West African fiddle like he was appreciating to the strange sounds."

"You're being goofy, Gibby. You make too much of him. He's just your normal sometimes annoying kid. You should have been here when he was whining about Lydia and Rex pelting him with slush. He had waylaid them with balls of what's left of the dirty snow out there and they retaliated. Of course. He was filthy, angry to tears and saying I wasn't 'sticking up' for him. I had pointed out he did start it, that didn't—"

"But he did understand later, I'll bet. I bet he did understand later. Right?"

"Jesus, Gibby."

"He thinks things over."

"But he's not—"

Gibby spotted her opening. "Listen. Seriously. Have you considered a different school for Paulie next year?"

"Different as in private?"

"For gifted children. There's one not far from you. In Evanston. It's a hands-on school, progressive education. He's got the inquisitiveness to fit right in. He's well over the IQ requirement. I've known parents who send their kids there. It allows for creativity, teaches problem-solving, has new methods."

"Stop. I can't afford to send him to a posh school."

"They have scholarships. He'll be with kids like himself."

"He's fine where he's at. I like Lydia and Rex." All she could respond at that moment. Then she gave reasons. "He changed school already this year when he came to Chicago. It's an adjustment, and not easy no matter how carefully it's done."

"I know. But he'd be challenged at a school for the gifted. He'd fit in better."

Gibby was resolute. "There's an intern teacher in every classroom, with the regular teacher. Only twelve to fifteen students—"

Janey shouted over her. "Gibby, you mean the best for Paulie. But he's not your son." Silence. "He is not your son."

Gibby jolted up, went to pour herself more coffee. Kept her back turned. "I'm sorry. Your son."

"…Not what I was going to say. He's not your responsibility. You're not the one who takes the blame if you make a mistake. Sometimes even if you don't you get blamed. A moment of carelessness, a bad choice, a mistake and you're branded. Any damn thing might go wrong. It wears you like a saddle. I don't ever completely relax. I made a choice about Braden and that's about all I can handle right now. Someone I love. Someone who I think will be good for Paulie."

Gibby came back, sat, swished her hand across her foolish, senseless, watery eyes. "I won't interfere anymore. Every other word I say I wonder if I've offended you. I'm like… I'm starting to act like Simon. Maybe I should stay away for a while."

"Not if you know what's good for you."

Gibby had picked up an apple slice turning brown on a dish, bit off a piece. "I've gotten too close to Paulie, I see. Swallowed the apple bit. "And to you."

"I know." Janey said. "It gets complicated.

∽

Hard-luck Hannah, what Janey called her hapless ex-mother-in-law, phoned in the morning to tell Janey before she read it in the newspaper. Arthur Kane was killed in an automobile accident. She listened to the poor woman sob, holding back her own press of emotions. Immense irony in Artie's demise. The famous race car driver, clever and talented, killed in a one-car crash on a quiet country road. The friend with him, in critical condition but conscious, had said they were making speed on a long stretch when Artie swerved to avoid hitting a dog in the road, lost control and smashed into a tree. After the call, Janey at the kitchen table, cradled her head in her hands until the painful thought whispered off. She wept a bit, felt a hollow in the pit of her stomach. Grief had startled her. Not before this had death crept in for one overpowering moment. She knew people who had died, but none close to her. Her wandering father was alive in South America from where he texted her often.

And that Artie had died in such a way. Not crashing at Indie in the race of his life after blazing compulsively around miles of oval track, not shaking off a cliff after dangling in frozen fear for eternity over oblivion, not dying in bed after a long life defying the black-cloaked skeleton with the scythe gripped in a hand of white bones.

Swerving to avoid killing a dog. Yes, he had to have had great skill as a driver to miss the dog. The dog had lived. Tassos had mentioned that because, of course, the friend not named with him in his car would have to be Tassos. Her tears squeezed through closed eyelids. Arthur Kane first and foremost worked hard to make his life as exciting as possible. She gulped down a defiant laugh, like shaking her fist at god. No one could deny his basic decency. Artie steered clear of places where inhumane people prowl.

She would explain all to Paulie someday. Now she had to find a way to tell her son that his absent father who so often seemed to forget him, the father he saw rarely but idolized, had died. She got up on rubbery legs to call Braden and Gibby, then when Paulie awoke, she would tell him.

He sensed bad news as soon as he sloughed into the kitchen, caught the fright on his mother's face.

"Paulie, something's happened."

A frizzle of cold fear thrilled along his spine. "Mommy, are you all right?"

"Yes, I'm fine. It's about your dad. He was in a bad car

crash. And…he died." There are not any euphemisms for a child.

She gathered him in her arms, he cried in soft whimpers. She talked about Artie as if he were still alive until the reality, such as a nine-year-old comprehends it, took hold. Then she called the school and her office. Through all this she hadn't absorbed that Artie was gone.

For a while Paulie lay shivering in bed, then found comfort digging out all the newspaper clippings of his dad's racing exploits and arranging them in a circle on the floor. He put his framed picture of Artie in a racer's suit plastered with auto product names in the center, and stared hard at it. As an adult Paul remembered little about his father's wake except that there were famous racecar drivers who came by and spoke to him. His mother and he stood at the back, but she took him up to the front before they left. There was a top on the casket. It was like his father hadn't shown up. Paulie had been speechless with fright when earlier his mother had said that it would look like his dad was sleeping. Still she had prepared him for that. However, the flower-strewn closed casket terrified him when he saw that the lid fit tight. He tried to cry out that his dad wouldn't be able to breathe. His own breathing turned shallow until he thought of something.

There must be air holes drilled into the bottom of the box. And decades later, as a very old man, when he had buried most of the people he loved, Paul would get a tug of painful grief each time he recalled his first funeral, and his panic at there being no way to breathe in a closed casket.

ELEVEN

THE news of Artie Kane's death refueled Simon Butler's hots for Janey Leduc. He had poured over the *Trib*'s obituary, one befitting a famous auto racer. An article which ironically brought back his good times with Janey. This is one of the ways the mind works to prompt us to reevaluate our feelings. However, Simon thought it meant Janey was finally free of That Jerk and would want him back. Would dump Braden — serve the dope right — and Simon could be his buddy, take Braden under his wing. Renewed friendship, renewed love life. Simon wasn't satisfied with his present romance. Tiffany did quirky little things that annoyed him. A deep inner voice nagged at him that he had worked it out all wrong — a faint, blurred and overwritten nag. But he was besotted with Janey and could not see past her.

Claymore glanced up from the collet that was setting the ruby's color. His eyes lit on Simon's impervious trot through his establishment. He put the neck socket aside and faced the inevitable. Simon came on as if he had no idea he could ever be a pest.

"What's going on, Clay?"

"What d'ya think goes on in a jewelry store, rumba lessons?"

"No customers?"

"Not at the moment."

Most of the time Claymore struck him as a bungling old goat. Still when he felt aggrieved, he chose Clay to listen to him bellyache. Today, he had also come to ask a favor. Even if Clay had lately been dismissive, he had to be sympathetic to Simon's latest trouble. So Simon thought.

A customer walked in. Simon waited until that mute clerk went up to a well-dressed matron with a vivid colored silk scarf. Leah began to show her a foxtail gold chain. Claymore had gone back to the ruby. A low murmur of the two women's voices, and the whir of the clocks. Simon had trouble getting started.

"Clay, man, I gotta talk to you. Did you read today's *Trib*?"

Claymore leaned a hip on his high stool, away from Simon's livid face. What had he done to deserve Simo?

Years ago he'd played poker with Simon's parents. It wasn't easy being alone after Lucille died. He had tried to make friends with people. And for that sin he had had Simon set loose on him.

"I didn't take time this morning to read the paper."

"Janey's husband is dead. Car accident."

"My god… In a race?"

"Ha, that's the beauty of it. On an ordinary road he crashed into a tree. The prick. How did a fancy car racer lose it on a normal country road?"

The jeweler stared at him. "You got a mean streak, boy, and it isn't pretty."

"Naw. I'm only saying it does seem funny." He corralled his snicker. "Hey, I'm meeting Braden Uptown later. Braden and I talked. The thing is, Claymore, I want you to go with me…to Rj Grunts. Braden wants to patch things up. Not let a woman get between us. I'm not surprised. He hangs onto people. Even after his mom died, he talked as if she was still around. So this is good… meeting up with him."

"Yeah, yeah, sure, that's fine. But why drag me along? I'm not your second in a duel. Braden doesn't want onlookers to your rapprochement."

"What in the hell are you talking about?"

"I'm not up for it."

"You gotta eat. You should get out a little, Clay, you need cheering up."

"You're cheered up enough for both of us. Go on, go to Lincoln Park." As if he were consigning him to the inferno.

"Listen to me, Clay. Leave your shop and your crummy apartment and that gloomy assistant over there and be a pal. It'd do you good."

The customer had left and Leah was starting the process of closing for the night. She overheard some of their conversation, not that it registered, merely slid off her consciousness into a stream of nothingness.

Simo persisted, "What d'you say, huh?"

"I'm not going anywhere with you." Claymore felt a deep animus for Simon creep into his voice. He choked on spittle draining the wrong way down his throat. Simon took offense.

"I only thought you being with might've taken a little pressure off Braden. But okay. Have it your way." He sauntered out into the street, disappeared in the sidewalk's foot traffic. Fact was he wanted Clay to be there when he met Braden because it would seem more natural, more like before. And if maybe Braden had asked along some of their other friends… But in truth, it would be easier to disguise that he had come to sabotage Braden's romance. He wasn't feeling malicious. He must stop Braden's wedding both to reclaim his friendship and win Janey for himself. All's fair in love and war, he thought not for a nanosecond sensing his venom. He had to get his own back. Without a scruple he planned to ambush Braden, demand the rites of friendship, reveal the true Janey. Square it with Braden first, then Janey would return to him.

When Simon got to Rj Grunts, Braden was seated by himself in a booth by the windows, tapping his fingers on the green-checked tablecloth and sipping a beer. With the brass chandelier, the skinny strings around the lit-up banana, the tucked away full bar, the place had a pub ambience. It was as usual packed with people and noisy. He sat across from Braden and ordered a drink, euphoric when he saw no one else there.

"Where's everybody?"

"Did you expect a crowd, Simo? Janey's gone with Gibby and Ben to the Royal George Theater—"

"Yeah, I know the place—"

"They're seeing Rosenkranz Mystery Magic… Medicine Show, or something nutty like that."

"Yeah, yeah, that's fine." He didn't know who Gibby and Ben were. New friends of his, guys who were taking Janey to something Braden wouldn't be caught dead at. Braden hadn't brought anyone else, he acted as if he had something he wanted to say to him. This plan to undermine and conquer was going to be easier than he imagined.

Throughout the meal, both men feigned their normal selves. When you've known someone a long time and have never lost touch it's easy enough to do. Even with the tension of harsh circumstance it was still possible to eat burgers and drink beer as if everything were normal. Pretending they were friends as they were before didn't hinder discussion, instead allowed them to sit together without being at each other's throat. So the veneer of civilization isn't a barrier to natural human behavior; it's a necessity concomitant upon it.

Less sensitive and aware than his friend, Simon let his mask drop to be able to articulate what he'd come for. He would sneak up to it.

"I thought I saw a 'sold' sign at your computer place. You going somewhere?"

"Yeah, Simo, I sold the business, the building and everything in it. I got a job at Avant, front-end software engineer. You wouldn't believe how many tech firms there are in Chicago. I got about a dozen offers."

Simon chuckled. "Front-end software. Sounds... interesting."

"I know what it sounds like. But I'll have time and freedom—"

"I would've guessed it's the other way around."

"Yeah, if you're a techy, but I'm not. Listen, Simon, you know I'm about to marry Janey. That's why I met you here tonight."

Braden gave him the perfect opening. With a derisive guffaw he pounced. "That would be a big mistake, Buddy. Big mistake." A frisson of intense antagonism zapped between them. Simon tried to back off when he saw Braden's brittle expression.

"I want us to remain friends." A question hung out there between them.

"Sure, sure, Braden. That's what this is all about." He waved his hand as if to include the entire Rj Grunts' interior. "As your oldest friend I had to come to warn you about Janey. She's a sorceress, a real bitch. You gotta listen to me. It's not good to be involved with her. She'll betray you, I swear she will. Take it from me." He thought he was tempering what he meant to say.

Braden reared up out of the booth, clenched his fists, a bewildered reality shredded. He had come to reclaim his part in Simon's life. Instead he felt repulsed by Simon, harried by his own defects.

Simon made it home, filled the entire drive with blaming Janey for the ugly changes that had been forced on him. Defeated, there was nothing he could do about it.

After they left the Royal George, Gibby and Ben drove Janey home. Gibby, who was worried about her friend's mood, hinted something might be wrong. Was it Braden?

"No, I wouldn't let the fact that Braden was meeting Simon put a damper on our fun." She sounded half in jest, and Gibby barked a laugh. Ben, who had flown in from Logan that morning, remained silent. He said he was tired, still he'd been too quiet all evening Gibby thought, a little worried about him, also. Benjamin Farrer, deep blue-eyed, dark-haired oboist for the Boston Symphony, had found Martha Gibson transposed into a different key when he arrived today. Their texts and phone calls hadn't given him a clue of how changed he'd find her. He knew all about her fondness for the child prodigy. He doubted that the boy could be all she claimed. He met Paulie that night and thought him a rather ordinary boy. She seemed overly keen on his mother as well.

"I'm going to go all therapishy on you, Janey," Gibby said. "Take a week off work, reschedule your clients or whatever. You got a shock when Art died, having to deal with your son, and then Simon intruding like he has. Too much piled on."

"I know, I know. I know. Stress points adding up. Don't patronize me, Gibby."

Gibby spewed before she thought, "You ought to listen to yourself, Ms. Leduc can't take a little tough talk?"

"You are annoying me with your cliché advice."

"What is advice but cliché?" She taunted. "The counselor must but listen and let the disturbed one figure it out for herself."

"It ain't that easy, honey." Both women sounded as if they were bickering now. Ben reached over and grabbed Martha's hand.

Janey unhooked her seatbelt. The car had brought her home. She reached from the back before she scrambled out and rubbed Gibby's shoulder.

"I will get it together. I plan to take some comp days next week."

Ben, as they drove away, needed to switch to regular, familiar subjects, their usual talk. But when Martha began rhapsodizing about some popular harpsichord player, he only wanted silence. Much later in the night, his lovemaking with Martha put all other desires out of his mind.

Simon slept late, awoke with pounding head and cotton mouth, defiant in his burning shame at the spectacle he'd made of himself last night to Braden. Many times over the years, man and boy, each had been mortified at some folly, predicament, indiscretion he had gotten into. They'd been at each other's throats before. But not like this. And over a woman.

As Simon made coffee, drew the drapes to block out the sun, he tried to sort out this new person he was but wasn't — to clear his head but not to think too deeply about it. He walked to the convenience store, movement of feet let random thoughts float in and out, specks of thoughts flicking on and off, easier to breathe. As he returned to his apartment, *Sunday Trib* tucked under his arm, a normal rhythm returned. Get it on with other women, get on with his life. Betrayed by Janey in one frame, Braden had to be put somewhere else. Looming, feeling better, settle with Braden. He came up with his next move. How strange it had never occurred to him that his misery would dissolve if he let go of Janey. It was a circular reasoning, a found spot to break out. Never would have come up with how, if he hadn't been willing to fix himself. He spent the rest of the day draped on the sofa.

When Gibby and Ben arrived at the door on Monday, Janey pulled Gibby aside. "Let Braden get to know Ben. I've got to talk to you." They sat on the porch in two deck chairs.

"Paulie's not acting like himself."

"Where is the little dickens? In his room?"

"Yes. He was cranky and shouted at Braden about something. Braden promised and reneged on. I don't know what." She shook her hair out of her eyes. "He's been easily upset since Art died."

"I would think that's normal."

"Yes." They listened a moment to the men in the house, talking politely like strangers, which they almost were.

"Still..." Janey stopped. She was out of answers. Nobody can influence the determined way fate dishes out life.

Gibby waited..." What exactly...how is he acting out?" A smile crept into her words. Paulie is a good kid. But he's going to be naughty.

"He's been mouthing off. Not to me, to Braden. He's never done that. He even got frothy with Lydia who just giggles back at him." Her mood lifted. "That might be the way to handle his sauciness."

There had to be more. Again, Gibby waited. When Janey remained quiet, she said, "It looks to me like a boy who never had much of a father, now lost what little of him he had. And whose mother will be married very soon to a man who will never replace him."

Janey looked her in the eye, "If I were talking to a client those would be my very words."

"You flatter me."

"I do."

Gibby slugged her arm. "There you are."

"Except…right before you and Ben showed up I heard noises. I went into his bedroom. He was kicking at his bed and shouting, 'Jesus Christ.'"

"I expect his hurt plays out as anger—"

"I know, Gibby, I'm the friggin' social worker." She lowered her voice then shouted the last three words.

"It's harder to see when it's your own."

"Jesus Christ, Gibby," she growled, "I'm at wits' end."

"Now, where could your son have picked up such language?"

A half-laugh half-shriek, "I've had it with everything."

Gibby nodded. She had nothing to add. "Come on, let's go eat. The men have probably run out of things to say to each other."

Paulie at dinner seemed normal to Gibby. He was quieter, which was likely because of Ben's presence. Although Ben behaved the way he thought adults acted with kids, his manner seemed to dampen Paulie's spirit further. Even with Gibby and Braden the boy seemed to be holding himself apart. Only with his mother was he more himself. It was an odd, off-centered evening.

Paulie had conflicted feelings about Ben coming into his life. The thought of Ben caused smudges of distress. At the same time, he was still dealing with his father's death, which he transposed into his thoughts about God. Since neither his mother nor any of her family were religious, he had picked up his Biblical knowledge like mythology and superheroes from television and conversations overheard. Also, he had read Bible stories in children's books, along with fairy tales and space adventures. He was bewildered by God, Ben and in a submerged way, Gibby.

After dinner, Paulie wandered off to his bedroom, listened to the voices muffled by his door, of his mother and these new people. Almost in tears, unaware of the dissonance that had come into his short life, he began to be afraid. He crawled into bed dressed, hid his face behind a comic book. He flipped over when he heard his door open. Gibby sat on the beanbag chair next to him.

"Hey, Kiddo," she whispered. "I think you might be awake… How about setting up your telescope on the back porch so we can view the craters on the moon? You can show us how many constellations you can pick out."

He scrunched to the side of the bed and dangled his legs over the edge. "I don't think I feel very good."

"Don't think? But you aren't sure you don't feel very good? I know how that is. Usually, I ask myself if I would like some ice cream. If I answer no, then I'm sick. If ice cream seems like a good idea, then I'm okay."

He gave a half-hearted smile.

"Maybe you can tell me why." She met his eyes, unsmiling. If she wavered even a moment and let him think about it, she wouldn't get a true answer.

Something cleared in his mind. "You know…huh…I went to Sunday school with Rex to his church." Gibby kept her eyes on his now lowered gaze. "And they talked about God. How he can do everything, and how he loves us. I heard a lot about Jesus… I wondered about what God does. The Sunday school teacher said he can do anything he wants. He created us…then…" He began to whimper. "I made a big mistake. I asked then why he let my daddy die in a car crash." Gibby didn't blink, let alone move. It was as if the boy was talking from far away, behind a veil.

"The teacher said there was a good reason for everything that happens. 'It's all God's plan. Only we aren't allowed to know it because we wouldn't understand.' I said I understand why my dad crashed because he didn't want to hit a dog in the road. Some of the kids laughed but Rex didn't. Then I said the bad thing, and everybody laughed even Rex and the teacher got real mad and made me leave the room." He stopped his narrative. It seemed as if he wasn't going to continue. Gibby stayed quiet. She hoped he wasn't finished yet.

"I can't tell my mom, or anyone…I said an awful thing." He stopped, wasn't going to tell Gibby either.

"Every scientist, Paulie, who's a real scientist has to be brave. Lots of times scientists ask questions that make people mad. But a brave scientist asks them anyway. I'm glad you asked your question."

"But the teacher said I was evil and going to go to hell."

"No, you're not evil, and sweet boy, you're not going to hell."

Something broke and he began to sob. "I said Superman was better than God." He rushed the words.

She almost laughed but was forever thankful that she didn't. Grabbed him in her arms and assured him that what he said wasn't evil at all and she could assure him of that.

The boy had told the class that Superman, if he had been there when Art Kane swerved off the road toward the tree, would have saved the racecar driver and the dog. Paulie knew that his father had done an instinctively humane act. The teacher had told him that God is everywhere. And that God is all powerful. If so, why hadn't God saved Art Kane's life? Superman would have. Logic dictated that therefore Superman was better than God. Perhaps others would be able to find holes in his reasoning. But she wasn't going to try. The boy went limp, he was so very tired. After she left, he changed into his pajamas and slept the sleep of the just.

There was more talk subtle and obscure that night of which Paulie asleep in relief was not aware. Gibby had followed Janey's movements the rest of the evening until she got her aside to give her a summary of what Paulie had confessed. Being ridiculed and humiliated, his grief, and his fear of being evil. Janey reacted like a mother. She got angry at the teacher, then had a leftover twinge of irritation at Gibby because her son had chosen her to confide in. But anger dissipated. The mean-spirited pious one hadn't been able to harm Paulie, and the professional Janey knew that children need other adults at times besides their parents. Often for Paulie it had been his grandmother. Maybe he had even talked freely to Artie during their irregular phone calls. She touched Gibby's cheek in gratitude when they were leaving.

Before Braden left — he tried not to stay the night anymore until after their wedding — and Ben and Gibby had taken off, he admitted being made uncomfortable about something Ben had said.

"Gibby's boyfriend, that Ben, he made me wonder…"

Janey didn't believe she could face another private unburdening. Her head was already spinning and not from the wine.

"Yeah, Gibby's boyfriend, go on—" Get it over with before she collapses.

"Well, he was talking about the burden of taking on fatherhood."

"His word "burden?"

"Yup, and I did say I didn't think of it that way. But I wonder…Janey… I'll never be Paulie's father, I know I won't."

"That's good. Freud wrote boys want to kill their fathers, and replace them in the affections of their mothers—"

"Stop it, don't be cute. It's not what I ever thought of, being a father."

"Not even with Carol, when you were almost married to her?"

"It's something abstract with men—"

"Lordy."

"Janey, you've got to listen to me. I never had a father. I was raised by women. I don't have a clue how to go about being one."

Janey brought her hands up prayer-like in front of her mouth. Nothing ever was easy. "Okay, I see what you're getting at…"

"Paulie and I don't have the same blood. These stories about young kids and older people having these great bonds seem to me nothing more than sentimental muck. Schmaltzy at best, suspicious at worst."

Janey agreed but said nothing. What was there to say? Time would work this problem out for Braden. She had confidence in Braden's good sense, trusted his basic decency. If she were wrong about Braden, it would kill her.

"How do you see yourself in my son's life?" Her lips were drawn into a straight line of hopeless intensity.

"I can't be a buddy, or a step-father, or an uncle…" His eyes seemed to twirl to the open window where moonlight made the leafy red branches dance. "Maybe, teacher?"

She dropped her loose hair over his hand. "Yes? Then be that, Braden. Be that."

∽

"Remarkable evening," said Gibby as she drove Ben to her apartment.

He grabbed at her fingers almost pulling them off the steering wheel. "Benjamin, watch it there. I like this drive, reminds me of Boston on nights like this."

He gave a short laugh the kind that means, if you say so, curt and unsubtle.

"You don't see the similarities?"

"Yes, the usual similarities that are there in most American cities, with some obvious differences." He had played in many places in the U.S. and abroad.

"I see. Philadelphia, for instance. What's it like?" She was teasing, lightly.

"Baltimore," he said and chuckled. A chuckle that meant, I can tease, too.

"Did you enjoy any of the evening tonight?"

"Braden's interesting. Interesting but limited, I can see him as…" he stumbled, "limited."

"And Janey?"

"She's your friend, Martha."

"So you don't want to say?"

"I don't think she does you justice."

"What? In what way?" He could mean anything, but she had a suspicion.

"You don't want to hear what I think about either one of them."

Could be I don't, she thought.

Benjamin Ferrar's week in Chicago ended in a proposal. He had flown in to audition as a soloist for the Lyric Opera orchestra. Often he was a guest performer for prestige symphonies, and Martha had assumed that was what he was hoping for this trip to Chicago. Instead, he had been invited to join the orchestra. There was a fortuitous opening in the oboe section and the offer was too good to pass by. He needed a change at this period of his career to keep his name vital and fresh. And so, he accepted the position, and then simply asked Martha to marry him.

Gibby couldn't wait to tell Janey. "I'm thrilled," said Janey Leduc in earnest, anxious Ben might take Gibby back to Boston where she would stay forever. Her son would be mighty upset if that happened.

"I've been hoping something would work out soon. Long distance relationships are such a strain." Gibby sounded melancholic. "So, hey, married next fall. I haven't much family except for my mother. Ben's family will come out, and we'll have a simple wedding at the courthouse…like what you and Braden are planning."

"It's best for our age."

"Come on, dopey. We're still young…"

"I guess, and with three of the four it's their first marriage." Unused words hung there between them. "Paulie's been a much happier camper since he unburdened himself to you."

"Are you going on a honeymoon? We'll go at Christmas."

"Yes, to Toronto. The family wants a reception there. Paulie is eager to see his grandmother, and my sister, too. Want to come?"

"On your honeymoon?" She tried to gasp.

"There'll be a lot of people on my honeymoon." Her friend's words of contentment sent a quiver through Gibby.

⁓◯

At the jewelry store, Leah was given more responsibility which allowed Claymore the time he wanted to create with gemstones. His almost dead passion blew into flame from cold ashes. Silver, gold, platinum, and a thousand colors of blue, a million colors of red, yellow, amethyst, the violets of a trillion stars all luminous and glowing, so many tints and blends that it would take a billion years to count all the colors bursting in the universe. And black, the absence of color. And sheer blinding white of all the colors, unspeakably beautiful. Beyond the word, and the world. He knew what he could never find, but that is the sorrow of the artist, the wordsmith, the musician. Blind Giovanni Gonnelli, deaf Ludwig Van Beethoven, visionary Virginia Woolf.

Leah was initiated into the lore of precious and semi-precious jewels — ever changing bits of color, blended shades of sparkled light. But she was also pleased to be learning watch repair. It was a skill that did not come easily, and it calmed her mind.

The old jeweler and the grieving woman came to be fond of each other. A bond recognized when Leah first came to work for Claymore strengthened into affection and mutual need. He admired that she remained upbeat and pleasant and didn't inflict her grief on other people. As Clay's congestive heart failure worsened, more and more he came to depend on his quiet assistant, his apprentice. Being in the store and listening to Clay's tutoring mitigated her throbs of mourning. She could pop the bezel out of the watch face, tinker with the tiny mechanism and find a spot of peace. She knew his heart was failing him, but all sorrows were one to her. All a cold numbness enveloping her like dank fog.

Dorrie came more often into her uncle's store as if she had an intuition that his life was closing and wanted to stay near him. Edwin might show up there with her on occasion, flaunting his bizarre guesses about who had expelled him into this world and then dumped him. He always pestered Dorrie to listen to him although Dorrie recanted on her silence about who his birthmother might be. Nevertheless, his hope along with his person clung onto Dorrie. She was the only one who pretended to go along with his fantasies and potshot attempts to locate this enigmatic figure. She played his game that there was a secret mother to be found. If she knew anything she was not giving a whimper of a clue.

Two weddings to come and perhaps a funeral. Births, deaths, celebrations, uncertainty, light, darkness and somewhere words and color.

TWELVE

THAT first spring in Chicago, Paulie got himself lost in an enormous, scary cemetery. And after finding his way out he landed amongst frantic goings-on. Adult Paul Kane did not recall how he managed to wander away, but his sense of the memory of it always made him uneasy. He had been frightened half to death by bleary apparitions in his active, imaginative child's mind which never totally left him. Recollected in tranquility, those scenes had the authenticity of reality. As real as a bright back-lit vibrant city illuminated by the enormity of the dark Great Lake.

He had contended with all the rapid changes in his life the previous months. Adult Paul conflated his — he called it running away— with his mother's remarriage, the trauma of his dad's death, as well as the dislocation of being transported from Toronto to Chicago which had taken an effort to get used to. And there was Gibby and amazing things he learned and saw and new friends and, of course, Braden. He knew all this as an adult, but very little of it was clear that afternoon he walked away from Rex and Liddy, not knowing where he might go. HIs life had been shaken up to uncertainty, bolting away was dealing with it.

Step by step, street by street, he was led into an entanglement of bustling residential streets and long strings of traffic, weaving noisy thoroughfares of metal-plated giant insects the cars seemed to have become. He decided to search the street signs for Ashland Avenue, but everywhere only confusion amplified his distress. He had no cell phone; Janey would get him one immediately after this ordeal. He knew better than to stop and ask strangers on the street. No police were in sight.

Mozart Street. A friend lived on Mozart Street. He remembered being taken there by his mother. He looked up at big Nativity Church where his mother turned up Mozart Street. His mother would hum Mozart every time they came, saying she remembered it from her flute lessons, for the flute and clarinet, she sang. A damp wind blew up his light jacket, tickled his neck. He began to shiver. Baffled about what to do next he ran higgledy-piggledy until he reached Ravenswood Avenue where he bent over out of breath. A cemetery materialized, jerking him up straight.

When he saw the huge cement gates of the cemetery and the quiet, leafy paths beyond, they seemed welcoming. The sun which was sinking below the skyscrapers made gloomy shadows over the crenelated castle facade. Rosehill Cemetery first chartered in 1859, he read, seemed familiar. He visited here with Rex and his family when they came to plant flowers. Lydia was there, too, and they played made-up games among the headstones and giant mausoleums. He and Rex had horsed around trying to scare Lydia who ridiculed their clumsy attempts, jumping out from behind some moldy tombstone. Once she had screamed and while they were mocking her, she admitted they had startled her but not for why they thought. "My momma told me there's not no reason to be 'fraid of ghosts, it's live people you should be scared of." Later, in adolescence, he would turn away from the simple wisdom of Lydia and Rex. Adult Paul would be troubled by a streak of willfulness that let him be selfish, blocking out how his actions affected others. But small Paulie that frightening day heard her words come back verbatim and heeded them. He walked under a stone arch into the fading light of the still graveyard.

Meandering along, he tried to find the spooky weird statues that had mystified him. He wended his way up and down the narrow asphalt drives, with a tad of well-being and no consciousness of how long he drifted. As yet he hadn't walked off the road into the uncut grass among the gravestones. Hesitantly, he ventured on tiptoe through a rough path and stumbled on the tomb of Lulu Fellowes: her statue, a young girl sitting on a bench inside a glass case. He'd seen it before. It marked her grave in such a sad way he had wanted to stand there forever staring at it. Rex had pretended to be freaked out and bolted down the lane. But Lydia had waited, her rounded eyes watching Paulie. Until she giggled and pulled him away. Someone had lost her, this Lulu he though, this time no longer fascinated by her, only frightened. He hurried past, knowing there was another glass case around here, larger… Here it stood, the monument to Francis Pearce, a woman sleeping on her side, a small child lying tucked beneath one arm, the other one curved over her pillowed head. Adult Paul might conjure up that recumbent figure although it lingered too wispy to be put in any specific place or time. He didn't connect it to his traipse through Ravenswood. Only within a free-floating aura of loss. It gave Paulie a creepy feeling, so he scuffled past. His shoe became untied. He was afraid to stop and retie it. At the firemen's memorial he stumbled, laced up his sneaker, and squeezed his brain to regain his sense of direction. He noticed the light fading, and started to quake a bit and whimper. The cemetery seemed immense. He had to think how they had gotten out when he'd been here with Rex's family.

Jogging past the nymph fountain so fast he didn't get a look at the naked body, he lurched and hurtled a small gravestone. Then he came upon the greyhound monument, long elegance lying stretched out with its intelligent head between its paws. Lydia had told them a sad story about how the dog was waiting on top of the grave of his master, waiting for him to wake up. She told it so solemn and earnest that he had believed her. Here was the dog, still waiting.

Paulie sobbed a little. An unbalanced lostness began to guide him down an open lane, which caught shreds of sunlight beneath fewer budding branches in the canopy of trees. At the end of the lane he found the way he had come in. He loped out in a wave of joy that he had left the dead. They had not done him any harm. But he was relieved nevertheless to leave them behind.

He was still lost. Streeterville, Clark Street, past a tavern where he heard cruel words, smelled the violence. The dark came but felt protective, instead of alarming.

He wandered cold, unconscious of the packed streets surrounding him, his skinny legs aching, nose running, red-eyed and so very thirsty. At last his adventure collapsed like a sine wave. A police car patrolling, an alert cop, and he was rescued and taken home.

"Did you run away?" His mother kept asking, even after he had explained to her.

"I got lost." At first it had been all he could muster.

"Why didn't you wait for your ride?"

"I wanted to walk…and I got lost."

His mother seemed far more scared now than he had been in the cemetery. Gibby was standing behind where they sat on the sofa. Braden talked for a long time with the cop. He wanted to hug Gibby and Braden, too, but his mother wouldn't let him go. Gibby leaned over and put her cheek on the top of his mother's head. When he turned his face up it looked like his mother had two heads. When the cop left, Braden was the only one to talk.

Adult Paul retained the vision of his terrified mother, running to him, flapping arms, hair flying, legs kicking out down the sidewalk in a panic of relief. The vision authenticated it — she loved him more than she could ever love anyone else.

Claymore and Leah, their heads dipped, leaned over sea glass their fingers were sifting through. Broken flakes, chips and shards and slivers of sand-scraped pieces washed up after decades by the tides, cast off broken to be collected strangely and end up as something else. Creation by flotsam and jetsam. Amazing, thought Leah, who never imagined in her ignorance what was happening in the world of contemporary art. With the warm weather and strong sun, consolations like sea glass had taken Leah's life a notch up from bearable. Gritty nuggets which caught the light when she washed them cleaned up to faint tints of lovely coloration. She and Clay were designing glass bead neck pieces.

Each morning Claymore felt his heart pumping harder than it had the day before. What mattered to him seemed daily, by increments, to become refocused, what counted now had substance, was right. Instead of selling a Rolex, he preferred to instruct Leah in the intricacies of old-fashioned watch mechanisms. Sales mattered but less and less, and what had been essential sank away. Whether it all held together— what he'd been or what he was — became less significant than what he might have become. He didn't rail in some big dissatisfied way. He queried fate in simple anticipation about the future.

Claymore had become a metalsmith years earlier and was reacquiring his flair for the craft. When the phone in the shop rang, he was polishing and buffing a sterling silver and gold cuff bracelet. He grunted at Leah to pick up the call. She flinched as the caller identified himself as Edwin. At the same moment a customer walked in, snaked along the glass display cases, looking down, waiting for attendance. Leah lost Edwin's words as she stared at the man. A thatch of dark hair stood upright on top, the sides buzz-cut which emphasized the way his cranium drew in at the temples. His head was shaped like a peanut shell. He must have stood six foot four. With the nattering Edwin on the phone, Leah almost panicked. Could this man be another friend of Dorrie? Apparently not.

Claymore went up to the peanut guy and pulled out a drawer of men's rings. Leah focused on Edwin's voice.

"You still there?" Edwin had realized he was talking to the phone.

"Yes, yes, of course."

"I said I need to talk to you. Clay, is he in? You didn't answer."

"Sorry. He's with a customer right now. I'll have him call you back."

Edwin was flustered. "Are you listening? It's you I want to — hell — I'll stop by the store." The connection went dead.

Claymore came up to her as the customer filed out, raised his eyebrows.

"It was that Edwin, that friend of your niece. He's coming here to talk to me."

"If it's not one thing it's another," snorted the old man.

Near six o'clock Edwin barged into the jeweler's, eyes seeking out Leah. He pranced around the center display cases and to the computer where Claymore was entering the day's receipts. Claymore shifted his eyes to the young man in an off-putting frown.

"Hey, Claymore."

"We're closing up, Edwin."

Edwin chuckled. "I'm not a customer. Is your assistant around?"

Claymore gestured a wide circle as if conjuring Leah out of thin air.

"In the back. What you want with her?"

"Nothing much," said with a meant-to-be-noticed smirk.

"Leave her alone." He turned to the spreadsheet on the screen. "What's with Dorrie? I haven't seen her in a couple of days."

"Me neither. It's this new job she has, a temp at the Sun Times. They work different days, get switched around, some days four hours, sometimes they're on eight. I call her but it's hard to catch her. If she's on a night shift she gets testy if you get her and she's been sleepy. She's gonna quit."

From the back room Leah came out wrapped in a light cotton serape, earth-toned umber and yellow-orange. Claymore glanced at her, if Edwin thinks he's getting anything from her, he's more delusional than I think he is. Edwin grinned at Leah, like a capuchin monkey Clay had seen in Brazil. Made him like Edwin a little more.

"I'm about finished here, Leah. See you tomorrow."

She headed to the door, where Edwin caught up to her. "Hey, wait. I came to see you. It's about my birthmother. We've told you how I'm searching… It's very urgent. I've got to ask you something. Want to go get a cup of coffee?"

"I'm too tired." She saw his face, gray with despair. "How is it possible that I can help you? I don't know your mother." It was like asking a perfect stranger on the street where his mother might be.

Leah stood astonished at the door. He seemed to totter. "Hold up a minute. I got to tell you about me." He paused to take some air. "Afghanistan…you lost your son. Bad.

Horrid. You understand. I want my mother back. Real mother, I mean... I never had her. Except—"

Leah's anger burst, flooded her with adrenaline, as if in an out-of-body experience she had come from nowhere. "Lost? Lost my son? He's dead. You can't find your mother, but she's probably alive out there. There's a possibility even remote you'll see her. There's an enormous, insurmountable gap between what you face and what I have to endure."

In one fierce motion, she yanked open the heavy door and darted away. Edwin heard Claymore scuttle up to him, felt his upper arm grabbed. "What the hell you think you're doing, Edwin?" The heavy heartbeats were making him wheeze. How many times over the many decades of his life had he encountered casual cruelty? Too often for him to pass this time off as his over-sensitivity, or today's culture. He had never believed in the idea of good old days.

Outside in the street, the heat meliorated by the lowering sun and lake breezes, fresh air, not air-conditioned, Claymore double locked his jewelry store. Edwin was still there. He blurted out to the jeweler, "Shit, I come for some advice. I didn't expect that. She really lost it."

"Go away, Edwin. You've done enough damage for one night. Don't make me..."

"Huh? What'd I do? I just wanted to talk to her. What if she holds the key to where to look for my mother. By the fact that she's lost her son—"

"Shut up. And go home. I've had enough of your goddamn obsession. And don't come back. You're not welcome here anymore." The old man hustled across the street against the light. Edwin watched him slowing down the traffic flow. He was thinking that Claymore knew something about his assistant that might help him. Why else had he gotten so mad?

Dorrie sat slumped at her kitchen table, one hand supporting her head which hung over the warmed-up leftover lasagna. She had heard the doorbell ring but was ignoring it. Again it rang, and then again. She hadn't the guts to pretend she wasn't home. Her car was in the apartment parking space. Maybe if she did have the guts…but then what if it was Edwin; he might camp outside her door until morning. She dragged herself up and walked to the peephole. It was Edwin.

Edwin crossed into the living room and fell onto the wingback chair, stuck his legs out and groaned. "You're never going to believe it. Your friggin' uncle is never speaking to me again. What I went through. And it wasn't my fault."

"Clay?"

Sarcastic snicker, "Yeah, that uncle. He hates me."

She squeezed her eyes shut. Brushed back a few tangles of hair. Unstuck her eye-lids and plunked on the sofa. "Well what did you do? Please no elaborations or circumlocutions, just what happened." There'd been a lot of words floating around the newspaper desks.

For a minute Edwin sat breathing hard, saying nothing. Building suspense; everything he did seemed calculated.

"What did you say to set him off?" She must get him to the point if that were humanly possible. Without obfuscation. She smiled inwardly at another word. If only Edwin knew words. He loses himself in concealing meaning, which is the opposite of the reason for words.

"No, nothing. I swear. I didn't say anything to him. I was talking to that clerk of his, Leah. And he lost it. Went ballistic, kicked me out of the store, like for good."

Edwin had insulted her so badly, the silent woman he'd barely met? To an ordinary stranger his mannerism would be off-putting, but not upsetting. His lies were benign, okay neurotic, foolish, but not malicious.

Dorrie gave an intuitive quiver. "You know her son got killed a few months ago…in Afghanistan."

"Once Claymore had told me that…he'd found her on a bad day like weeping…and she explained to him." Dorrie worried he would start making up a scenario about the soldier's violent demise.

"Clay's become sort of protective of her—"

"But I hardly said at all, nothing really."

"You said nothing about her dead son, right?" Ominous silence.

"No. I mentioned the bond between her and me. How she lost her son and I lost my mother. You know, Dorrie, I think there's a clue she might have because we've got this same suffering."

Appalled, all she managed was "A clue? To what?"

"I got this feeling Leah could help me reunite with my mother, my birthmother. Come on, Dorrie, what else would I be after?" He pulled his legs in and straightened up in the chair, its wing sides looking like they were sprouting from his back. Edwin's face when he was fabricating a falsehood took on an angelic air. "That woman could hold the answer to who my birthmother is."

"My God, Edwin!" He finally had stunned her to outburst. "I am telling you this much, Leah has no, none, nada knowledge, not any connection to you or to your birthmother. Nothing."

"How would you know? You lost contact with her for years and years. You say you don't even know if she's still living."

"I never said that."

"But I have clues, and hints and...and a lot of true suspicions, indications like movie scenes I could describe to you. She's out there waiting for me to find her. Maybe years ago she met up with that Leah woman and now that her son's dead, she'll tell me because there's this bond—"

"Stop it, Edwin, stop it."

His voice took on a distilled anger, "And she'll help me because she knows how I feel."

"None of that—"

"She told my mother to reclaim me before it's too late. I might die like her son did. And my mother would be so sorry." He sucked in his breath, almost lost his train of illogic. "I think my birthmother has secretly kept track of me and the link here is Leah. I've got to get her to admit it to me. She's on my side, don't you see? Because of her son." He stopped, had run down.

"Right now, Edwin, I would tell you who your mother is and end all this crazy stuff. If only I could... I was set up and used by a desperate young woman into taking this damned vow of silence that I have to keep. No matter how much I hate to and resent it, I can't help you." She closed her eyes, her pounding headache making them water. "My relief would be tremendous if I could... But this clerk of my uncle's, you're barking up the wrong tree."

"How can you be so sure?" That gap of years when

anything could have happened. A more rational Edwin suspected Dorrie of holding some vital piece from him that he might trick her into revealing.

"I am sure. But, Edwin, what you're doing is like picking some woman at random walking down Michigan Boulevard and deciding randomly for no reason that she's your mother or knows who your mother is."

He tossed his head as if her explanations were ever nothing more than pandering. Rocked back into the chair against his salmon-colored angel wings, crushing them. "You don't get it, Dorrie. You don't get it at all."

Dorrie whisked herself up and coaxed him to the door. "You gotta leave now. I have to go to work in the morning."

Edwin disappeared into the darkening moonlight, sure that he would soon make a discovery that would reveal his mother to him.

With summer about to blow the hot winds across Chicago, school was out and there was a question of who would take care of Paulie while Janey and Braden were at work. In Canada, Janey's mother had taken charge of him which had been great. But the older woman hated to leave her garden and her friends, activities, her own home for a few months, not even to be with her beloved grandson. So early in June before the vacation started, Braden quit his new job. He had hated it and was relieved to have found a reason to chuck it and arrange to take back his computer business. Work at the corporate level appalled him. So he'd never be rich. He didn't want to be and that was lucky because, he said, he wasn't smart enough to be. He found a shop for rent near enough to their house so that he could watch Paulie. In the event, the boy went to day camp, took summer courses for kids at the Field, and rarely spend a full day with Braden. Even adult Paul felt a residue of how as a boy he struggled with Braden being in their life. His discomfort at the intimacy of having him hanging around strained some boundaries. Braden and his mother kept him out of things, but then Paulie began to see that he and his mother were set apart from Braden. So things had worked out in the end to little lingering effect.

With Gibby, when she didn't come around for a while, the boy felt a sense of loss of which adult Paul had no mental record. Gibby had become so a part of him that she seemed irreplaceable. And therefore never in his life was she totally gone. If he was forced to learn there was no magic in the world, she gave him the key to see that there was something greater. To stretch himself into the mysteries of nature, the universe, the human predicament, his wonder as a child enriched his life forever. His memories of childhood, colored by nostalgia and the softening of time, were not, of course, all happy. But the traumas he suffered as a kid never left him stunted. They annealed his spirit.

Adult Paul could summon up Gibby sitting in a diner as they did years ago, dipping French fries in little paper cups of ketchup, trying not to get their greasy fingers on her photos of globular clusters and the astounding cauldron of Mercury's molten surface. He had asked her how the planets formed, whether Earth had been created in the same way. She would give him theories instead of facts. It always made him smile if he thought of Gibby, freckled upturned nose, eyes with shards of glittering green crystals, often she hid a solemn, lurking smile. His mother, always in the shadows of these memories, as a subtle reality, part of Gibby as Gibby was of Janey. No man wants to marry his mother. It's this illusive variable star he seeks.

Little boy Paulie groused at Gibby in fall when she picked him up at school. He hadn't seen her in two whole weeks. With a little boy's candor he whined about the new marriages and vindictively proclaimed that his mother and Braden fit together better than she and Ben did. Gibby didn't rise to the bait.

Paulie pressed on. "He doesn't like me, Ben doesn't. He doesn't like any of us."

"Oh, Paulie, sure he does. He's new here and a bit shy."

"He hollered at Rex."

"What was Rex doing to provoke him?"

"Rex didn't poke him."

"That's a kind of pun, sweetie, good for you.... Know what a pun is?"

He hurried on, eyes down. "There's this kid at school, his mom got married three times to three husbands…"

"That's not going to happen to you—"

"I don't care if it does."

"Listen, you and your mom and Braden are one family. I promise you, that's the way it will stay." Not theory at all, but fact. He lifted his head caught by the unaccustomed certainty of her phrase. Its sound eased the stomach ache he had felt coming on.

"My dad…"

"That was a different thing. So, here are Ben and me in our condo, and not too far away you guys in your house. Sticking together."

"Forever?"

"Nothing's forever, sweet boy, but for a long time." Not even the universe is forever, the boy knew that. He began to laugh.

"You're a hoot, Gibby." Hoot was a favorite word of Braden.

There's a seamlessness to life that can be disconcerting. Without knowing how it began, Simon was insinuating himself back into Braden's life. When Janey recognized the signs, she needed help to contend with the consequences, so she turned to Gibby, even though Janey thought Gibby knew little about personal relations and less about complications of the heart. To Janey, Gibby was very smart, but hopeless about human motivations. Her friend was naive. Janey didn't, however, hesitate to confide in this brainy type, knowing she'd get honesty. People don't offer honest answers as a matter of course. By honest Janey meant what went on in a person's mind. As a therapist she knew it was difficult to extract truth out of a client. With Gibby she would at least get an honest answer and that's all she wanted.

"At first Simon would call Braden and talk a few

minutes." Janey said. "Then Braden told me Simon had been texting him off and on. I shouldn't have a problem with that. But he's trying to wheedle Braden into something."

"Sure, resuming the friendship they've had since kindergarten."

"So, I should say nothing. Let it resume."

"Why not? Observe what's going on. Is Simon still following you around?"

"Well, no, but clinically…"

"Yes, I understand. But if we view this not clinically, but empirically… What does Simon say when he talks to Braden?"

"Not much. He brags to Braden about his new girlfriend. Wants Braden to go for a drink with them and meet her. I know, don't look at me like that. I think Simon has some idea about spreading discord."

Like on the oval of a racetrack their words flew round and round.

Gibby folded her arms, lifted her crossed hands beneath her chin. "It's so easy to see folly and evil these days." She felt puzzled; there was a wrong sense about it.

"Gibby? What are you thinking?"

"Why worry about Simon when you don't have to?"

"You're saying Simon's not a problem?

"I don't know what I'm saying." But Janey had snatched at that, it would be greedy to deny Simon his buddy. It would be wicked.

"You do know, Gibby — ungenerous. That does help me see—"

"I'm so glad...I could help. Using the scientific method." It was at moments like this that what is said is what is meant.

Braden held a grudge. He wasn't about to renew a soured friendship for the sake of old times. He had made no attempt to return Simon's calls or answer his texts. He figured Simon would get the hint. Simon got the wrong hint. He accosted Janey on her leaving her office after work.

"Wait, hey." He darted across the street in the middle of streaming traffic, horns blared. He caught her in the parking lot and slammed his fist on her car's hood.

"Give me a minute, Janey. Can't you spare five minutes?"

"Get away from me, Simon." She glared at him. "We settled it. We're not going to talk or see each other."

He grinned. He wanted to sting her, he needed to win. "I don't give a shit about you. But you got Braden on strings like a puppet. He can't have a life of his own. He won't pick up my calls and it's because you won't let him. You're jealous so you can't let Braden hang out with any of his buddies. You've…you, you're a controlling bitch."

"You better get a grip on yourself." A quickened volt of anger at the sound of her own voice. "Braden does what he wants. If you two are on the outs, take it up with him. Leave me the fuck out of it." She clicked the lock and opened the car door. "You better not have put a dent in my hood." The engine surged. He jumped aside as she drove off. If he'd had a gun he would have shot her.

⁂

Benjamin Ferrar made himself uncomfortable at times thinking how his new wife could turn an argument inside out. Ben sang in a rich baritone. He had auditioned to be a cantor at Beth Hillel Temple. When he believed another person had been chosen over him, Martha had commiserated. When it turned out he was selected, she was thrilled. In both instances, he couldn't find a difference in her attitude toward him. It bugged him that she could seem so disinterested. She didn't seem to get his point. So, his anxiety on his first Sabbath stemmed from his need to impress on Martha how he wanted her to notice his significance.

Many years later, adult Paul comforted his frail mother at Gibby's funeral, watched Ben, in an old man slouch, his head floating in his spotted hands, weeping and mumbling in Hebrew, and he remembered Claymore Mandebrote. Surprised, he felt himself mourning for Art Kane, the illusive, disappearing father. Braden was buried only a few years ago, grief for him surged like new. But Gibby, a wholly different loss, an unexplainable breach. The hot and muggy summer that his mother married Braden, he had been left for a few days with Gibby. She had taken him to hear Ben sing as The Cantor which had conjured up a white horse prancing. More vague was the memory of Gibby holding his hand, but this part he was unsure of because she rarely did. Ben in a colorful silky scarf, his dark curls quivering, sang, *Eilu D'varim*. These are all the things we do that have no measured worth…

THIRTEEN

EDWIN angled around a corner and slid behind a double-parked delivery truck being unloaded at Odd Fellows Convenience Store on the lip of Claymore Mandebrote's business. Down the road stood St. Michael's Episcopal Church, its carillon bells tolling twelve round clear tones. Mrs. Campion was about to leave for lunch, and Edwin had planned to join her at the little cafe where he had a few times ambushed Claymore. Unaware she was about to be disturbed, Leah took her usual small table and comfortably pulled a novel out of her purse. She didn't look at the menu since she had decided earlier what she would eat. Her appetite had awoken, found not dead but only hibernating. Edwin followed the waitress who brought Leah's coffee. He plunked on a chair opposite her. Silent, she focused her eyes on the interloper.

"Hey, Mrs. Campion. Here on your lunch break? Me too. I've been helping a friend out in his bodega, stocking groceries. Not far from here. Just temporary, y'know."

Leah concentrated on the sound of a pretty black woman on a cell phone in a nearby booth, "Mom?… Mom?…" Laughter. "Mom?… You need to start learning to turn that TV down." Laughter.

"I saw you coming in. I thought why not join you? Claymore likes it here. I come in with him sometimes." She began to drink her coffee, not averting her head. "We should get to know each other better." He didn't care if she wouldn't speak. "Like, I'm writing my memoirs. Plenty of awful things in my childhood to fascinate readers. I can tell them what it's like, dysfunctional family life, abuse… and the redemption part, when my biological mother and I are reunited. Now that part's what you can help me with.

The waitress came to take her order. Edwin grabbed the menu and pretended to peruse it.

Ignoring the waitress who stood pencil poised, blank look on her face, Leah said, "I like to read while I eat my lunch."

"But not today, huh?" It was obvious he wasn't going to leave.

"Goodbye, Edwin." She pulled out money to pay for the coffee and fast-walked out of the place. After her came Edwin at a clip. He hounded her to the door of the jewelry shop, streaming talk at her, until she escaped inside. He knew better than to follow her in. Claymore's recent outburst had scared him off.

Braden whisked past the kids playing on the porch and banged into the house, his news practically choking him. Lowering the newspaper Janey winked at him.

"Yo, Braden, hey man, you look about to pop."

"They arrested Simon Butler." He sat next to her on the couch.

"Whatever for? It can't be."

"I'm flabbergasted. He was out with the old group and some guy tried to put the make on Simo's new girlfriend. Tommy was there, a reliable witness. Some of the other guys thought it was funny and exaggerated it. Archie for instance. He played it up for effect." Braden tried not to grin.

"So, what did Tommy tell you happened?"

"They were all fooling around at a sports bar. Dozen televisions showing every sport in the world, big racket, you know. So, some guy Simo thinks is messing with his date, and he starts pushing and shoving him. The guy takes offense and clobbers Simo. Then Simo goes nuts and jumps the guy. A few people pull him off but not before he's already bitten the guy badly, ripped open his cheek and took a chunk outta his nose."

"I can't believe it. This is what comes from stalking."

"Biting. That's what's crazy."

"Thank God there weren't any guns."

"No. This isn't the kind of place people go with guns."

"Oh, sure."

"No knives either."

Braden felt bad; she took his hand. He was mystified by Simon biting. "Listen, it'll be okay. This kind of thing isn't unknown in my business. The thing is if Simon loses his job because of it."

"I called down to the dealership. The owner went to bail Simo out." He snuggled up to her and nuzzled her neck. "Think it's my fault?"

This was a serious question, not to be blown off. "No. Simon seems to have developed an anger management problem. And, before you even think it, I'm not to blame, either."

He aped seriousness. "Yes, I was about to accuse you."

"I wonder what his new girlfriend thought."

"Uh huh, when they carted him off with someone's blood in his mouth. What would you have done, Janey, if

I had gone off like that?"

"I know an excellent anger management shrink."

While Janey served dinner, Braden stepped outside to call Paulie in. Paulie seemed glum, staring down the empty street.

"Come in for dinner, Kiddo."

"Braden, just now Rex hurt Liddy's feelings. He hollered at her to go home and wash her mouth out with soap. He made her cry."

"That's rude." He could smell the roast chicken through the screen door.

"Why would he tell her that?"

"Did Lydia use a swear word or something?"

"Of course not. Liddy went like 'I can't find the ball, you guys. Jesus H. Christ where is it?'"

"Yes, that would do it. Paulie, to religious people like Rex's family what Lydia said is taking God's name in vain."

"No, she only said Jesus' name."

"In vain."

"I don't know what that means."

Braden thought maybe they should not have turned their noses up at Bible School when Rex asked Paulie to go. "In vain...this expression Lydia used...sounds insulting to the name of Jesus."

"Names are important," said Paulie.

"Yes, they are."

"What's the 'H' stand for, Braden, Jesus' middle name?"

"Let's go eat. Dinner smells really good."

The boy followed him into the house. He heard Paulie mumbling, "Heaven, maybe his middle name is Heaven."

Claymore was putting costume jewelry under the glass of the center floor display counter. He was pleased with the look of the ormolu pieces. Some of the glittering jewelry had woven a colored mosaic into the bright sunshine. He held up a bangle to Leah when she came in. "Ormolu, come see it. It's well-fabricated." She took up the imitation gold-leaf bracelet. "I finally got that order you had to call in twice." He seemed cheery and lighthearted this morning. Better not to bother him about her lunch time run-in with Edwin. But anger got the better of her good resolve.

"That Edwin, Dorrie's friend—"

"Don't worry about him. I told him not to come around here again. He's a pest."

"He found me at the cafe yesterday when I went to lunch. You'd gone to Shiller's when I got back."

"He has no right to go following you places. I'm going to talk to my niece. Not that she has any influence over him. He's a nut case."

"Maybe. But I don't think he means any harm."

"I'm going right now to call Dorrie. That may be, but harmless isn't always harmless."

Dorrie stormed off to Edwin's rooming house and pounded on his door. Under her breath she whispered, "The little bastard better be home." When Edwin opened the door she howled, "So you've finally taken leave of your senses."

"Looks like you've totally lost it, Dorrie." She followed him in. He kept his small room and its connected bathroom clean but messy. He had a silly smile on his face which made her bellow.

"I told you to stay away from my uncle's clerk. I told you there wasn't one speck of evidence that that poor woman knows anything about your mother."

"I'll run out and get us some coffees. Sit down. Only take a minute." She plumped down on his rattan sofa.

"I don't want coffee, Edwin."

He settled his thin shanks into a wooden rocker. It squeaked when he leaned back; he steadied it, knowing its creaking would annoy the already angry Dorrie. Let her have her say, then he'll sort it all out after she vents. He never had a doubt he could settle whatever upset her. Since it never bothered him to use deceit, he wasn't tied down to any annoying line of thought.

Dorrie disliked having to accuse him, to be going over the same drivel, to belabor the obvious. She held back a genuine sob.

"If you keep bothering Leah, you will get yourself into trouble. I mean what I say, Edwin. You'll get hounded by the cops—"

"Oh, yeah, for what? Jaywalking?" This last threat was way off, to Edwin's mind, beneath contempt. He admired the police and prided himself on being law-abiding. He'd never even gotten a traffic ticket. He hadn't really lost his license. Only quit the job driving the flower truck because he hated it.

"Okay, okay. Tell me. What's the real reason you've chosen Leah to pester?" Let him tire himself out making up convoluted reasons. Then she'd try to divert this latest mania down a different brain pathway.

"She's very nice. I like her. She's very sad."

"That's not an answer."

"She's mourning her son, name of Jonathan, and I am mourning the untimely loss of my real mother."

"So? So what? Millions of mothers all over the world

are suffering the losses of their sons. Why choose this one? Why Leah?" An image flitted, the marble Pietà, the fluid form of her shrouded son, the Virgin with harrowed face.

"It's, you see, Leah Campion that tipped me off so I know where to look next. The story of my birth and why my mother…left me. The lead to my mother is somewhere hidden in the Convent. The Benedictine Sisters up by Rogers Park. I think Leah got a vision and I sensed it, like she'd relayed it without words. No matter if she doesn't even know she did it. Claymore's clerk somehow managed to transmit this info. I take it from there."

Dorrie got up and nudged herself toward he door. What he said assured her he was ready to go off in a different direction. That was enough for now. Edwin followed her into the hall, but he felt queasy. Dorrie seemed to be drifting away from him.

"No more messing around at my uncle's jewelry store," Dorrie said, thinking, now he's going to be bothering the nuns.

∽

Janey called Simon from her office, a professional rather than personal call. If she spoke to him she might determine how bad off he was, mentally. When later

Gibby asked her why she felt obliged to call Simon, Janey tried in a self-deprecating way to blame it on the fact that she had slept with him. She did not take having had sex lightly. There remained a responsibility after intimacy. That belief, or ethic, had kept her from having had very many sexual encounters, and none taken thoughtlessly. Gibby had said, "Not me. I've gone to bed with only a couple of guys, and I'd rather not ever see them again." Neither woman realized they were actually alike on that point after all.

"Simon? It's Janey. I'm calling because I'm a little concerned about you." She knew he was listening although he hadn't said a word.

The call vindicated him, in a way; he compromised by answering her civilly.

"Yes. I have to go to court, but my lawyer says it'll be a fine and a warning. Maybe community service, some kind of anger class."

"That's good… I mean, the courts have lots of leeway for first time offenders…"

"You think I should've gotten more?"

"No. No. How are you feeling?"

"Bit bruised and battered." He joked.

"I mean, have you thought about what started the fight?"

"Quit analyzing, Janey. I'm not going to go out and do

it again. I feel lousy."

"Well, Braden—"

"Yeah?"

"We wondered if you'd stop by tonight for pizza. Braden will bring it home. He knows all the stuff you like on it."

Like a kick in the stomach, he caught his breath…then told her he'd be there. A surge of triumph. He might have won that fight. Braden was his buddy and it was getting easier to pretend Janey wasn't around.

Braden wasn't happy when Janey told him the dinner plans. He hadn't gotten over the way Simon had humiliated himself by biting a man. No harm done, though, he began to believe. Better that things between them get back to normal. And anyway, Simon had done some stupid things when they were kids, too. He was probably built that way.

After pizza, Braden helped Paulie set up his telescope, a cloudless evening, the moon full, and craters, shadows, mares and canals visible. And alongside the moon a little below it, bright pinpoint of Jupiter. Simon wandered out, coffee mug in hand, trying to be knowing about the night sky. His blurts about astronomy were clumsy attempts which made the boy uneasy. They scanned the sky where over the lake it was dark enough to see Jupiter. Paulie had sensed the tension when the interloper first showed up, but by the end of dinner, Braden and Simon had slipped back into their old ways and were joking around and telling stories as usual. They acted like brothers who had had a big fight but had never been estranged.

After Paulie went to bed, sitting in the living room while Braden and Simon sipped beers, Janey said, "I suppose you're surprised why I asked you here, Simon." Both men stared at her.

"We hadn't exactly parted friends." Simon thought he had put that well. Braden switched his glare to him. Many times he had heard that swagger tone from his old friend when Simon tried to squiggle out of a bad place.

"I think it's important I say this to the both of you."

Simon half-smiled. "Sounds too friggin' serious."

"Artie Kane loved nothing so much as going as fast as he could. In a car. He died slamming on his brakes for a dog in the road." She shaded her eyes with cupped hands. Simon felt an itch of anger at the one whose existence started his misery. Janey's damp hair clung to her forehead when she dropped her hands. It became clearer to her how she would continue.

"I worried how Art's death affected Paulie. But I never gave a thought to me. Art and I together survived the biggest thrill of all, tempting death. For hours trapped in a car hanging like a ruined ornament on crippled trees rooted to a sheer cliff. The car swayed and we saw our death coming over and over. Artie prayed; I didn't. I remember asking my mother to come and save me. We clung to each other speechless. Sometimes I didn't breathe for minutes at a time. But we survived." Her voice had hardened. Braden took her hand, began stroking it. Simon, eyes lowered, watched drops of beer dribble down his mug.

"Art shouldn't have died." Janey said. "It shouldn't have happened."

Simon looked up, seemed stunned, frozen there, voice icy. "You invite me here to tell me about your dead husband — first husband?"

"Simon, if I had told you about Artie right when we met, I'd have had to tell you about why I divorced him. You see…the terror, the risk, the waiting for death, not just fearing it, stuck in the place where I was dead already but still living, waiting to die. I couldn't handle it. But Artie did die. He shouldn't have but he did. Such a stupid way for him to die. And so saying anything doesn't matter anymore. I can talk and I want to tell you both. I can admit it was unfair not to tell you about Artie. Not unfair to you, but to him. I was married once to Art Kane and it counted. "

Simon's body seemed to break up in waves as he moved to get himself out of the house. He looked over his shoulder and saw Braden stroking Janey's hair.

"You two deserve each other." He spat out his parting words.

Paul as an adult had a distinct memory of the first time he saw the banded planet Jupiter with his new bigger six-inch reflector telescope. Its Galilean moons four tiny specks of light. He had danced around jubilant. His mother and Braden had come out so he could show them Jupiter's satellites. They had been jubilant, too.

Later, Simon drove past Claymore's house and saw him sitting in a wicker chair on his stoop, porchlight on and gazing at the dark. Simon climbed out of his car and sat on the cement step.

"You looking at the moon?"

"Simo, what the hell you doing here?"

"I was at Janey's place. Her goofy son looks at the stars."

"He's a smart boy. What were you doing there?"

"Nothing. Clay, I think I haven't been myself ever since I got mixed-up with that ditsy woman. What do you think?"

"Listen, Simon, I don't give advice. Don't expect me to say anything. Go ahead and crab as much as you like, but you're not going to hear squat from me. Don't take it personal. I never kibitzed."

"She had me over to their house to tell me off. In front of Braden. That is low."

"I designed their wedding rings. Matching." He drew pleasure from how he'd accomplished it. Two engraved gold circles.

"Big fucking deal."

"Exactly why I don't waste my words telling people what I'm thinking."

Simon wasn't listening. He was coming back to himself in the light-shifted realities that had changed from red to blue. "Janey wasn't ever the one for me," he said.

Whenever Simon was forced to admit that he had once been arrested for assault, he told himself that it was because of a shoving match on the number seven train to Wrigley Field. The entire year and a half of his involvement with Janey condensed to a memory of an unlucky affair. His unhinged actions dissipated into floating particles of memory. He never had to remind himself of what a jerk he had been again.

Skimming through the *Tribune* before work, Janey's eyes lit on Edwin Blake's name under a picture taken at a convent. She grabbed the phone and caught Dorrie on the run.

"Dorrie, did you see today's *Trib*? Front page of section two."

"Didn't look at it yet. I'm going to be late." The phone jiggled between her chin and collarbone. It sounded as if she was eating something.

"Look now."

"What's so important in the paper?" She caught the phone as it slipped down her neck and managed to open the door.

"There's a picture of Edwin with a group of nuns."

"What?"

"Can you hear me, you're cutting out."

"Yes, yes, good lord, what did the monkey turd do now?"

"Saved a sister from choking. On a piece of meat stuck in her throat."

"That is astounding. Edwin. Was it a Benedictine nun?"

"I think so, I'd have to look again."

"Chicken?"

"It doesn't say what kind of meat. Honestly, Dorrie." Started to giggle.

"He was going there… I suppose they must have invited him to stay for dinner."

"Then you think she would have choked on one of his lies."

"Oh, Janey." A giggle from Dorrie now. "Swallowed his lies easily enough then choked on a piece of food."

"He's got all the publicity he could want. The article recounts the whole story of his search for his birthmother. The entire concocted scenario of his birth as he fabricates it."

"Am I mentioned in it?"

"Of course you are—"

"Oh, my God—"

"First you're the false lead, next the phony plant, then the blameless dupe, always though the loyal friend."

"Oh. My. God."

"But you're not mentioned by name."

"Thank you, Lord. Really. He holds back my name? Oh, Lordy. Where did he find the discretion…" She thought, saddened. "Putting a name to me would have ruined his fantasy."

FOURTEEN

PHONE calls today made Dorrie nervous. Claymore had suffered another heart episode and had been taken to the hospital to undergo a procedure. The hospital, when she ran over there, explained that he was being given tests and she should come back another time. Later a hospital call informed her that he would be released early the next morning. She stopped by the jewelry store where Leah said he had made arrangements with a valet service to bring him home. "Independent old cuss," thought Dorrie. She said nothing to Leah.

Dorrie visited her elderly uncle the day he was released. Comfortable at his home Claymore wanted to give her the doctor's prognosis. She had a brother, Roger, working on an oil rig in Houston whom she hadn't heard from in years. For a while she'd tried to keep in touch with him.

He didn't seem interested in holding up his part. This elderly uncle was her closest living relative. Sitting there drinking red wine with him, she glimpsed what her life would be without him, and felt lousy.

"No one at the hospital would tell me much. They're on a privacy kick."

He made a face. "I would've had them call you right away, but when I went in the ambulance I knew I was probably going to be all right."

"That's nice," said Dorrie, "I'll get alerted when you think you're going to die."

"What the cardiologist doctor told me you ought to know." He leaned back into his soft leather chair and sighed. "What's happening, Dorothea, is I'm suffering from congestive heart failure." He pronounced each word as if it were a death sentence which she supposed it was.

"But there's a treatment for it?"

"Oh, yes, I have pills. Several kinds of pills as a matter of fact. Added to my digitalis. Do you know Ginger, the dog next door takes digitalis, too? The dog and I take the same pills."

"Well, see there, the doctors have drugs. You'll be fine." She drained her wine glass, plunked it down.

He knew Dorrie would be the one who buried him, got someone to sing Kaddish and give a damn that he was gone. Wicked to think that at his end most of his mourners would have gone before him.

"You'll be all right as long as you take your pills. Everyone I know takes scads of meds. Keeps them going." She herself didn't take any pills although she sometimes reasoned she probably would be, if she went to a doctor. Which she didn't. She left him when he began to doze, saying she'd check on him at his shop since he insisted on going to work. Her annoying temp job was over.

Claymore ran his shirt sleeve over his perspiring brow, coughed while he explained to a persistent young woman whose bangles and heavy rings clanged on the glass showcase. "Pearls, Mrs. Tottenfelt, are weighed in facets, just like diamonds are." His face had turned gray, Leah thought as she walked from behind the computer when she heard his coughing. She'd been trying to get him to rest in the back for an hour.

"Sounds funny to me. Is that why the necklace costs—"

"No, no. Nothing at all to do with comparative price." The woman lost interest and unenlightened wandered out of the store.

Leah suggested he go home for lunch and sleep awhile before coming back to the shop. There had been few customers this morning. He didn't argue, left out the rear entrance into the alleyway.

In the event, Claymore didn't return all afternoon, only showing up at closing time, still drowsy. He asked if there'd been a hoard of customers while he was home sleeping.

Leah, leaning over the day's receipts at the cash register, said, "Browsers mostly. And not exactly a hoard of them." They looked up at the buzzer to see the latecomer — Janey Leduc with what seemed like a swarm of kids on her tail.

Leah saw Leduc's son, the one who had asked for the butterfly pin, another small boy, and a little girl. The kids broke for the glass cases which Leah had minutes before wiped clean of smudges. But Janey called them over, warned them not to touch anything. They trailed back to her, suddenly appearing shy. Leah stopped herself from saying the shop was about to close. Claymore never minded the stragglers who came at the end of the day.

"I'd like my wedding ring made smaller. It was a tad loose when we bought it. In the cooler weather now, I'm afraid it'll slip off."

Clay became more animated. "Sure, Janey, I can resize that for you. Let me get the ring measure." He bounced away smiling. Leah paused a few feet away while the kids bumped each other and giggled at nothing.

Janey said, "About to close, huh? Sorry to hold you up. I've been trying to get here to have this done for weeks."

Leah kept one eye on the rambunctious children. Back came Claymore, measured Janey's finger and placed her ring in a velvet bag. He began writing out a receipt. "I can have that for you by late Monday afternoon." Janey nodded acquiescence.

In an awkward moment of silence, Paulie had stopped fooling around and stood staring up at Leah.

Leah was caught in a moment of remorse. "You're the boy who wanted to buy the butterfly cloisonné pin for your mom. I'm sorry I didn't hold it for you. It was my mistake." She smiled tentatively at Janey. "I hope you weren't too disappointed." Remorse dissipated, the taste of humiliation drained down her throat.

Paulie balled his hands into fists, both angry and ashamed. "It's okay," he mumbled. Both Lydia and Rex were looking up at Leah, mouths opened. Paulie's gaze fixed on the ground.

Janey frowned. She'd seen Leah many times but not paid her much attention. She knew the episode of Edwin accosting the woman. Janey spoke up now from that spark of intuition which had made her an invaluable therapist. "Hey, we're meeting Braden and my friend Gibby at Fat Freddy's Diner for hamburgers, why don't you both come along? We'll make it a party."

Ever excitable the three kids cheered. Rex shouted, "Braden calls Freddy 'the fattest of men!'" They hooted uncontrollably. Claymore turned one palm up signaling how can they turn such an invitation down.

At a big round table in the diner, Braden entertained and supervised the three children while the others chatted. When the kids began to squabble, Braden offered to take them home. Claymore left with them. He found Braden to be amiable and restful.

For a few minutes while the waitress refilled their coffee cups, the three women sat a little puzzled what to say next. Janey was trying not to guide the talk and Gibby was hoping her disconnected observations weren't putting Leah off. Leah contented herself with answering the others' questions. Little by little the talk opened up.

"Paulie," said Gibby who had taken him recently to a science program at the Montessori school in Evanston, "is the most discriminating little runt, I mean, first, he observes differences. And that leads to discoveries when he recognizes analogies. It's amazing in a child his age… I think…" She watched Janey for confirmation.

"You make too much of him. I know he's smart, but Lordy, Gibby, he's not a genius or anything."

"I didn't say he was. No. No, he's not. But he has an interesting mind."

"You admire that because you didn't change his diapers when he was a baby."

"You're purposely goading me, too aggravating."

Something roiled in Leah, a left-out, rejected-by-God, horror. As they stopped ragging each other, in a moment's lull, Leah reached the critical mass, and like an infinitesimal neutron bomb, she exploded. "Pretend all you want. That ordinary life is…normal. I saw your son standing there with the cloisonné pin, and he was like my Jonny, same way he'd be glued to something when he was small. All the talk and praying and good causes and patriotism, it's a rotten game that goes on forever. It will go on forever. It's like everybody, people god the devil all want it to go on forever, with all the rest of the miserableness in the world. Nobody cares because they can't care. It gets wasted who we are…and it's all a waste." Her dry tears had wetted into puddles under her eyelids. She put her hands to her eyes and sobbed quietly.

Gibby took Leah's arm and Janey led them stumbling out of the restaurant. In Janey's car, they mourned together. It wasn't for them to console her. Both women knew Leah would hate it. Instead they let her weep and rage at God. Until without a word spoken, Leah straightened up, regained her strength. Later at her home she began to accept her void, the nothingness. She had cried at last in front of strangers. She knew Jonathan was dead. She would never see his face again on this earth. She crawled on top of her bed and sank into a forgiving sleep.

Before she got out of Janey's car, Gibby whispered, "Poor woman thinks it's all for nothing. It isn't, look what's in the clear black sky, look at it." Janey kissed her gently and let her go, not saying a word.

At home Janey told Braden about Leah's meltdown, admitting she hadn't acted at all like a therapist. Braden's concern reflected the pragmatist he often portrayed himself to be.

"Where do you think we go, when we die?" He had felt very sorry for Leah.

"Nobody knows. Least of all me."

"Somewhere," said Braden, "or nowhere."

When Janey returned on Monday to retrieve her resized wedding ring, Claymore Mandebrote was alone. She slipped the ring on her finger, then flinched as a figure came up behind her. Edwin. He widened his eyes on purpose when he saw her, in the best tradition of overacting.

"Hey, Doctor Leduc, what's happening?" Donned his cocky persona since his exploit was in the newspaper so he didn't need to lie. He would embellish it, though, Janey assumed. He might think made-up heroics generated more esteem.

"I read about how your quick actions saved the Sister's life. Good for you, Edwin. That's commendable." Sounded awkward to herself, but the words were sincere. They wouldn't sound heartfelt, but she meant them.

"The nuns could not find ways enough to thank me. So they've decided to induct me into their order as a Holy Brother." There it is, she smiled, the preferred whooper to a wholesome truth. She broke away, needed to make a quick return. "Wait, wait a minute." He set a pick with Claymore's frail body and cut her off as she headed toward the door. "I was telling Claymore here, and I want to tell you, too. You along with everybody else had no faith I would find my birthmother. In fact, you stopped hunting right away and never gave the search a real shot."

She turned on him. "That's not true, Edwin. I worked for months on your case. How do you think we found Dorrie? She didn't just drop out of the sky. And she solved part of the mystery of your birth, and she claims to know who your mother is. It isn't my fault she won't tell anyone.

"Dorrie," he chuffed. "She doesn't know anything. That song and dance she gives about a sacred promise to someone she would never betray. Big fat nothing. Her name on my birth certificate…she offered to take a DNA test. And I had her do it. But she always stood in my way. The same like you did. I had to go find my birthmother by myself."

"Yeah, that's good, Edwin. Let's go. C'mon…" Claymore seemed bothered by them, was tipsy, as if he needed to sit down in the quiet.

"My niece, leave her out of this. You better get wise. That birthmother doesn't want to be found. She believed you'd be better off without her."

Edwin's red-streaked face distorted. "Shut up, you old bastard."

Claymore flinched. In Edwin's mind Claymore had set off shrill alarms. Danger, if his birthmother had assumed he would find a better life without her. He most definitely hadn't. If he believed what Clay implied, he must blame his birthmother for his miserable childhood, his unhappy life. Intolerable thought, never to reach the surface of consciousness. And it never did arise as he wiped the last few minutes from his consciousness. He did it by the clever expediency of not absorbing Clay's words. Intolerable, also inconceivable. In momentary terror at Clay's words, Edwin simply did what he had done most of his life, adjusted, refined, did over, worked in a way to satisfy his desires.

Edwin left the store with Janey; he complained all the way to her car how mean of Claymore to insist that Edwin's mother had died at his birth. When he left she sat thinking before she started her car. Hornswoggled was the word she wanted, "I'll be hornswoggled" like the old-time cowboys who probably saw life a lot clearer than she ever had.

At the time he saved the Benedictine sister from choking, Edwin had been eating dinner at the convent with the nuns as a result of his visit to the Prioress. He had charmed her with a story about how he believed his birthmother might have come to St. Benedictine's for sanctuary. After she gave birth to Edwin she meant to recuperate before she went to reclaim him. But when she left to go retrieve her son, the social services people had already had him adopted by the Blakes. The kindly and curious Prioress had promised to investigate, but she assured him that St. Benedictine Convent had never had such a person. However, she did invite him to break bread with the monastic community and to worship with them at the Monastery and pray for guidance. It was at that dinner after he used his CPR training to resuscitate the sister that another sister had approached him. A middle-aged, slender woman in a simple white blouse and black skirt. She had light brown hair and round, deep brown eyes. She wanted to thank him personally for his heroic action. In the evening light they had walked the labyrinth and viewed the garden, acres of fall-colored flowers and green quietude. As he later told Dorrie, he sensed a spiritual bond with this nun. She is called, he said, Sister Diana.

"How does he keep coming up with these stories?" Dorrie said when she had again burst into Janey's office to unburden herself of Edwin's latest version of his birth. She no longer thought of Janey as a social worker but as a confidant. With all the Edwin shit they had gone through, she trusted Janey to hear her out and not pass judgment.

"I didn't think it was possible to live delusion after delusion as long as he has…if you're sane," Janey mused.

"You don't believe Edwin is…crazy."

"He's not, but he's emotionally disturbed and Clay almost tore a hole in his cover. But Edwin didn't falter."
"Janey, will he keep on this way, telling lies like this the rest of his life?"

"Nope. He'll either get worse or get better."

Braden stayed home with a beer watching football on television while Paulie accompanied Janey and Gibby to his school's open house. Paulie showed off a bit, then wandered away while the teachers talked to his mother. Gibby had the pleasure of poking Janey with her elbow every time a teacher proclaimed Paulie to be exceptional. And a good kid, his teachers assured Janey when she asked. Gibby linked arms with Janey, and Paulie let her slip her other arm through his as they walked to the car afterwards through the dark. He loved the night, wasn't afraid of the dark, it felt so good that evening he remembered it the rest of his life.

When Janey and Paulie got home, Braden had Dorrie sitting next to him, drinking a beer on the sofa.

He went off to ask Paulie about the open house, and let Dorrie speak to Janey since that's what she'd come for. The two women sat at the kitchen table, drank coffee.

"I took Edwin to a nice dinner tonight, told him to dress up for it, and I put on something special myself, like we were having a celebration. I thought about what you said at your office the other day. It's my fault playing along with Edwin. But after you all dug me up, I felt kind of responsible. It's been what…two years and he isn't getting better. It's worse if anything. And now he thinks this Sister Diana herself might be his mother."

"Did she tell him that she was? His mother?"

"He said she only smiled at him when he asked. Didn't say yes or no. Damn nun, he's gonna go off that this is his mother. She's very kind, gentle spoken. She didn't say no—"

"How did he seem, happy? Was he euphoric? Triumphant?"

Dorrie seemed taken aback. "Oh, happy, glad. She's everything he imagined his real mother would be."

"He made her up and brought her alive…"

"What are you saying?"

"This Diana couldn't be his mother, could she?"

"No, no she isn't. Hell, no."

"Did he positively say, this is my mother?"

"He didn't. At least not yet."

"That could be a good sign if he evinced a doubt about her."

"He fudged a little, maybe because she wasn't all joyful, crying and hugging on him."

Dorrie went on to recount the rest of their dinner conversation.

"He had told me this Sister Diana had been twenty-five years at the convent. How did he jive that with her being his mother? A naive nun. His mother was wily. She had tricked the hospital, came to them in the last stage of labor, gave them a false name and was gone a few hours after his birth. I don't see her hiding out in a nunnery. He decided that his biological father had probably threatened her life. I don't believe the biological father even knew a baby existed. But Edwin has a lie for every occasion. I don't know why I humored him. All along I haven't wanted to leave him defenseless. People are fragile, aren't they?"

"I don't know. I don't know if they are or not anymore."

∽

When Leah came to the jeweler's early she caught Claymore humming *O Mio Babbino Caro*. He told her it was from the opera *Gianni Schicchi* by Puccini and laughed when she looked surprised. "You don't believe I like opera? I'm not uncultured. I have loved it always, but don't listen much anymore. The Lyric costs a fortune. Sometimes I hear on the radio an aria and it rips my heart up."

"Janey Leduc's friend Gibby's husband plays oboe for the Lyric. Maybe we can ask her to get us free tickets. I've never listened to an entire opera, all the way through."

"And maybe you'd like to?"

"I think I would."

Claymore did not make it to an opera. By November his heart gave out and he died in his leather chair. He left his entire estate, savings, house, store, all the jewelry, his business to his niece Dorothea Pounce, the daughter of his sister Elvira. He would have been surprised at the crowd who came to the funeral service. He had been in business a long time, had acquaintances who admired him, even a few grateful people showed up for whom he had done favors. In a private room in a cozy restaurant, they had gathered afterward to take refreshment as Dorrie had invited them to.

Paulie stayed at Rex's house, almost unaware that his mother's errand was a good-bye to the old man at the jewelry store. When he was late into middle age, he remembered the jewelry store clearly and Claymore became a character in the penumbra of long ago.

The bereaved who had gathered at the restaurant broke into subgroups. Dorrie hung around Janey and Braden. She enjoyed teasing Gibby and looked with awe at Ben whom she never guessed would come. Near the end of the evening when she went to get the small casket of her uncle's cremated remains, Edwin slinked in. He looked downtrodden and gloomy. She gave him credit for showing up. He did, after all, feel something for Claymore.

Gibby was trying to wrangle a confession about Paulie's recent rebellion out of Janey who was playing it down. Braden was fueling their fussing.

"So," said Braden, "Paulie waltzes in and announces to his mother that he is going to be a racecar driver like his dad. And Janey says, 'Oh, no you're not going to waste a first-class brain.' Which infuriates Paulie who can be the devil to argue with. He declares that she has it all wrong. His dad didn't die because of racing, but swerving not to hit a dog." Janey wisely gives up at that point.

"For a while," said Janey. Gibby wiggled her eyebrows, an affectation they all ignored.

"Then a couple of days ago," Braden smirked in admiration at Janey, "she told the kid, why not go a hundred thousand times faster than your father and live a hundred times more dangerously? Paulie, who's astounded says, how? Be an astronaut, says Janey. End of rebellion." Ben was impressed, he and Braden wandered off, and Gibby slipped her arm around Janey's shoulder, whispered, "You think he'll become a scientist, maybe in physics or astronomy, but there are astronaut payload specialists, you know."

Janey nudged her ribs, "Shut up." At that moment they saw Dorrie hurrying to the entrance where Edwin stood, as if on watch. "I better help out Dorrie."

"Wait," said Gibby. "What, I wonder…what's wrong with Edwin? Why do you let him get to you? I think it's strange. What's his problem anyway?"

"I don't know exactly. He shows damage from growing up with alcoholic parents. Abandonment—"

"But what is it? Chemical imbalance?"

"Probably. I don't—"

"Is he a sociopath?"

"Gibby…ask till the cows come home, I can't explain him. As a therapist I could tell you the way a client is, but that isn't an explanation, like you want."

"And they call it a science."

Janey grabbed her hand, "Come on, let's go bail out Dorrie. Look at the face on Edwin." He had pulled down the mask he always wore, and she feared his skin would rip off with it.

Dorrie was babbling to Edwin how pleased she was that he had shown up. He was about to say something when Janey and Gibby joined them. He fell into a sulky silence.

Dorrie said to them, "I'm so glad Edwin made it here."

Edwin perked up. "I came to tell you something important. It's good that Janey can hear it, too." Gibby, although not named, decided not to walk away. He glared at Dorrie, then switched his focus to Janey. "You disrespected me, but I got it done. Did it myself, because I had faith, even when you, Dorrie, didn't have enough. I never gave up since I never had one bit of doubt I'd find her. That's real faith. The sisters in the convent have faith." Paused as if he needed to take a breath. This sham was new to Gibby who took in the melodrama innocently. Dorrie, already emotional in her grief, seemed overwhelmed. Edwin was incensed by their lack of responses.

"Did you hear me? I have located my birthmother—"

"Again," said Janey.

"And…and she admits that is who she is." He backed off, tentative now, "It was uncanny."

"Admits it," said Dorrie.

It was late, the private hall was empty. Leah came up and asked Dorrie if she needed a ride home. They left together, Dorrie awed a little at how she would have her uncle's car now and didn't have to take the El. As if she'd turned off a mental switch, she no longer seemed interested in Edwin's problems and his instability. He had found a birthmother that he approved of. As long as this woman played the part, for whatever reason, in whatever way, he would be satisfied. Dorrie was well out of it. Her uncle would be glad — she could not hear him saying how she was safe from Edwin at last. But he would have told her so if he were here.

FIFTEEN

NOT long after Claymore Mandebrote died, Edwin brought Sister Diana to meet Janey. They caught her after her last client had left as she was heading to her car. Edwin in a dark suit and tie, his hair trimmed and neat, looked like a young barrister in London. The nun dressed in plain white blouse and black skirt, her light brown hair two quarter-moons each one limning the sides of her smooth face. Like many women who take religious vows she had unlined skin and farseeing eyes. Hers were dark brown, moist, pensive. Janey suggested they go to the Palmer House lounge. It was late afternoon and they could have tea. Where else might a middle-aged nun care to be entertained?

In her car Janey phoned Gibby. "Hang on to Paulie when you pick him up. I won't be home until later after all. I'm taking Edwin and his current birthmother to the Palmer House for tea."

"Really? I don't like this, Janey. I don't like him. There's something freaky about all of it. Are you heading there right now?"

"Yes. Sister Diana has her own car. I'm meeting them."

"I'll see you in ten minutes. Your son and I will be there." She clicked off her phone.

In the plush luxury of the Lobby Tea Room at Palmer House, Sister Diana did not feel out of place. They sat at a round table on red velvet upholstered oval-backed chairs. The frescoes, Damask linen, wall mirrors, glittering chandeliers, the ambiance of it all seemed to entrance Diana. However, Edwin hadn't brought them here for pleasure, he had plans. Edwin had found it intolerable to have Janey and Dorrie disbelieve that he had captured his prey, that he had located his birthmother. Dorrie refused to have anything more to do with him. And in fact he had yet to cajole Diana into a declarative admission. He needed someone besides himself to believe he had found his mother, or he would continue on shaky ground. So Edwin had turned to Janey to confirm Diana was she. Janey had expected a crisis as an opening to Edwin feeling better. Important too if she could obliterate this case in her own mind. It would be freeing.

Diana was willing to discuss nearly any topic, her subdued, tempered mind was up to conversation. When tea came, she said a small prayer before she gleefully tucked into the cakes, scones, cucumber and shrimp dip. If Janey asked anything about her past, she was polite, but clever at evading a significant answer. Gibby, who had joined them five minutes after they were seated, was silent and concentrated on Paulie who, overly chatty, seemed impressed to have been brought along for tea. Sister Diana showed affection for Edwin, but then she seemed to be including the whole table in her benediction, and not only the people but the elegant surroundings and all the goodies, too.

Edwin broke into these easy dynamics with his manic need to have this enigmatic woman identified.

"Sister Diana Peters..." he began. "Janey Leduc here was my social worker. She helped me trace my birthmother...as far as she could. She was supposed to find her. She's here because she didn't complete my case to close it, as the law requires. You need to confirm with her that you are indeed my birthmother."

Momentarily, Janey was too appalled to speak. How do you combat treachery, trickery, unabashed, bold-faced lying?

"Nothing of the kind," she sputtered out. "I'm not here to bully you, Diana." She sent Edwin a wicked stare. "He hasn't been my client for months and he's good at playing people. Don't fall for his manipulations."

Sister Diana sent out an understanding smile encompassing everything, even the unlucky shrimps. Her crystalline eyes made no distinctions. She might be a Buddhist nun rather than a Roman Catholic one.

Diana's undisturbed gaze reached first Janey, then lingered on Edwin.

"In a sense, I am your mother. What more needs to be said?"

"I'll tell you what I need." He pointed at Janey. "I need you to say to her what you told me before."

"What, Edwin, what is it you think I said?"

"We were talking about when I was born, my adoption…"

Leading the witness, thought Janey. She put a restraining grip on Edwin's arm. "Don't do this to—"

He shook her off. "Shut up, Janey. I brought you here to listen not talk." Diana shied away, pushing backward slightly. But she remained upright, her face glistening.

"Go ahead, you can tell Janey how we figured it out." But Diana remained silent, her irises receding into slits. Janey sensed she was wary now as well as puzzled.

"Remember, I was your newborn then you came to the convent. You stayed to serve the Lord. You're beautiful and holy. And now I've found—"

Diana blinked, her eyelids flittered, she clutched the table edge as if she were about to tumble off her chair. "I am the Immaculate Conception," she quoted. Her cheeks were flushed, beads of sweat crept along her hairline. Then her manner settled as if she'd returned unharmed. "And I am not. I'm Diana Peters and you are my son—"

"Did you hear that, Janey, did you?"

"And these two young women are my daughters. And most precious of all is the boy there, who is my child." Edwin sat stunned. It was enough for Paulie to want to scramble under the table.

Gibby raised halfway up from her chair. "Edwin, I know who your mother is. I know and I'm going to tell you. There will be no doubts anymore. Dorrie Pounce is your mother. She won't admit it but she is. I can do a simple DNA swatch in my lab at the Field anytime you want."

Gibby saw Paulie out of the corner of her eye. He looked frightened and confused. "You've tormented Dorrie long enough. And you've moved on to tormenting this woman." Janey stood up beside Diana and motioned the nun to leave. "And you Janey, my clever friend, you've known about Dorrie all along, haven't you? Not suspected, you've known. He's denying Dorrie and for some reason you won't take him on, and it's destroying Dorrie. Lately, lately, it's not been good for you at all." Gibby lifted her face to Janey, "You can stand up to anything, why not this lying bastard?"

Then Edwin fled, knocking into the waiter who was coming fast to their table. Janey led Sister Diana out of the Palmer House by one arm. Her son stumbled with her, tucked under the other arm.

"Like an experiment gone very badly," Janey said sotto voce. She gave the waiter her credit card to cover the entire tea. It was an ungodly amount.

It was formless what adult Paul remembered of the tea fiasco, nothing about Edwin that day, and no memory at all of a nun. Gibby's trembly voice, his mother incongruously in the wrong, a phantom who looked half-alive and hidden away, a creep who made Gibby furious. A memory squelched before it could encase him in devouring blue flames. Burning spindles of fear accompanied the brief, half-remembered incident. What happened at the Palmer House had made his mother argue with Gibby. So awful an argument that he didn't see Gibby for weeks.

Janey had been appalled that Gibby brought Paulie to the Palmer House and subjected him to the bizarre scene. Janey retreated away from her. Gibby, made miserable by how Janey had slashed at her, kept her distance and suffered.

⁓◎

Since Claymore had passed away, Dorrie had done some serious soul-searching. She wasn't sleeping well — she'd dredged up some sunken demons to wrestle with. In the early morning clarity, caffeine, eggs and bacon, and her determination to rid herself of this hag-driven fear, took her to Leah Campion with her decision made. She pounded on the door of a white shingled bungalow.

Dorrie heard Leah's footsteps approaching, heard her ask who was there? Dorrie shouted her name. Her uncle's apprentice welcomed her in. "I just made myself some coffee so I can offer you fresh." She led Dorrie to the kitchen, divested her of her coat. In a moment they were settled at a teak table eating hot blueberry muffins. Dorrie's anxiety about coming here evaporated. But the task she'd come about hung over the friendly conversation. Leah gave her condolences, poured the coffee.

"I liked the simple service. It fit him."

"Yes, he wanted no fuss. My uncle wasn't one for showy ceremonies."

"It was low-key, and dignified."

"He never married. Or maybe he did… My mother thought when he was overseas in Korea he married a Korean girl, but the army didn't let him bring her home. She had got lost when he went back for her… Mama was never sure. Though he liked to go out, never got married."

"In the store he didn't talk about the past. Didn't get personal. We had companionable, understanding ways."

Talked flagged. Dorrie seemed hesitant. Each attempt Leah made with neutral topics fell flat. Yet on she stayed, accepting more coffee, blundering into conversational dead ends. Dorrie struggled with how to get to her point. Reels of images from Claymore's funeral service unwound silent-movie-like in memory, in memes, maybe stopping articulation. No matter, she knew what she meant to ask Leah.

"Listen, I'm Claymore's heir…heiress. He made me sole beneficiary in his will. My mother was his sister. You see…he designated me — I've inherited his whole estate, jewelry store, house, all kinds of savings accounts.

It amounts to more money than I could ever believe."

Leah gave an appreciative laugh. "Oh wow, my god. Good for you."

"I don't know what to do. I could sell the house and the jewelry store, buy a condo and go live in Arizona or Florida. Where I can lie on the beach in the sun, and do nothing. Swim if I want, pick up seashells, eat shrimp in garlic oil…do nothing. I worked since I was fourteen and I'm almost sixty. What I want to say is, my uncle thought a lot of you."

Leah shook her head. "Did he?"

"I lost sleep over this decision. What I mean is, what if I stay here in Chicago… Then will you manage the jewelry store, take charge of it? I'll be glad to come in and kibbitz. I'd like that. But the running of the place would be yours."

"How can I handle it? I'm not sure I'm capable. Claymore taught me a lot, but the accounting part?"

"Didn't he say you were in business once?"

"Not like this would be."

"How hard could it be if Clay did it?" She enjoyed a chuckle. "I could sell the store, lock stock and barrel, but I've been at odds with myself. There's something wrong about doing that. Maybe I'm kidding myself. Anyway, these last couple of months with him so ill, you've been great. My uncle trusted you. And he didn't trust that many. I won't have anyone else to be manager. I'd be robbed blind. Don't give me your answer right away. Think about it."

"It's flattering you're asking me. I will consider it." She smiled. "I like the jewelry business."

"Take your time. Hey, if it becomes too much for you, well then, I can always sell. I can always do that. What do we got to lose?"

Leah had found a career in Claymore's store. She would continue to study gemstones, appraising, watch repair, even years later, jewelry design. She had undertaken the apprenticeship because it had carried her through the long, unspeakable grief when Jonathan died. It had tempered her and let her survive.

Dorrie, for her part, left Leah's home pleased that she had handled a perplexing dilemma rather well.

SIXTEEN

APRIL chill in Chicago didn't put a cramp in Paulie's baseball excitement. All winter Braden had been teasing him about the tickets he bought for opening day at Wrigley. After school Paulie practiced his skills for when the great day came.

Janey yelled out the backdoor, "Hey you guys. You promised we'd go to Fat Freddy's for lunch."

"One more out." Braden was great at pretending they were the battery in an actual game. He threw a knuckleball that dropped under and away from Paulie's outstretched glove.

"Bray-den," he wailed. "I said no curveballs."

"That was my World Series class knuckler. Come on, Sport, I'm hungry, and your mother awaits. She might get testy from starvation. Not unlike my own mother who would suffer no tarrying."

Paulie was startled. "Where's your mother at, Braden?"

"She died. After giving birth to my baby brother. I was sixteen."

Paulie shied away from this sudden stranger. Some fragment from his father's dying caught in his throat like a tiny perch bone. Moments of unfolding joy in childhood can be sullied by wisps of prescience. Not listening to Braden's babble, desultorily sauntering through the back door into the kitchen, a foreign, unpleasant recognition gripped Paulie that he might someday need to be comforted and no one would be there. A poignant moment of helplessness…but…safe again when his mother appeared. He followed Braden and Janey to her car. Maybe Gibby would be at Fat Freddy's waiting for them. He hadn't seen her in weeks. His mother had hardened herself to the loss. Paulie expected any minute that everything would be all right again. But Gibby was not at Fat Freddy's. She wasn't going to be taking him to Jurassic World at the Field. He had no idea why.

∽

Dorrie dropped into the jewelry store with the taxes her accountant had prepared and electronically filed. It was all new and exciting, and she wanted to go over the store figures with Leah and crow about how in their first few months in business they had turned a nice profit.

"Edwin's been in here a couple of times today, looking for you," said Leah. "In fact, he left only a few minutes ago."

"What'd he want?" For two years Dorrie had stunted her emotions, isolated the struggles within her, absorbed punches, and survived. But she was not going to take it anymore. "He's got his nun mama. I never hear from him. I haven't seen him in weeks. If something's come up to upset his applecart, I'm not available. You know what he can do with his pathetic search—"

"Yeah, I sure do. He didn't tell me what he wanted. Just hung around, waiting. I put him off badly once, so normally he stays his distance."

"Did he accuse you of being his mother?"

"Not exactly. It was more fraught even than that."

As fate would have it and fate always has it, Janey Leduc hustled into the store, in bright new sandals which it was still too chilly to be wearing. "I came to see how the new owner was getting along, not to buy. You've spiffed up the place."

"We worked a little on interior design," said Leah. "The new owner had a few chic and stylish ideas."

Dorrie tried to seem lighthearted and join in. They were teasing her, but she felt detached.

"Edwin came around today looking for Dorrie." Leah left the remark pointed, hanging there.

"Can you close up the store?" asked Janey. "This might be a good time to talk." She had made an intuitive split-second decision that she must confront Dorrie. The game was up and Dorrie didn't know it. Throw in her cards, she should — the metaphors got worse, call it a day.

In Claymore's back workshop, stuffed into the small space on clustered stools, Janey gathered her professional resources and began.

"Dorrie…you are Edwin's birthmother. You are, and I know it. Edwin's been told you are, outright. Whether he believes it, who knows? But I think he does. I think at some level he's always known. That's a clinical opinion." Janey waited. She would wait until the cows come home, as her mother would say. It was Dorrie's time to talk.

Dorrie let out her breath. "Yes, I am Edwin's mother. Should I say, 'for my sins?'" I'm Jewish. No absolution for me. I gave birth to him, then ran away in the dead of the night when no one was around to stop me. Half-naked. What I said when your agency tracked me down after all the years was a lie, as bad a lie as Edwin ever told." A moment of defiance surged out from her squinting eyes.

"I always meant to tell him—"

"How'd you fake the DNA test?"

"I paid some woman where I was working to go take it for me. Gave her my driver's license. They barely gave her a look."

"Oh, my God, did Claymore know?" Leah was about to tilt off her stool.

"Of course not. I could have had a quiet abortion, but no. I was afraid. Afraid of doing anything, afraid of doing nothing, afraid, afraid, afraid." She sobbed, stopped herself.

"Why, why?" Janey asked in awe. "Why the deception all the years later? Why this rigamarole?"

Dorrie struggled to her feet, wheeled on the two women. "You won't understand. So what, I'll tell you. It's simple. I was all ready to confess when I met him. But then I saw it, in his eyes, in the way he looked to the side. I didn't come anywhere near up to his high 'Mother' expectations. He was so obviously relieved when I made up that pathetic story. Pitiful. He would hate for me to be his mother. How could I let him down again?"

"What are you going to do?" whispered Leah.

"Listen to me, Dorrie, he has been told who you are." Had Dorrie heard her the first time she said it? "You can leave it at that. If he's disappeared that probably means he's hiding from the reality. Maybe he's discarded the news like an uncomfortable fact. He does that easily enough."

"That's what I am, an 'uncomfortable fact.'"

"That's not what I mean. To Edwin on some days the sky being blue is an uncomfortable fact. He prefers his fantasies."

"Do you think there's a chance he might take it like a rational person, Janey? Will he recover his wits?"

"That's hard to say. We don't know what he's been up to since he was told the truth. Anyway, he did accept that Sister Diana is not his birthmother. He never made an attempt with me to get to the root of his problems. But I think you should talk to him. For you. So that you can get better."

"Afterward, come in and help me in the jewelry store," said Leah, a healing place to her.

"I'll go to him. One way or the other I have to see him."

The three women left the building together. Dorrie stopped abruptly in the cooling dusk. "You guys know about the wisdom of Solomon? What drivel. The woman who stopped Solomon's bluff to cut the baby in half wasn't necessarily the baby's mother. She was the woman who had love and humanity for all babies."

Janey giggled. "Yeah, but she was obviously the right one to give the baby to."

Leah gasped. "Solomon was wise for the wrong reason."

"I always thought so," said Dorrie.

―✧―

Gibby dunked her donut into her coffee unaware that she already had. The donut end fell into the cup with a soft, squishy thunk. "Damn," she mumbled and grabbed her spoon, fished out the caky blob, no longer appetizing, and dragged the drippy mess onto her napkin.

"I hoped I'd find you here. Seemed a likely place to find you at lunch." There stood Janey Leduc, pulling out the chair opposite her. Without asking she joined Gibby as if they were still on speaking terms.

Gibby asked herself if the Field Museum cafeteria had trembled. She scraped for something to say. "I'm bemoaning the fact that I dropped the damn donut in my coffee cup." She clinked her spoon on the cup lip to hide her dismay.

Janey sighed, slightly smiling. "Can… I wonder if things could be the same…between us, friends where we see a situation differently, but it won't ever matter."

"I shouldn't have told Edwin, huh? Even though it was intellectually dishonest to hold it back, and you were being drawn into a dark place that frightened me—"

"I was perfectly in control. And…" she would not squabble. "Paulie got scared."

"Okay, alright. I do understand why you got mad at that. To me you were vulnerable, open to abuse, I couldn't watch it anymore… But you couldn't pull yourself away."

"You were…I didn't know you. As if you were someone else right then. I'm not going to analyze myself."

"The thing is…the situation at the Palmer House was distorted. I could see the damage it was doing to you. I wasn't thinking of Paulie being there at all."

"My god, Gibby… I came here to find you. This is the place we met…the right place to tell you. I don't care that you told Edwin—"

"I couldn't stand the tripe anymore. But, Janey, I am sorry Paulie was there, what a horrid mistake I made, exposing Paulie to that. How could I have done it?" Artie, Simon, Edwin, as Gibby saw them, an unholy trinity. Not solvable with limited empirical data.

"Must be your science shielded you, logic and reason. The observer, experimenter, analyzer, so simple."

"What simple? — you try it sometime." They were themselves again, beginning with a laugh. "Now let me tell you how I see it, empirically. In no part of your mind can you imagine a scenario where you surrender up Paulie, ever, for any reason. So you have no reference and not a ray of empathy for Dorrie. So, Edwin, in a way, got to you."

"Would I ever have given — give Paulie away, if the circumstances gave me no other choice? I don't know... No." Her eyes intensely lit on Gibby's face, searching. "But at that critical moment, we can only say how we truly believe we would act. I would never..." She bowed her head. Gibby stroked her hair, making a tacit understanding complete.

∽

Braden had not completely broken with Simon Butler. At odd times he would run into Simon when he met with his old friends. Braden had seen Simon at a fundraiser they had organized to help their buddy, Jack, whose youngest daughter had leukemia. Braden had been horrified by the little girl's disease and barely mentioned to Janey that Simon had been there. Clearing up after dinner when Paulie had gone outside to pitch his baseball at Rex's glove while Lydia took awkward swings with a too-heavy bat, Janey asked Braden how Simon had seemed at the fundraiser.

"Simo? Same as usual. Jack's barely hanging on. God, that poor little mite, Brittany."

"I know, Sweetheart. I was wondering about Simon."

"He's the pinhead he's always been." Finished at the dishwasher he was loading, he looked out the back window. "I've known Simo since we were Paulie's age. Like Paulie and his friends out there in the yard. And you know what, Simo never in his life would have thrown a sinker to get Lydia out like Paulie's trying to do right now." That about summed up Simon Butler. If Janey didn't get it, there was nothing more he could say.

∽

Dorrie flew into the jewelry shop, florid from the heat, breathing in chunks of air conditioning. Leah called her over to where she stood drooping over a FedEx package ripped open, contents glittering on folds of protective layers.

"I raced here to see with my own eyes. I can't believe it."

"It came from Thailand," said Leah, "Look at the billing and shipping papers. Look at what it's been insured for." Both women gasped.

Dorrie grabbed the sheets out of Leah's hand. "It's an untreated Burmese ruby. Clay spent a fortune on it. Shit, it's gorgeous."

"Claymore must have had a reason," said Leah.

"My uncle had his ways," murmured Dorrie.

"Someone must have commissioned him to design a setting for it. But he never mentioned it to me."

"Did someone order and pay for it, or did Clay buy it?"

"The receipt is made out to him. We'll keep it in the vault. If a person comes in with proof it's theirs, okay. If not, it's yours, Dorrie. I kind of think no one's going to claim it."

"If someone did want him to create a design for it?"

"If so, Clay never mentioned it. Never wrote it down. Nothing to account for it. The master jeweler is gone. The person would have to take it somewhere else to have it set."

"Oh, Uncle Clay," she raised her hands in prayer. "You were too generous to me."

∽

Janey dozed in the backyard lounge chair while in the warm air kid noises were afloat. Paulie and his friends rooted around plucking worms from the rain-soaked ground. Rex wanted to set up a business selling earthworms to the bait shops at the river. Braden banged out the screen door and plunked down in the canvas chair beside Janey.

"So, you made it up with Gibby." He wished he had a

cigarette although he'd stopped smoking ten years ago.

"It wasn't that big a deal." She closed her eyes again.

"It was a very big deal to Paulie. You didn't ever really explain, I mean, I never did get what happened at the Palmer House that set you two off."

"Leave it, Braden. A tiff between friends who have different views about confrontation. Mostly, I was angry because she dragged Paulie into a tense, adult situation."

"You told me that. But it doesn't explain everything. Did Gibby hit a sore spot—"

She flashed open her eyelids and glared at him. "You want the whole story? I'm not sure I'm ready to give it."

"I wonder if you trust anybody, Janey?"

"Oh goodness. Has Simon gotten to you?"

"All right, I'll leave it be. I'm glad you guys settled. I missed Gibby, too, and Ben. He's quiet, but when he does talk it's like listening to his oboe solo, real relaxing."

When the note has been reached, a pure clear, unworldly note of encapsulated moment of the divine, a moment of reality is breeched and the word is worth a thousand pictures and the music a background to a million words. Poetry is all of this, but one word with another becomes a unity. With a rift.

"Braden, okay. See if this makes sense to you." It came to the point where she must tell him, or it will return again and again like a sour aftertaste for the rest of her life. "We had left our baby with my mother and gone off on a road trip. Artie and I — he loved to drive fast better than anything. Then the accident, the bottomless, dark pit, staring for hours into the abyss. The two people who loved me, needed me, far away, and only Art. He laughed sometimes when the branches swayed and acted as if it was impossible we would die. When we were rescued, in the hole where fear had sat, emptiness descended. I returned to the living from the frozen lake in hell that immobilized Satan. I sat next to my mother and suckled my baby and never let anyone else in, Braden." She sang, "I love you dearly more dearly than the spoken word can tell."

Janey had let in one other, Martha Gibson. Braden was her man, forever and truly. But Gibby was the gulf in the heart.

⁓

Adult Paul didn't know such soul-shaking was happening. He reveled in spring evenings, his fertile mind filled with magic. In that time when they sold earthworms and his grandmother came to stay, he got

Gibby back. Summer trip to Stanley Field Hall for the official debut of the new 122-foot dinosaur, Máximo. The biggest dinosaur discovered to date, the boy crowed. On the way home along Lakeshore Drive, Gibby stopped to show him a ship dipping down over the horizon. She said it was a phantom ship. After he took in the sight, she said that it was an inferior mirage. Moist warm air over cooler waters created a mirage of a ship going over the horizon. He lifted his glittering eyes to her in appreciation.

The only shade in that sunny summer was when Rex broke his arm.

"Rex can't be normal outside," he complained to his mother, "because of that stupid cast. And now Liddy's mom said she shouldn't play so much with us because we're too rough."

"What? It was Rex who broke his arm, not Lydia."

"I know. It wasn't our fault, Mom," he wailed.

"That's true, Paulie, but I did tell you not to climb those weak-limbed Aspen trees."

"He didn't jump right. He didn't flex like we did and he sorta tumbled down when the big branch went too low. It was a hell of a fall."

"Heck, heck of a fall, Paulie. It's politer than saying hell."

"Well then tell that to Braden."

"It's different with Braden." The boy didn't see how it could be.

⁓

Another half-forgotten, dim-cast memory, of a drive past the jewelry store, car air conditioner on too cold, Paulie feeling muggy, his mother brought up the butterfly he had never gotten. A shadowed conversation…holding grudges and not meaning to hurt others. He heard her name for the first time. "Mrs. Campion felt bad about it."

"No, she didn't" Anyway, he had switched to another interest. "I'm gonna be an astronaut when I get big."

"Then, my darling boy, you can give me the stars."

SEVENTEEN

CHANGE is all you can count on, it's the only permanence, so say all. Nothing stays the same. If you put your logic and skepticism to work, you might see a paradox in this truism. If change is the only permanence, there is nothing permanent, so therefore how can change be permanent? Follow it now: for there to be nothing permanent, permanence can't be permanent either. Permanence is a something, a noun, an idea, a person, place or thing. It can't be outside the mind. We've thought of it. Therefore, permanence could live in some universe. Read Descartes. Read Tagore. Read as if life depends on it, because it does.

Up the long stairway, on the landing, Dorrie knocked boldly on Edwin's rooming house door. She heard

Edwin's footsteps tromping over. He jerked it open in front of her face. He was expecting the Chinese food he'd ordered. They stood for a few seconds staring at one another. Dorrie asked if she might talk to him.

"Sure," he stepped aside and let her in. "I'm waiting for my supper to come. I didn't order enough for two."

"No problem. I've watched you eat lots of times." She followed him to his seating area, and dropped into an overstuffed leather chair. "I heard a rumor that I need to address with you."

He sensed a grimness about Dorrie. At that moment Edwin was in a quandary, worse than any he had ever faced, or would ever face again. Here sat his birthmother. So he'd been told unequivocally. He had clung to her denial these two years and was desperate to believe her again. But he could not. Because he was not insane. He recognized her, in her voice, in her eyes, in her walk. He hadn't allowed who she was to enter consciousness before now because he simply did not want to. One look at the Nazi supporters after World War II will explain how that works. This matronly, wild-haired, red-headed, freckled, loud and sometimes abrasive woman he would never accept. In his heart he needed his mother to have inner beauty as well as outer beauty. To Edwin, Dorrie had neither.

Since the Sister Diana episode, he had yearned for, craved an answer to why, why had his birthmother not gone out to find him. He answered the bitter question with a wrong-headed assumption. She had tried but had been unable to recover him because of circumstances beyond her control. To Janey's assertion, "or she's dead," he might have been reconciled, but because that didn't suit his dream reunion, it was easy to reject. His birthmother wasn't dead, but somehow wad held against her will from reclaiming him, that he could live with. He could script any plot. But never one about a mother who was Dorrie.

There she sat, rubbing her knuckle across her chin. The words gushed from her large mouth. "Edwin, all this foolish searching is done with. You heard it. It's true. I gave you birth. I'm your mother. I left you to be adopted, signed you away, because I believed you'd get a chance for a better life. More than I could ever give you. I was single, ashamed, had run away from home, fell into some unsavory company. I went back home but I couldn't have gone back home with a baby."

He said nothing, only looked at the door as if he expected the Chinese food order soon.

"I would have told you right away, as soon as Janey approached me, but there you were. You had such a face on you. When you saw me walk in, it was like the biggest disappointment of your life. If I had kept you and raised you, you would never have looked at me that way…"

"And you want me to believe that cockamamy story? Shit, what a pile of bullshit. You aren't my birthmother. I don't have any idea why you decided to drop this on me, but I'm not falling for it. It ain't gonna get me, understand. I don't want to go looking for her, I found that out with my bust, huh, Sister Diana, big bomb. But someday I know she'll show up, come walking up to me, somewhere. And then, then…" He swiveled his head to the side, stared at the carpet. "It'll all be right."

A knock on the door shattered the deep quiet. Dorrie shoved past a delivery on her way out. Edwin's Chinese food had arrived.

⁓

Sneaking into Mordecai's, Janey joined Gibby and Ben at their table. "You two got here early. Ben's parking the car. I've never eaten at this place before." She helped herself to oyster on a half-shell from the appetizer plate. "A thought came to me just now. I don't like these late-night outings much anymore. That must mean I'm entering middle age."

"No, it doesn't," said Ben. "I normally go home exhausted from a concert." Gibby smiled at him, rubbed his bared forearm. "Martha and I were talking about an opera, the Met, where eight years ago we heard the definitive Carmen. Elina Garanca. Each time a soprano sings, or tenor or musician plays, nothing will never be heard like that again. The music is there in the notes, underneath, close to infinite in their different syntheses. And the human voice gives …" He looked at Martha.

"Gives music its most beautiful instrument." He tilted toward her.

Janey found Ben's wide-open silky brown eyes half-hidden by long, curled lashes. "You, Benji, must have acquired self-actualization early."

Gibby laughed. "Don't talk dirty to him, Janey."

"I'm not sure I know what you mean."

"She's teasing you, Sweetheart."

"Then why are you poking her with your elbow?"

"Here comes Braden." Braden's arrival always made things go well.

༄

Adult Paul recalled that in his childhood he had missed his father. Missed him in a generic way, how people miss what they've never had. He didn't put Braden into that role. Braden had been in every way good to him, but after Artie died, Paulie considered himself fatherless. He loved Braden and had no emotional link to Art Kane. Never mind, he had no father. Whether in myth or modern metaphor, may we get rid of the angst? Paulie the curly-haired butterfly boy flourished.

༄

An evening at Mordecai's is a time to relax the nerves. Background tones and murmurs were mellow as Ben seriously explained to Braden, Massachusetts meant nine-pin bowling. In an aside to Gibby, Janey said, "I'm considering changing careers. I'm a burned-out therapist."

"I have to take this in. It's…a big decision, even to contemplate."

"It's not drastic. There are other places I could use my degrees."

"Sure, I know that. But I believe the work you do is critical—"

"I don't see it that way."

"Come on, Janey. You help the woebegone. Help the helpless with a capital H."

"Don't be an idiot."

"And don't put me off with a wisecrack. You're serious?"

"Yes, I've lost my calling." Shocked by admitting out loud what hadn't yet entered her thought. "I go on without being good at it."

"Now you're doubting your ability, I would never doubt your ability. This crisis…whatever…is because of Edwin isn't it? I knew it."

"I'm after something else now. Something absolutely—"

"Absolutely what?"

Janey's shoulders rose up, she shivered, and said, "Something significant."

Ben who'd been half-listening to their conversation said, "You want to switch to another profession?"

Janey smiled. "I don't seem to be very good at this one."

"You are, you're very good at helping people." Gibby shook her head.

Janey wanted a change of topic. "I'm looking in a different direction."

"Hindering people," said Ben. "There's always that."

Braden leaned over, his arms flailed across the wineglass-strewn table. "It's time to go home, gang. We've partied into a whole new day."

The couples walked into the deepest, darkest part of

night to begin the way home. Gibby, beside Janey, leaned against her shoulder. Janey's dim smile pressed her lips. Tacit understanding embraced the two women.

༄

Paul Leduc Kane, payload specialist, sits atop a rocket that will take him to the International Space Station. He will reach the ISS in six hours where he will work for two months on neutron-scattering techniques. Far below him his family waits, watching, thrilled and frightened, full of optimism and hope.

Right before lift-off, there's a lull. A quiescent vapor floats as in solid form, through zero gravity, lasting only a moment. Paul's mind slips off his coming research to wait for the final countdown. At the speed of thought, which might slow time as the speeding-up of light does, he sees them there, his mother young again, Braden alive and joking, Gibby amid the fluttering Monarchs and Swallowtails. The massive rocket's deafening roar begins, it makes the earth tremble, it shakes its enormous finger at the sky. It curls itself into the blast of dark exhaust. Still, for a stroke more, it does not rise. When it seems as if its shuttering self will break apart, the behemoth awakes unaware and achieves lift-off.

Gibby had shown him one night how to find the space station in the clear night sky. She will take him near enough to the stars.

CPSIA information can be obtained
at www.ICGtesting.com
Printed in the USA
FSHW012255290919
62511FS